# SHAKESPEARE

# Shakespeare

BY

MARK VAN DOREN

NEW YORK
HENRY HOLT AND COMPANY

IN CANADA, OXFORD UNIVERSITY PRESS

TO

RAYMOND WEAVER

# ACKNOWLEDGMENTS

THESE chapters are indebted not only to Shakespeare but to many books that have been written about him, and to many things I have heard said about him by persons who did not claim to be critics. Anyone familiar with the recent literature of Shakespeare will recognize my obligation to Sir Edmund Chambers, H. B. Charlton, Walter Clyde Curry, Harley Granville-Barker, G. Wilson Knight, William Witherle Lawrence, George H. W. Rylands, Caroline F. E. Spurgeon, Elmer Edgar Stoll, Charles Williams, J. Dover Wilson, and Frances A. Yates. Anyone at all will see that my favorite among the older critics is Dr. Johnson. But no one unless I tell him, and I hereby do, will appreciate my debt to those students of Columbia College with whom I annually read and discuss the complete works of Shakespeare. The text I have always used is that of William Allan Neilson, prepared in 1906 for The Cambridge Poets. Scene and line references are to the third edition of that text, permission to quote from which has been generously given me by Houghton Mifflin Company, Boston.

M. V. D.

*New York, 1939*

# CONTENTS

viii CONTENTS

# INTRODUCTION

I HAVE imagined the reader of this book to be a person already acquainted in one degree or another with the poems and plays of Shakespeare, and willing now for the first or hundredth time to consider them as human documents and as works of art. The knowledge I have assumed is a reading knowledge, since that is the kind we habitually have. Further knowledge in a theater is finally necessary, but the interest of the plays as they stand in print would appear to be without end, and I have counted on that. I have made each chapter as brief as I could, my endeavor being always, with neither novelty nor convention as my guide, to say the things that seemed to me essential. The quotations, many as they sometimes are, have been kept as short and few as possible. They will need attention even when they are familiar, for they carry the discussion; but I have assumed in the reader an awareness that Shakespeare was never writing quotations, and that the force of anything he said was in a peculiar sense relative to the force of other things. As a whole can be greater than the sum of its parts, so a complete poem is richer than the sum of all the things that can be said about its passages. Twice as many quotations as I have used, and ten times as much critical wisdom as I may chance to possess, would still provide no substitute for Shakespeare.

I have ignored the biography of Shakespeare, the history and character of his time, the conventions of his theater, the works of his contemporaries, and, with respect to the plays themselves, most questions having to do with their text and authorship. These matters are important, but it was more important for my purpose, and more practical, to proceed on the

1

theory that the interest of the plays as they have come down to us exceeds the interest either of the individual who wrote them or of the age that produced him. That he was an individual I have no doubt, but he exists for me wholly in the work he did, and I often fail to recognize him in pictures painted of his time. He had too much poetry, and—the same thing for him—too much sense, to be the slave of fashions in human being. He is typical of any world that can be understood, and he is the kind of story-teller who can be judged by the most general standards we have. The "Poetics" of Aristotle will explain him more readily than the unique literature of his age will explain him. It is difficult enough for such literature to explain itself; nor does Shakespeare seem to call for explanations beyond those which a whole heart and a free mind abundantly supply.

I have no other theory about Shakespeare unless further ones appear, as doubtless they will, in the chapters that follow. I have none at any rate about the order in which the plays were written. I have followed an order, violating it here and there for convenience in discussion, but I do not insist upon any chronology. Dogma in these matters is difficult in view of Shakespeare's variety, and it is absurd when it depends upon conjectures about his moods. I seldom assume that I know what those were, and I always assume that he was greater than they, both as artist and as man.

If the plays of Shakespeare had not been easy to write they would have been impossible. If their solutions had once been problems they could not have been arrived at in a dozen lifetimes, let alone one lifetime in which two or three plays were often the output of a single year. The great and central virtue of Shakespeare was not achieved by taking thought, for thought cannot create a world. It can only understand one when one has been created. Shakespeare, starting with the world no man has made, and never indeed abandoning it,

made many worlds within it. Some of them are more interesting than others, and a few of them are merely sketched; but
each of them tends to be internally consistent, immediately
knowable, and—at the same time that it is familiar—permanently fresh and strange. He may never have said to himself
that this was what he had done, and if he talked to himself at
all there were other excuses for congratulation. As a poet,
considering the term in the narrower, verbal sense which is its
commonest meaning now, he had written so well that any
kind of poetry and any kind of prose can be found in him at
its best. This has its lasting importance, being one of the reasons that the words he used have become so widely known.
But a reason of deeper importance is the context of those
words in the worlds they helped to make.

How these worlds came into being cannot be plainly said.
If it could be, the criticism of Shakespeare would at once
reach an end. Criticism grows desperate from time to time and
denies their existence. Shakespeare was merely a poet, a word-
magician; or merely a carpenter of plays; or merely an Elizabethan; or merely a man who wrote for money. He was all
those things and more things like them, but to be satisfied with
saying so is to be thrown off the scent of his distinction. At
the opposite extreme criticism grows fanatical in the definition
of devices by which the miracle of creation was performed;
performance assumed, the investigator looks for tricks. The
styles of Shakespeare are studied—the styles, for it is true that
he had no style, no special way of writing beyond the way of
writing well, and that he is not to be imitated except by one
who will say things both as clearly and as interestingly as he
did. But his success is not a matter of devices; or if so, they
are secondary to a larger method which ordered them instinctively to the ends of unity and delight. The unity of any play
is not alone a matter of images, though the coherence of its
metaphors may be amazing; or of diction and syntax, though
the monosyllables of "Julius Caesar" and the involutions of

"The Winter's Tale" have much to do with the natures of their respective universes; or of atmosphere, though the difference between the environment of "Lear" and the environment of "Antony and Cleopatra" is so palpable that one may well become lost in the exercise of feeling it; or of character, though Shakespeare's people live forever; or of plot, though he is inimitable at story-telling. Beyond all these, worthy of study and praise as of course they are, there is in any of the successful plays a created or creature life, a unity of being which reveals itself with every step of our progress into its interior.

It is literally true that while we read a play of Shakespeare's we are in it. We may be drawn in swiftly or slowly—in most cases it is swiftly—but once we are there we are enclosed. That is the secret, and it is still a secret, of Shakespeare's power to interest us. He conditions us to a particular world before we are aware that it exists; then he absorbs us in its particulars. We scarcely say to ourselves, this world exists; nor do we pause to note how consistent each thing in it is with every other. Our attention is on the details, which we take in as details should be taken in, one at a time. Meanwhile there is for us no other world. The great world is not forgotten—Shakespeare indeed knows best how to keep us reminded of its greatness—but it is here confined to a single mode of its being. He is not telling the whole truth in any play, nor does he do so in all of them together, nor could he have done so had he written ten thousand. But the piece of truth with which he is occupied at a given moment is for that moment eloquent both of itself and of the remainder. It seems to be all. It is satisfactory and complete. With each new line a play of Shakespeare's lights its own recesses, deepens its original hue, echoes, supports, and authenticates itself. The world is not there, but this part of it is so entirely there that we miss nothing; it is as if existence had decided to measure itself by a new standard. And the secret of that standard is shared with us. Shakespeare, who denies his reader nothing, denies him least of all the excitement of feeling that he is where things are simply and finally alive.

Only a remarkable artist could have done this, and only a remarkable man—a man, moreover, in whom the balance was well-nigh perfect between understanding and observation, between intellect and instinct, between vision and sight. It has long been recognized that his characters, while irreducibly individual, partake of that nature which belongs to all men, and seldom desert the types in whose terms they were conceived. Hamlet is young, melancholy, courteous, brilliant, and moral. Falstaff is old, fat, drunken, untruthful, and witty. None of those traits is new, and it would almost appear that nothing in either man had been invented by Shakespeare. Each, however, has his unique carriage and voice, and will not be mistaken for any other man on earth. He is first of all a member of the human race. After that he is himself, saying things which Shakespeare knows how to envelop in a silence so natural that for the time being we hear no other sound than that of his discourse. Yet the act of being himself never takes him beyond the range of our understanding. We hear him with our ears and we see him with our eyes, but he is most valuable to us because we can think about him with all the mind we possess. He is not that monstrous thing, an individual undefined, any more than Shakespeare's worlds are irresponsible constructions, or any more than Shakespeare's poetry is idiot-pure. Sometimes this poetry struts on cumbrous wings when it should go by foot, but seldom is it being written for its own sake, as if poetry were the most precious thing in the world. To Shakespeare it was apparently not that. The world was still more precious—the great one he never forgot, and the little one in which he knew how to imprison its voice and body. What he dealt in was existence, and his dealings were responsible, high-hearted, and humane. The reader who places himself in his hands will not be protected from any experience, but he will be safe from outrage because he will always know his bearings. What is supposed to happen in Shakespeare's plays does happen; and what has happened anywhere cannot be finally hated. Shakespeare loved the world as it is. That is why he understood it so well; and that in turn is why, being the artist he was, he could make it over again into something so rich and clear.

# POEMS

THE poems of Shakespeare are seldom perfect. The songs that shoot like stars across his plays are brightest at the beginning, and often burn out before the end. Few of his sonnets are powerful at the finish. And neither of his narrative poems has mastered its stanza. He seems to have been without interest in the relatively unimportant matter of mechanical form. Perhaps he was without skill, but his possession of all other skills renders this doubtful. It is more likely that the duty of a poem in his mind was to be as good as possible whenever possible; once the thing had been said, the impulse satisfied, the target hit, he could walk indifferently away, for conclusions were arbitrary.

When the stanzas of "Venus and Adonis" are weak it is the concluding couplets that have failed, usually through a forcing of the rhyme:

> Dismiss your vows, your feigned tears, your flattery;
> For where a heart is hard they make no battery.   (425-6)

> This way she runs, and now she will no further,
> But back retires to rate the boar for murther.   (905-6)

But there may be a forcing of the fancy also:

> This beauteous combat, wilful and unwilling,
> Show'd like two silver doves that sit a-billing.   (365-6)

> For from the stillitory of thy face excelling
> Comes breath perfum'd that breedeth love by smelling.
> (443-4)

> Which seen, her eyes, as murder'd with the view,
> Like stars asham'd of day, themselves withdrew.   (1031-2)

7

And there can be flatness falling into bathos:

> For, by this black-fac'd Night, Desire's foul nurse,
> Your treatise makes me like you worse and worse.
>
> (773-4)

Nor is it only the couplets that permit themselves to be stuffed
with laborious nothings. One of the lamest lines,

> His short thick neck cannot be easily harmed,      (627)

comes third in its stanza. And anywhere at all there may be
desperate rhetoric for filling:

> Tell me Love's master, shall we meet tomorrow?
> Say, shall we? shall we? Wilt thou make the match?
>
> (585-6)

Desperate, indeed, is the word for "Venus and Adonis" as
a whole, and for "The Rape of Lucrece" in its duller fashion.
"Venus and Adonis" has its rush of melody and its forest-
morning freshness of color. The dive-dapper, the milch doe,
the snail, the horses, and the purblind hare are flawlessly and
joyfully observed. But most of the ideas are overdeveloped;
there is strain, there is conceit, there is exaggeration, there is
bad taste. The dimples in Adonis's cheeks which Love has
made for his own tomb, the neighboring caves which echo
for three stanzas the groans of Venus's heart, and the loving
swine that intended a kiss for Adonis are ridden beyond all
bounds. Sometimes the overstatement is quickly achieved:

> My boding heart pants, beats, and takes no rest,
> But, like an earthquake, shakes thee on my breast.
>
> (647-8)

More typically, however, it is achieved at an unmerciful
length, as when the conceit of Venus's drunkenness sweats on
to this ultimate stanza:

> Upon his hurt she looks so steadfastly,
> That her sight dazzling makes the wound seem three;

And then she reprehends her mangling eye,
That makes more gashes where no breach should be.
    His face seems twain, each several limb is doubled;
    For oft the eye mistakes, the brain being troubled.

                                              (1063-8)

To say, justly enough, that Shakespeare's narrative poems
are Ovidian exercises is to say that at their worst they are
coldly clever. Their play with opposites (lifeless life, cold fire,
wanton modesty) and their love of the riddling, compendious
line—

    My love to love is love but to disgrace it,          (412)

    She's Love, she loves, and yet she is not lov'd—     (610)

are signs of a desire to be verbally striking, just as their conceits are signs of a determination to press more poetry out of
an idea than it ever held. To be reminded of Ovid, however,
is also to be given a clue to much that will be important
henceforth in Shakespeare's behavior as a poet. If he needed
to learn it anywhere he learned from Ovid the art of making
poetry out of all things—high and low, big and little, plain
and pretty—whether or not they were personal to him, and
whether or not they had ever been made into poetry before.
He learned how to say a given thing over and over, always
differently and always ingeniously, so that the interest of the
reader might come to center in the subject not as experience
but as pure subject capable at any moment of being rarefied
into further statement, of being rendered still more real to the
mind. It is to the mind, the wit, the thinking heart of the
reader that Shakespeare steadily addresses himself. It is not to
his specific experience or his senses, just as it was not from
Shakespeare's experience and senses that the poems and plays
derived. The biography of Shakespeare is the biography of his
art, his intellect, and his imagination; and if he writes better
as he grows older it is because they too have grown older,
along with a heart which there is no reason for supposing to
have been otherwise than normal.

> He had the dialect and different skill,
> Catching all passions in his craft of will. (125-6)

This couplet from "A Lover's Complaint" describes its author, if Shakespeare was its author. In "The Rape of Lucrece" the passions which he catches in his craft of will are heavily caught, like those in the early plays. There is the rhetoric, for instance, of Lucrece's grief as she contemplates the grief of Hecuba and the rest at Troy.

> For sorrow, like a heavy-hanging bell,
> Once set on ringing, with his own weight goes.
> (1493-4)

Sorrow rings ponderously, to the tune of many words, through all of the Histories before "Henry IV," and rings even there in the mind of the sleepless King. Lucrece is the first of Shakespeare's wailing women, just as the poem in which she appears is stiff with the harangue which was Shakespeare's first method in dramatic dialogue. By comparison the music of lamentation in "The Phoenix and the Turtle," after the melody of its gnomic opening, is frigid and brittle. But "The Phoenix and the Turtle" comes later, and, minor masterpiece though it is, Shakespeare did nothing else of its metaphysical kind.

The mechanical imperfection of the sonnets has more than mechanical importance. It is an imperfection with respect to the virtue of evenness, if evenness is a virtue; the sequence is radically uneven, and so is the average sonnet within the series. Only the 71st maintains its music to the ending syllable. The others die as poetry at the couplet; or cease somewhat less suddenly at the close of a quatrain. Again it is as if Shakespeare had recognized that once his burden had been discharged the remainder of the journey could be made by a substitute. Or he may not have recognized this; he may have labored every line. What he was conscious of matters less than what he did and what he did not do. He wrote some of the finest poetry in the language, and he did not write perfect poems. The importance of the twofold fact is that we have a twofold answer to the question concerning the sincerity of his sonnets.

The question whether he wrote them to one or more specific persons with whom he was in love can be answered, for all criticism cares, in the affirmative. Criticism in fact does not care greatly about these persons, because it is not to them or about them that the poetry of the sequence was composed. The man writing may have meant every word he said, even when the words were lame, and possibly most so then. The poet writing brings up, however, a different question, or rather a series of questions. What interested him most as he proceeded? What was he writing about when his deepest imagination was engaged? What are the best sonnets, or the best parts of them, actually saying to the reader?

The man, let us admit, is saying that he feels humbly and sincerely towards the recipient of his unworthy words. Words of any sort would scarcely tell the tale of his unprecedented devotion, least of all these dumb, naked words whose very muteness is but testimony to their speaker's truth. The beloved person is in fact his own poetry. "You alone are you" (84), and there is no more to say. Rival poets may break their brains in an effort after new hyperboles, and for a term you may be impressed; but you will recover your pleasure

> In true plain words by thy true-telling friend. (82)

For I am your slave (57), your vassal (58), I cannot sleep for thoughts and images of you (61); and even when you despise me I shall agree with you,

> With mine own weakness being best acquainted. (88)

But do not despise me because my Muse is tongue-tied (85), or because my praise of you is monotonous.

> Why is my verse so barren of new pride,
> So far from variation or quick change? (76)

There is but one thing to say, and it is absolute.

> Therefore my verse to constancy confin'd,
> One thing expressing, leaves out difference.          (105)

The man in the sonnets speaks thus, and speaks, let us admit, sincerely. But only once does he achieve that kind of excellence which is interesting to criticism. The 71st sonnet is one of the perfect English poems, though it is not among the mighty ones:

> No longer mourn for me when I am dead
> Than you shall hear the surly sullen bell
> Give warning to the world that I am fled
> From this vile world, with vilest worms to dwell.
> Nay, if you read this line, remember not
> The hand that writ it; for I love you so
> That I in your sweet thoughts would be forgot
> If thinking on me then should make you woe.
> O, if, I say, you look upon this verse
> When I perhaps compounded am with clay,
> Do not so much as my poor name rehearse,
> But let your love even with my life decay,
>     Lest the wise world should look into your moan
>     And mock you with me after I am gone.

What, then, is the great poet of the sonnets writing about—unmistakably, whether he knows it or not? He is writing about the world, the largeness of which he has perhaps only recently discovered, and his power to release which in a line he may be only now discovering. The sonnets are not, finally, love poems. They are poems. Their subject is the greatest possible subject, existence: beautiful or ugly, near or remote, celestial or domestic, and sometimes so awesome that its force can be no more than hinted at.

On a certain level Shakespeare would seem to be entertained by a variety of subjects satisfactory in themselves. He is clearly in love with the word "golden." He ranges after faraway images: the lion's paws, the fierce tiger's jaws, the long-liv'd phoenix (19). He considers the stars in their secret influence on the shows of men (15), and he looks forward to the crooked eclipses that foreshadow death (60). Music, the theater, the law, the state of the times—these hold him here and there. And human life has caught his eye: the painful warrior (25), the decrepit father who takes delight in his active child (37), the rider of a tired horse (50, 51), the fancier of hawks and hounds (91), the dyer's hand (111), the misery of lust (129), the transparent deceptions of lovers (138), sick men (140, 147), the careful housewife with her babe (143), and conscience that is born of love (151). The multiplicity of the world has become enormously interesting to the poet of the sonnets.

But on another level there is a single subject. The great single subject of the sonnets is Time, swift-footed, terrible Time that writes death on faces, roots out the work of masonry, fades roses, brings winter after spring, and makes in general the music to which all the world marches groaning to its end. Under the wing of this bloody tyrant (16) Shakespeare has composed the sonnets which the world knows best; in so far as the sequence has unity it is organized about the theme of Time's decay. The deaths of days and seasons, the springing and the withering of plants (and of men as plants), ravaged faces and ravaged shores, the chronicle of wasted time, the poet's own decline and death, the loss of precious friends, woe, loneliness, and doom—these are the grammar of the poet's finest language, a language which he is using to say what has never been said better or with profounder love. For the universe which Time has revealed to Shakespeare is given to the reader in its fullest glory, in rich forms and colors, and to the accompaniment of sounds now as loud as drums but now as gentle as one string, sweet husband to another (8).

> So is it not with me as with that Muse,
> Stirr'd by a painted beauty to his verse,
> Who heaven itself for ornament doth use

> And every fair with his fair doth rehearse,
> Making a couplement of proud compare
> With sun and moon, with earth and sea's rich gems,
> With April's first-born flowers, and all things rare
> That heaven's air in this huge rondure hems.          (21)

So is it not with the poet of the sonnets? So nevertheless it is, whatever the man insists. The man has human love for his subject, and one or more persons for the object of that love. The poet has nothing less than "this huge rondure."

The failure of the couplet in the following sonnet has more than technical significance.

> When to the sessions of sweet silent thought
> I summon up remembrance of things past,
> I sigh the lack of many a thing I sought,
> And with old woes new wail my dear time's waste:
> Then can I drown an eye, unus'd to flow,
> For precious friends hid in death's dateless night,
> And weep afresh love's long since cancell'd woe,
> And moan the expense of many a vanish'd sight:
> Then can I grieve at grievances foregone,
> And heavily from woe to woe tell o'er
> The sad account of fore-bemoaned moan,
> Which I new pay as if not paid before.
>     But if the while I think on thee, dear friend,
>     All losses are restor'd and sorrows end.          (30)

The first twelve lines are an introduction to the last two, which make the statement to which the sonnet has apparently been tending. But only apparently. The twelve lines, with their burden of woe and their slow, mournful movement through foregone sorrows which it is both dreadful and delicious to remember, and their music so skillfully constructed on the ground bass of the letter "o"—those are the lines that Shakespeare has been interested in writing. Not the two others which run with such perfunctory and absurd rapidity to fabricate a concluding statement. The sonnet was not written to say what they say, at any rate by the great poet in Shakespeare. That poet is truly personal in the body of the poem; he is dealing with what interests him, namely his own flowing sorrows and the sweetness of still thought.

So in another case:

> Not marble, nor the gilded monuments
> Of princes, shall outlive this powerful rhyme;
> But you shall shine more bright in these contents
> Than unswept stone besmear'd with sluttish time.
> When wasteful war shall statues overturn,
> And broils root out the work of masonry,
> Nor Mars his sword nor war's quick fire shall burn
> The living record of your memory.
> 'Gainst death and all-oblivious enmity
> Shall you pace forth; your praise shall still find room
> Even in the eyes of all posterity
> That wear this world out to the ending doom.
> > So, till the judgement that yourself arise,
> > You live in this, and dwell in lovers' eyes.　　(55)

Here again the couplet quickens out of step with the poem as a whole, which ends for all practical purposes with the word "doom." Not even the conventional boast that the poet's work will live has been the theme of the sonnet. Shakespeare has been interested in the things that will not live so long—in them, and in the stern music of their crumbling, as if they marched like armies to destruction.

In the 64th sonnet there are two changes of tone and pace.

> When I have seen by Time's fell hand defaced
> The rich proud cost of outworn buried age;
> When sometime lofty towers I see down-razed
> And brass eternal slave to mortal rage;
> When I have seen the hungry ocean gain
> Advantage on the kingdom of the shore,
> And the firm soil win of the watery main,
> Increasing store with loss and loss with store;
> When I have seen such interchange of state,
> Or state itself confounded to decay;
> Ruin hath taught me thus to ruminate,

That Time will come and take my love away.
This thought is as a death, which cannot choose
But weep to have that which it fears to lose.

Not only does the couplet sink into comparative voicelessness, as if one were using it to say what might after all not be true, though it should be said somehow; the twelfth line also falls away, into thinness, into plantiveness, and into a personal key far other than that in which eleven great lines have been written. It is a fine line in its kind, but what the poem says by placing it where it is—at the end of three sonorous quatrains whose rhythm has set a wave of change roaring across the face of the great world—is that the great world is a very different thing from the little world of any man, and that it is vastly more interesting for poetry.

By so much does the caliber of the sonnets at their best surpass in interest the crux of their occasion. At their poorest they are perhaps quite personal in the biographer's sense of that term. At their richest, when the volume of their sound suggests a deep, an almost subterranean hum of energy coming from the dark center of all the power there is, they may be personal too; but they are personal at such times rather to the artist than to the man. Shakespeare had found his subject. It was the universe, pulsing under change.

# HENRY VI

THE three parts of "Henry VI" taken together are a massive and masculine performance. They are built with blocks, as befits the youth of their author. Shakespeare—assuming, as it is still permissible to assume, that he was substantially the sole author—must have learned invaluable lessons from the experience of writing so busy a work, with so many people in it, so many individual and group actions, so many documents from Holinshed to study and trim, so much sheer weight to move. One lesson he had already learned, for "Henry VI" is continuously interesting, not to say exciting. He was to know more, however, about the concealment of machinery and the manipulation of motives.

Here all is explicit. The spring of every action is exposed; each person tells the audience at the top of his voice both what he privately intends and what he means publicly to be understood as intending. Enmities are confessed and clear. Conflicts are obvious, as of large bodies moved up to each other and palpably colliding on an open field. There is no mystery or ambiguity of purpose, there are no uninterpretable acts. The fifteenth century is for Shakespeare a time filled solidly with faction; parties split, feuds rage, and oversized heroes growl at one another's tough throats. Hatred is elementary and theatrical, whether it is the hatred of Gloucester for Winchester, Talbot for Joan of Arc, Margaret for the Duchess of Gloucester and the house of York, Suffolk for Gloucester, York for Clifford, Somerset for York, Warwick for Edward IV, Jack Cade for the nobility, Vernon for Basset, or Red for White. No sounder apprenticeship could have

17

been served by a playwright whose destiny it was to be subtle. Subtlety counts most in one who is capable of plainness. Shakespeare was to have had his plainness, as indeed he was to keep a necessary portion of it to the end. He could have traveled toward his later plays from no better direction than "Henry VI." Toward, for example, "Othello," where the theme of witchcraft taints a whole play from sources somehow hidden, and is not, as here in the persons of Joan and the Duchess of Gloucester, merely an aspect of intrigue or an excuse for calling names.

"Henry VI" assaults both the eye with tableaux and the ear with choral effects. Color is recklessly splashed—Blue versus Tawny, Red versus White. The son who has killed his father and the father who has killed his son (3-II, v) rush on the stage and declare the grossest irony. Mortimer dying in gaol (1-II, v) and York baited like a bear at the stake (3-I, iv) are lugubrious and horrible spectacles. The first part begins with a dead march and the bells of Westminster Abbey tolling for Henry V.

> Hung be the heavens with black, yield day to night!
> Comets, importing change of times and states,
> Brandish your crystal tresses in the sky. . . .
> England ne'er lost a king of so much worth.
> England ne'er had a king until his time. . . .
> He was a king bless'd of the King of kings.

And the tolling of the verse is interrupted only by three messengers from France who enter one after the other with news that runs from bad to worse to worst. The three plays everywhere are plangent. Talbot and his son (1-IV, v, vi, vii) rant to each other in high rhyme, their oaths and their boasts falling antiphonally on our ears until their deaths soon after; when the French take up the chant in their praise; though it is Joan's privilege to end the passage, when its end is due, abruptly.

*Lucy.* But where's the great Alcides of the field,
    Valiant Lord Talbot, Earl of Shrewsbury,
    Created, for his rare success in arms,
    Great Earl of Washford, Waterford, and Valence;
    Lord Talbot of Goodrig and Urchinfield,
    Lord Strange of Blackmere, Lord Verdun of Alton,
    Lord Cromwell of Wingfield, Lord Furnival of Sheffield,
    The thrice-victorious Lord of Falconbridge;
    Knight of the noble Order of Saint George,
    Worthy Saint Michael, and the Golden Fleece;
    Great marshal to Henry the Sixth
    Of all his wars within the realm of France?
*Joan.* Here is a silly stately style indeed!
    The Turk, that two and fifty kingdoms hath,
    Writes not so tedious a style as this.
    Him that thou magnifi'st with all these titles
    Stinking and fly-blown lies here at our feet.

                        (1-IV, vii, 60-76)

Joan for this instant anticipates the criticism of his own heroic style which Shakespeare will delegate in later plays to the Bastard Faulconbridge and to Hotspur, not to speak of Ancient Pistol. But the criticism goes in large part unheard. The enemies of York yell a chorus of insults at him as he dies; King Henry wanders over the battlefields singing endlessly of the shepherd's life which he envies:

    Would I were dead! if God's good will were so;
    For what is in this world but grief and woe?
    O God! methinks it were a happy life,
    To be no better than a homely swain;
    To sit upon a hill, as I do now,
    To carve out dials quaintly, point by point,
    Thereby to see the minutes how they run,
    How many makes the hour full complete,
    How many hours bring about the day,
    How many days will finish up the year,
    How many years a mortal man may live. (3-II, v, 19-29)

Henry's long woe sounds forward to the exquisite elegies of Richard II, but it is not so exquisite, or so nicely adjusted to

dramatic necessity. And the stichomythia of the wooing scene
between Edward IV and Lady Grey (3-III, ii) is permitted to
become monotonous as never again in Shakespeare.

The prevailing style of the verse is stiff, in harmony with
the "antient, unlettered, martial nobility," says Dr. Johnson,
who deliver it with undifferentiated voices. The unit of utterance is regularly the line; each of the lines stands sturdily like
a tree, and falls as stolidly. Breath is taken at measured inter-
vals; the drums never tire of beating; and the poet seldom
hesitates to pad for the sake of rhythm, which means that
most of his dialogue is undistinguished:

> One drop of blood drawn from thy country's bosom
> Should grieve thee more than streams of foreign gore.
> Return thee therefore with a flood of tears,
> And wash away thy country's stained spots.
>
> (1-III, iii, 54-7)
>
> Speak, Winchester, for boiling choler chokes
> The hollow passage of my poison'd voice.  (1-v, iv, 120-1)
>
> Hast thou not worldly pleasure at command,
> Above the reach or compass of thy thought?
> And wilt thou still be hammering treachery,
> To tumble down thy husband and thyself
> From top of honour to disgrace's feet?        (2-I, ii, 45-9)
>
> What louring star now envies thy estate,
> That these great lords and Margaret our queen
> Do seek subversion of thy harmless life?     (2-III, i, 206-8)
>
> But that the guilt of murder bucklers thee
> And I should rob the deathsman of his fee,
> Quitting thee thereby of ten thousand shames,
> And that my sovereign's presence make me mild,
> I would, false murd'rous coward, on thy knee
> Make thee beg pardon for thy passed speech
> And say it was thy mother that thou meant'st.
>
> (2-III, ii, 216-22)
>
> The gaudy, blabbing, and remorseful day
> Is crept into the bosom of the sea;

And now loud-howling wolves arouse the jades
That drag the tragic melancholy night;
Who, with their drowsy, slow, and flagging wings,
Clip dead men's graves, and from their misty jaws
Breathe foul contagious darkness in the air.    (2-IV, i, 1-7)

"Come, 'the croaking raven doth bellow for revenge,'" cried
Hamlet to the player ten years later. Hamlet had outgrown
this stuffed verse, these labored lines that drag their way so
wearisomely up a stubborn hill. But the personages of "Henry
VI" insist on speaking so, and there is a certain grandeur in
their will, even though their accents are all alike and sincerity
can never be distinguished from insincerity. Henry means his
rhetoric over the death of Gloucester, and Margaret does not
mean hers (2-III, ii), but the verse of neither would tell us
this, just as the epithets which the style of the play makes so
inevitable—"Thou ominous and fearful owl of death," "Obscure and lousy swain," "Rebellious hinds, the filth and scum
of Kent," "Outcast of Naples, England's bloody scourge"—
fail to identify their speakers in the way that Othello, Lear,
Timon, and Coriolanus are identified by theirs. There are ex-
ceptions to the rule. Suffolk and Margaret saying farewell
achieve a surprising concentration:

> Even as a splitted bark, so sunder we;
> This way fall I to death.
>                         This way for me.
>                 (2-III, ii, 411-12)

But the rule is the rule of Marlowe, and Shakespeare honors
it like law. So in the same sign he packs his pages with the
names of animals—bull, mule, mouse, dog, lion, bee, dove,
sheep, wolf, horse, ox, leopard, owl, deer, cur, fox, lamb,
raven, calf, eagle, kite, chicken, spider, snake, wren, heifer,
partridge, lizard, ostrich, bear, crow, falcon, adder, tiger,
toad, bug, hare—and with fine figures out of classical story—
Venus, Astraea, Adonis, Rhodope, Memphis, Darius, Cyrus,
Tomyris, Hercules, Hector, Hecate, Icarus, Calydon, Asca-

nius, Dido, Jove, Agamemnon, Achilles, Ajax, Nestor, Ulysses,
Diomede, and a dozen others.

Certain themes, however, that in the future are to be very
much his own are announced in "Henry VI."

> How irksome is this music to my heart!
> When such strings jar, what hope of harmony?
>
> (2-II, i, 55-6)

So the King speaks of civil discord, which Shakespeare is always to present as musical discord; unless he presents it, not
only here but in "Richard II," through another medium, the
image of an infested garden. Weeds and caterpillars, but particularly caterpillars, are here a potent symbol of disorder and
political disease, as in "Richard II" the worst name that the
King's favorites can be called will be "the caterpillars of the
commonwealth." And then, significantly early in "Henry VI"
(1-I, i, 51), comes the line

> And none but women left to wail the dead.

The burden of grief which Lucrece bequeathed to so many
women in the plays is taken up first of all by Queen Margaret,
who in her youth is possessed of a fatal and brilliant beauty
which is magic and death to Suffolk, and who in her prime is
a mighty contriver ("She-wolf of France," "O tiger's heart
wrapt in a woman's hide!"), but who will wail throughout
"Richard III" as indeed already she wails here.

> Oft have I heard that grief softens the mind
> And makes it fearful and degenerate,    (2-IV, iv, 1-2)

she cautions herself as she commences her outcry over the
head of Suffolk. But she is no more sure than Shakespeare ever
is that grief corrupts the spirit. It is one of his favorite questions. So is it one of hers; and meanwhile she gives herself over
to lamentation for her dead lover, as later she rears like a
Fury at the disinheriting of her son, and as still later she

howls upon the stabbing of this son by Edward, Richard, and Clarence.

> Why should she live, to fill the world with words?
>
> (3-v, v, 44)

asks Richard on the last occasion. For his own comfort he should have killed her, because his own play will be filled with her bitter words, and men will stand aghast at what she can utter, as better men will stand aghast at Constance in "King John."

King Henry here is woefully out of place, an ageless lamb among the gray wolves of his generation.

> No sooner was I crept out of my cradle
> But I was made a king, at nine months old.
> Was never subject long'd to be a king
> As I do long and wish to be a subject.    (2-iv, ix, 3-6)

The longing has perpetuated his infancy, so that he can express himself only with sighs, tears, and prayers, and with protestations against strife which nobody heeds. Margaret, coming from France with Suffolk, had expected Henry to be such a man as wooed her in the tournament at Tours:

> But all his mind is bent to holiness,
> To number Ave-Maries on his beads.
> His champions are the prophets and apostles,
> His weapons holy saws of sacred writ,
> His study is his tilt-yard, and his loves
> Are brazen images of canonized saints. (2-i, iii, 58-63)

The contrast between him and his colleagues in the play is all too plainly marked, as when for instance his pious plaint that Vernon and Basset should be quarreling in his presence:

> Good Lord, what madness rules in brainsick men . . .
> Good cousins both, of York and Somerset,
> Quiet yourselves, I pray, and be at peace,

is balanced by Gloucester's stout rebuke:

> Presumptuous vassals, are you not asham'd
> With this immodest clamorous outrage
> To trouble and disturb the King and us?
>
> (1-IV, i, 111-27)

Carrying in his frail body a "heart drown'd with grief" and
practiced in self-pity, Henry is a study for Richard II; but
only a study, a faint sketch. He luxuriates like Richard in
thoughts of himself as other than what and where he is; as a
shepherd perhaps, with

> His cold thin drink out of his leather bottle,
> His wonted sleep under a fresh tree's shade;
>
> (3-II, v, 48-9)

and he delights to argue in gentle images:

> Look, as I blow this feather from my face,
> And as the air blows it to me again,
> Obeying with my wind when I do blow,
> And yielding to another when it blows,
> Commanded always by the greater gust;
> So is the lightness of you common men.
>
> (3-III, i, 84-9)

But he exists only for contrast; his weakness, unlike the weakness of Richard, has no fascinating, no dramatic force.

There is nothing but difference between him and the pungent Talbot who scatters epithets and oaths across one portion
of the cycle:

> Pucelle or puzzel, dolphin or dogfish,
> Your hearts I'll stamp out with my horse's heels,
> And make a quagmire of your mingled brains;
>
> (1-I, iv, 107-9)

and who takes a fierce pleasure in spectacles of his own de-
vising:

> Bring forth the body of old Salisbury,
> And here advance it in the market-place,
> The middle center of this cursed town.

Now have I paid my vow unto his soul;
For every drop of blood was drawn from him
There hath at least five Frenchmen died tonight.

(1-II, ii, 4-9)

Or between him and the sturdy logician Jack Cade, who in
his rebellion against the nobility argues from the fact that
poor men have been hanged because they could not read
(2-IV, vii, 47-8) to the principle that all who can read shall
lose their heads. Or between him and "dogged York, that
reaches at the moon," who locks his counsel in his breast and
bides his time in silent secrecy until his house shall have two
kings on the English throne. York's motto is "I must dis-
semble."

My brain more busy than the laboring spider
Weaves tedious snares to trap mine enemies.

(2-III, i, 339-40)

In which respect he is only a patch on his son who will be
Richard III, and whose brilliant emergence as a character from
this crowd of persons who are so appallingly alike is the most
interesting thing about the second and third parts of "Henry
VI." He has the power to make them prologues to his own
play, so that the trilogy proper is "Henry VI 2-3" and "Richard III." At his first appearance he is struck at like a snake:

Hence, heap of wrath, foul indigested lump,
As crooked in thy manners as thy shape!

(2-V, i, 157-8)

He is the first character in Shakespeare to achieve his own
form, to have sinuous and purposeful movement controlled
from within. His being hunch-backed and a "foul stigmatic"
makes success relatively easy. Yet the success is real. Richard's
force is felt from the first as something mysteriously and ma-
lignly different from that of the stuffed heroes who stand so
erect around him. He is picturesque:

For you shall sup with Jesu Christ tonight.

(2-v, i, 214)

He is melodramatic with a vengeance, as when he brings Somerset's head into Parliament (3-1, i) and waits for the most
effective moment to give it in evidence of his prowess during
the recent battle. His eloquence, unlike that of the other
heroes, has an intellectual edge; he can prove the impossible
(3-1, ii, 20-1), and there is always something in his speech
that can revive the spirits of his family; he can make anybody
believe anything. His epithets may not roar, but they really
cut. Margaret has art enough to call him "a foul mis-shapen
stigmatic," a "toad," and a "lizard." He has the deadlier art to
call her "Iron of Naples hid with English gilt" (3-11, ii, 139).
He can crouch and lie with the smoothest smile of irony on
his face. We know what he thinks of Edward's marriage to
Lady Grey and how he intends to use it for his own advance-
ment; yet when Edward asks him in public whether he is offended he puts his brother off with misleading mockery:

> Not I.
> No, God forbid that I should wish them sever'd
> Whom God hath join'd together; ay, and 't were pity
> To sunder them that yoke so well together.  (3-IV, i, 20-3)

His hatred is brilliant, his guile diabolical; and his next move
is never apparent to those who watch him. "He's sudden, if a
thing comes in his head," says Edward (3-v, v, 86) when
Richard has disappeared to make his bloody supper of old
Henry in the Tower.

Richard is of course a roaring devil in an old play. He has
his set speeches in which he assures the audience of his villainy; he will "set the murderous Machiavel to school" and
frame his face to all occasions; he has neither pity, love, nor
fear; because he was born with teeth he will snarl and bite and
play the dog. "Why, I can smile, and murder whiles I smile."
"I have no brother, I am like no brother." "I am myself

alone." He is as much of the stage as Aaron the Moor, and on another level as Iago. But it is not his set speeches that measure his force. It is his suddenness when things come in his head, it is his serpentlike appearances and disappearances, it is his way of moving. With him wriggling under his hand Shakespeare is ready to write the youthful masterpiece of "Richard III."

# RICHARD III

RICHARD is a brilliant villain, and he is all the more brilliant because he is seen and heard against a wall of stone music made by the many other persons in the play whose constant opposition to him is massed and loud. The individual who emerged so slowly from "Henry VI" now moves swiftly under his own power. But the choral tendency of "Henry VI" comes also to its climax here, so that the spectacle is of a lithe serpent coiling and uncoiling along the gray base of a masonry not to be weakened at last even by all the poison he can set working. The conduct of the drama is simple and every effect is pursued to the extreme; the play is long and sometimes laborious; but the total achievement has its magnificence.

The chorus against Richard consists chiefly of women's voices. The heavy-hanging bell of sorrow starts ringing in the second scene, when Anne's curses accompany the actual bells that are tolling for the funeral of her father-in-law, Henry VI.

> O cursed be the hand that made these holes!
> Cursed the heart that had the heart to do it!
> Cursed the blood that let this blood from hence!
>
> (I, ii, 14-16)

Each line is a full swing of the metal, and the notes—curse, heart, and blood—echo one another within the passage. Anne is wooed on the spot by the object of her curses, and cleverly won; but the dire sound of bronze is to be all the deeper in her life as a result. In IV, i, she remembers how she had wished for Richard a sorrow-haunted bed; and realizes that it is her own sorrow which haunts it:

28

> For never yet one hour in his bed
> Did I enjoy the golden dew of sleep.   (iv, i, 83-84)

The worst of all woes is now befalling her: she is to become Richard's queen, and his "timorous dreams" that have interrupted her rest will give place to venomous nightmares; for Richard III, like Macbeth, never sleeps.

Elizabeth, Edward's queen and soon his widow, can say as early as the third scene of the play:

> Small joy have I in being England's Queen.
>
> (i, iii, 110)

For Gloucester has baited and scorned her from the first, and he has just ended a series of insults which will motivate her outbreak later on:

> Ay me, I see the ruin of my house!
> The tiger now hath seiz'd the gentle hind;
> Insulting tyranny begins to jut
> Upon the innocent and aweless throne.
> Welcome, destruction, blood, and massacre!
> I see, as in a map, the end of all.        (ii, iv, 49-54)

Nor are we permitted to forget that the old Duke of York had had a wife. The mother of Edward, Clarence, and Richard, absent from "Henry VI," comes howling in to be the Hecuba of this shambles.

> O my accursed womb, the bed of death! . . .
> Eighty odd years of sorrow have I seen.  (iv, i, 54-96)

She contributes the hoarsest note to several choruses which she helps to raise, either against Richard or for the victims of his ambition. The first of these is for Clarence and Edward, and it is Elizabeth who begins it:

> Give me no help in lamentation,
> I am not barren to bring forth complaints. (ii, ii, 66-7)

Elizabeth like all the other women speaks of herself as barren of everything save misery; she is fruitful only of death, her womb is a seed-bed of woe. But the help she refuses comes in a chanted abundance from the old Duchess and from Clarence's children:

> *Elizabeth.* Ah for my husband, for my dear lord Edward!
> *Children.* Ah for our father, for our dear lord Clarence!
> *Duchess.* Alas for both, both mine, Edward and Clarence!
> *Elizabeth.* What stay had I but Edward? and he's gone.
> *Children.* What stay had we but Clarence? and he's gone.
> *Duchess.* What stays had I but they? and they are gone.
> *Elizabeth.* Was never widow had so dear a loss!
> *Children.* Were never orphans had so dear a loss!
> *Duchess.* Was never mother had so dear a loss!
> Alas, I am the mother of these griefs!
> Their woes are parcell'd, mine is general. . . .
> Alas, you three, on me, threefold distress'd,
> Pour all your tears! I am your sorrow's nurse,
> And I will pamper it with lamentation.
>
> (II, ii, 71-88)

The strength of this is primitive, like that of the later scene in which the Duchess and Elizabeth assist Anne to recognize the calamity of her having to be Queen. And it would make itself felt only if the actresses in the roles maintained high, monotonous, unaccented voices, the voices of women possessed by grief alone, hollow of every happy growth.

Their music, full enough already for all ordinary purposes, is still however to receive its shrillest addition from the voice of Margaret, the fatal beauty of "Henry VI" who survives in "Richard III" as a "foul wrinkled witch," a lady "altogether joyless." Her apparition in the third scene is so terrible that the "wrangling pirates" of the house of York, who until then have been cursing one another, turn on her as a pack. But they are impotent by comparison. Her imprecations against Rivers, Grey, Hastings, and Vaughan are to be remembered when those men die; Buckingham is rendered utterly helpless:

> My hair doth stand on end to hear her curses;
>
> (I, iii, 304)

Richard she nominates "abortive, rooting hog," "the slave of nature and the son of hell," "that bottl'd spider," and "this poisonous bunch-back'd toad." And for the time being she is Elizabeth's unfeeling enemy—"poor painted queen." Her worst wish is that Elizabeth may survive to join the company of wailing witches of whom she herself is head:

> Long die thy happy days before thy death.
>
> (I, iii, 207)

The prophecy, of course, is amply fulfilled, and the recognition by all the women of its fulfillment leads on to the great lyric scene of the tragedy (IV, iv), following the murder of the young princes in the Tower. Margaret opens the scene gloating over the woes of others:

> So, now prosperity begins to mellow
> And drop into the rotten mouth of death.

To her enter Elizabeth, crying for her tender babes, her unblown flowers, and the old Duchess, who cannot stand under this new weight of agony:

> Dead life, blind sight, poor mortal living ghost,
> Woe's scene, world's shame, grave's due by life usurp'd,
> Brief abstract and record of tedious days,
> Rest thy unrest on England's lawful earth.

Sitting down, she is joined on the earth by Elizabeth; when Margaret, who has remained out of sight, creeps forward to make a third,    If sorrow can admit society.

Their instinct is to curse her as the ancestress of their sorrow; but their judgment is to beg that she now instruct them in the art of which she is so awful a mistress. Elizabeth does the begging:

> O thou well skill'd in curses, stay a while,
> And teach me how to curse mine enemies!

The lesson is simple, however much self-torture it involves:

> Forbear to sleep the night, and fast the day;
> Compare dead happiness with living woe;
> Think that thy babes were sweeter than they were,
> And he that slew them fouler than he is.
> Bett'ring thy loss makes the bad causer worse;
> Revolving this will teach thee how to curse;

and Margaret disappears from the scene. But the secret has been communicated. "Why should calamity be full of words?" asks the Duchess, whose comprehension is still incomplete. Elizabeth explains:

> Windy attorneys to their client woes,
> Airy succeeders of intestate joys,
> Poor breathing orators of miseries,
> Let them have scope! though what they will impart
> Help nothing else, yet do they ease the heart.

The rhyme on which she closes expresses her new-found certainty, as does the direct, clear power of her metaphors, so different in their effect from the mechanical contraries of which the Duchess has delivered herself. The Duchess, however, has learned the lesson too; for when Richard enters with troops bearing drums and trumpets she becomes the occasion for his ordering the instruments to strike up so that the heavens may not hear "these tell-tale women." She only waits for silence to begin her dreadful biography of him; which to be sure he answers with a pun, as later he is to meet Elizabeth's curses with his second tour de force as a wooer—for now he has the ultimate audacity to ask for the hand of Elizabeth's daughter. And he has the ultimate brilliance to obtain it; though the princess Elizabeth is to fall not into his hands but into Harry Richmond's.

The wailing women of "Richard III" are its principal chorus, and there is none more powerful in Shakespeare; but the play has others. The princes pipe briefly but in harmony, small voice to voice. The apparitions which appear to Richard

and Richmond in the last act, and the orations which they deliver to their armies on Bosworth Field—these come in sets,
palpably paired against each other, and spectacularly successful. And the end is a duet by Richmond and Derby in which
four unions are prophesied: York with Lancaster, White with
Red, Richmond with Elizabeth, and Peace with Plenty. Everywhere the forces against Richard are musically massed. The
women carry the burden, and it is stone within their hearts;
but no portion of the play is without its wall of voices at
whose foundation he licks with his serpent's tongue.

The famous soliloquy—"Now is the winter of our discontent"—with which Richard opens the play is an advance upon
any rhetoric so far written by Shakespeare, and it has the further virtue of describing its speaker's special brand of villainy;
we shall hear him expand this initial statement in the scenes
to follow, telling his moves before he makes them and working at all times to induce in those he is about to destroy the
belief that he is their best, their only friend. It is from the
actual exercise of his power, however, that we learn most
about him. He is what no one was in "Henry VI" except
himself, witty; his energy, like that of Shakespeare's best
heroes, is mental. He is therefore both fearful and fascinating.
In his most heartless moments we feel the pulse of his intelligence beating in its hidden chamber, and there is a pleasure,
perhaps guilty, in such intimate recognitions. The cleverness
with which he parries Anne's accusations can be admired in
spite of the fact that it is unscrupulous; the man is without
legitimate defense and he is alone in the world, so that his
repartee comes all at once to seem the one thing that can
save him.

*Anne.*    No beast so fierce but knows some touch of pity.
*Richard.*  But I know none, and therefore am no beast.
*Anne.*    O wonderful, when devils tell the truth!
*Richard.*  More wonderful, when angels are so angry.
                                                    (I, ii, 71-4)

The fallacy of his rejoinder has escaped her; he hastens to cover it with a compliment, and the compliment is so beautiful that we are blinded along with Anne. His wit appears by extension in others: in the second murderer of Clarence, who promises that his mood of mercy will not last long—"this passionate humour of mine . . . was wont to hold me but while one tells twenty" (I, iv, 120-2); and in the "little prating York," Richard's nephew, whose emulation of his uncle's quickness renders his death even more pathetic than that of his brother, who is merely charming. "So cunning and so young is wonderful," remarks Buckingham (III, i, 135), who soon will be himself cast off with Richard's most cutting line:

> I am not in the giving vein today.     (IV, ii, 119)

Nor does Richard fail to divine in what terms he should woo Elizabeth for her daughter. Not only should he be clever; he should refer to that seat of life which for the elder women of the tragedy has come to seem a bed of barrenness, but which the vigor of his imagery may with luck restore:

> *Elizabeth.* Shall I be tempted of the devil thus?
> *Richard.* Ay, if the devil tempt you to do good. . . .
> *Elizabeth.* Yet thou didst kill my children.
> *Richard.* But in your daughter's womb I bury them;
> Where in that nest of spicery they will breed
> Selves of themselves, to your recomforture.
>
> (IV, iv, 418-25)

The fanaticism of the voice and the sweetness of the image conceal the fiendishness, not to say the nastiness, of the intention.

The form of hypocrisy in Richard which keeps him constantly asserting his innocence is so obvious that one would expect it to fool nobody, compact and impressive though the assertions are:

> My tongue could never learn sweet smoothing words.
>
> (I, ii, 169)

Cannot a plain man live and think no harm?        (I, iii, 51)

I am too childish-foolish for this world.         (I, iii, 142)

I do not know that Englishman alive
With whom my soul is any jot at odds
More than the infant that is born tonight.        (II, i, 69-71)

Will you enforce me to a world of cares?          (III, vii, 223)

The last of these lines, however, spoken on a balcony between
two bishops whom at Buckingham's suggestion Richard has
placed there as stage properties proving his disinterest in the
imperial theme, is a reminder that Richard is more than hypo-
critical. He is histrionic. The assertions of his innocence are
always supported by elaborate acting; as much as Hamlet or
Iago he has a genius for entrances and displays. In the scene
of the bishops, as well as in the scenes which have prepared it,
he has Buckingham for an assisting cast. But Buckingham is a
coarse amateur, and Richard elsewhere plays alone. The bar-
ing of his breast to Anne (I, ii) is so gross that it should not
succeed; but his manner of announcing the death of Clarence
(II, i), entering as he does on the heels of a "united league," is
ghastly in its effectiveness, and the startling request for some
of my Lord of Ely's strawberries (III, iv, 32-5) is more than
a device to make his exit with Buckingham appear innocent,
it is talent for acting in its highest and most professional degree. In an aside (III, i, 82) Richard tells the audience that he
is "like the formal vice, Iniquity," who used to gesticulate on
an older stage. But at his best he is not an old-fashioned actor,
as Buckingham finds to his sorrow and as Elizabeth can tes-
tify when to her own amazement she discovers herself willing
that her daughter should marry the devil. He loves his art too
well not to know its finest devices. And his spirits are infec-
tiously high. In spite of themselves people desire to travel with
him in his moods. When he feels thus or so there is no other
way to feel. His merriment before Clarence (I, i) on the subject of Mistress Shore is one of the things that make it im-

possible for Clarence to doubt his good will; and that deepen,
incidentally, the pity we shall feel for Clarence in the Tower
as he recites his dreadful dream.

With all this there is no refinement in Richard's character
viewed as a whole. He is called the devil as often as Iago is,
and as much as Macbeth he suffers from an incapacity for
sleep; like Macbeth too he is visited by visions, and trembles
at the remembrance of prophecies. Superstition is ever-present
in the play; Hastings knows why his footcloth horse stumbled thrice and started when he looked upon the Tower (iii,
iv, 86), and Margaret's curses are everywhere recalled as having enjoyed supernatural sanction. Richard partakes of such
terrors no less than Macbeth partakes of the witches' world.
Yet the effect remains external; it is after all a rather rigidly
constructed villain who falls suddenly, with all his weight, before Richmond's righteous sword. Attractive as his brilliance
makes him, and close to us as he sometimes comes through the
sheer lonely force of his wit, he is nevertheless a murderer by
nature, he likes to kill. Shakespeare has not yet discovered the
secret of a true success in fables of this kind. For true success
the villain must be a hero too, must be a better man than we
at the same time that he is worse. By nature he must be incapable of inflicting death, as Othello and Hamlet are, and as
Macbeth must once have been. That is why his doing so will
terrify us—why Othello, for example, will seem so much more
destructive than Iago. The great stories of murder are about
men who could not have done it but who did. They are not
murderers, they are men. And their stories will be better still
when they are excellent men; not merely brilliant and admirable, but also, in portions of themselves which we infer
rather than see, gentle and godlike. Richard is never quite
human enough. The spectacle over which he presides with
his bent back and his forked tongue can take us by storm, and
it does. It cannot move our innermost minds with the conviction that in such a hero's death the world has lost what once

had been or might have been the most precious part of itself. Richard is never precious as a man. He is only stunning in his craft, a serpent whose movements we follow for their own sake, because in themselves they have strength and beauty. Even the wall against which he curls is not a proof of his reality. It stands impregnable, and it gives forth in its choruses a volume of sound hitherto unmanageable by Shakespeare. And the total result is a magnified answer of effect to effect. It is not, however, a mature achievement in tragedy, nor is Shakespeare for a number of years to be capable of such achievement.

# TITUS ANDRONICUS

"TITUS ANDRONICUS" is no tragedy at all if pity and terror are essential to the tragic experience. Aaron the Moor is the kind of villain concerning whose character there can be no curiosity, and whose deeds therefore cannot be felt as horrible. They do not violate his nature, for there is no nature in him. Nor is Titus an object of increasing pity as his misfortunes mount; he is himself bloody-minded and insensitive, and in fact his misfortunes, rather than mounting, stretch along in a simple series which nothing save ingenuity prolongs. Monstrosities and absurdities abound. Not only is there the butchery of Bassianus, and the descent of Quintus and Martius into the pit, and the mutilation of Lavinia, and the piglike squeak of the nurse as Aaron stabs her, and the amputation of Titus's hand, and the meal of human flesh; there is also the absence of any reason why Chiron and Demetrius in v, ii, should come to Titus's house—any other reason, that is to say, than the author's will to bring them where they can have their throats cut over a basin.

The lack of feeling with which the play is written may have been part of a prescription: the tragedy of blood as a form called only for heaps of death, and sentiment was as much out of place as it is in the modern equivalent, the detective story, which fails as soon as the reader is permitted to have any pity for the victim of poison, bullet, or dagger. The spectator at a tragedy of blood wanted only new shapes of death, and novel devices for revenge.

On the other hand the uniqueness of "Titus Andronicus" among Shakespeare's plays as being the only one that is inhuman may be attributable to the inexperience of its author; if we could at any rate be sure about the time of its concoction we might say that it was a first attempt to do as much as was well done in "Richard III." Or, chronology failing us, we might point to the alien Roman scene, and note the greater success with which Shakespeare, studying under Holinshed, had absorbed a portion of the English past; and suppose that the finer saturation in the Roman scene such as appears in "Julius Caesar," "Antony and Cleopatra," and "Coriolanus" could have come only with maturity. Or as a desperate resort we might dally with the proposition that "Titus Andronicus" was a conscious parody of the tragedy of blood considered as a current form.

The burial of Titus's sons in the first scene is not without a certain smoky splendor, and the play is not without its successful lines:

> What, man! more water glideth by the mill
> Than wots the miller of; and easy it is
> Of a cut loaf to steal a shive, we know.       (II, i, 85-7)

This rare excursion into the vernacular follows Demetrius's echo, or anticipation, of Richard III as he watches Anne walk away from the outrageous scene of his courtship. Richard's words are:

> Was ever woman in this humour woo'd?
> Was ever woman in this humour won?

Demetrius multiplies the phrase perhaps too far:

> She is a woman, therefore may be woo'd;
> She is a woman, therefore may be won;
> She is Lavinia, therefore must be lov'd.       (II, i, 82-4)

But he has the accent of a better villain than himself; and elsewhere the verse may be said to surpass itself.

> Some say that ravens foster forlorn children.
> (II, iii, 153)
> Rome is but a wilderness of tigers.       (III, i, 54)

What fool hath added water to the sea,
Or brought a faggot to bright-burning Troy?

(III, i, 68-69)

I'll to thy closet, and go read with thee
Sad stories chanced in the times of old.
Come, boy, and go with me; thy sight is young,
And thou shalt read when mine begin to dazzle.

(III, ii, 82-5)

But let her rest in her unrest a while.        (IV, ii, 31)

Why, what a caterwauling dost thou keep!
What dost thou wrap and fumble in thine arms?

(IV, ii, 57-8)

For all the water in the ocean
Can never turn the swan's black legs to white,
Although she lave them hourly in the flood.

(IV, ii, 101-3)

But we worldly men
Have miserable, mad, mistaking eyes.        (v, ii, 65-66)

The second of these passages carries more than a suggestion of Shylock's "wilderness of monkeys," as does the third of Salisbury's sermon on the painted lily in "King John," and the seventh of Richard II's claim that not all the water in the rough rude sea can wash the balm off from an anointed king, or for that matter of Macbeth's apostrophe to the multitudinous seas. And the sixth, spoken by Aaron, is a surprising exception to the rule of his speech, which never elsewhere is the speech of an audible man.

In general the style, however, is as coarse as burlap. The phrases are from a common stock, and images designed to summon horror summon only the memory of similar images, particularly since the writing in its prolixity keeps the reader reminded that he is a reader:

Here nothing breeds
Unless the nightly owl or fatal raven. . . .
No sooner had they told this hellish tale,
But straight they told me they would bind me here

Unto the body of a dismal yew,
And leave me to this miserable death.        (II, iii, 96-108)

There's not a hollow cave or lurking-place,
No vast obscurity or misty vale,
Where bloody murder or detested rape
Can couch for fear, but I will find them out.   (v, ii, 35-38)

There are shameless tautologies:

That I may slumber in eternal sleep.        (II, iv, 15)

Hath hurt me more than had he kill'd me dead.
(III, i, 92)

The names of animals—tiger, dog, gnat, eagle, bull, lamb, boar, tadpole, lioness, swan, snake, sheep, calf, raven, lark, owl, toad, adder, panther, hart—are employed without either the rough pertinence of "Henry VI" and "Richard III," where the buzzard, the boar, the rat, the cur, the spider, and the toad are at least good rhetoric, or the refined rightness, the indeed perfect pertinence, of the later tragedies. The feigned madness of Titus is without a vocabulary to give it the literary or dramatic force of Hamlet's so much debated mood. Marcus says of his brother:

Alas, poor man! grief has so wrought on him,
He takes false shadows for true substances.
(III, ii, 79-80)

But the presence of "false" and "true" is sign enough that the theme of grief has not yet taken hold of Shakespeare's imagination; when it has, as for instance in "Richard II," Richard and Bolingbroke will not pad their "shadow" and their "substance" with epithets excessive to the theme. The appearance of Lucius as Rome's savior at the end yields no such relief as that which Richmond yields in "Richard III" or Malcolm in "Macbeth"; we are jaded beyond the need of relief, and again Lucius lacks vocabulary. Aaron's technique as a villain is faintly like that of Iago, for he works whenever possible through the desires of other men; but only faintly, since he cannot inspire terror even though he foams at the mouth and blasphemes every virtue. And there is the business of the hounds in ii, ii. Titus begins it:

> The hunt is up, the morn is bright and grey,
> The fields are fragrant and the woods are green.
> Uncouple here and let us make a bay,
> And wake the Emperor and his lovely bride.

And Tamora takes it up in the next scene:

> Replying shrilly to the well-tun'd horns,
> As if a double hunt were heard at once.

Neither Titus nor Tamora achieves anything but the flattest approximation of that music which Theseus and Hippolyta will ring to its last full note from the hounds uncoupled in the fourth act of "A Midsummer Night's Dream." But this only brings us back to the truth that the author of "Titus Andronicus" is as yet an undeveloped poet.

There is still the possibility, though, that he was parodying his contemporaries and himself. If he was, the signature beneath the cartoon is a series of anticlimaxes such as few poets have ever perpetrated. The anticlimax can be, of course, a sign of puerility, of an untrained imagination, of a pen that slips and slides beyond its goal. But it can intend its absurdity, it can tell us that the author is clowning. What principle, if any, determines the order of compliments in Aaron's apostrophe to the absent Tamora?

> This queen,
> This goddess, this Semiramis, this nymph,
> This siren.
>
> (ii, i, 21-3)

Why does Quintus at the pit add that last ineffable line?

> What subtle hole is this,
> Whose mouth is covered with rude-growing briers,
> Upon whose leaves are drops of new-shed blood

> As fresh as morning dew distill'd on flowers?
> A very fatal place it seems to me.          (II, iii, 198-202)

Is it with or without art that Titus descends from high to low and scorns transition?

> I am the sea; hark, how her sighs do blow!
> She is the weeping welkin, I the earth;
> Then must my sea be moved with her sighs;
> Then must my earth with her continual tears
> Become a deluge, overflow'd and drown'd;
> For why my bowels cannot hide her woes,
> But like a drunkard must I vomit them.          (III, i, 226-32)

And could the writer of the following passage, the climax of many anticlimaxes, have been unconscious of the direction it takes? Aaron as usual is boasting of his badness:

> Even now I curse the day—and yet, I think,
> Few come within the compass of my curse—
> Wherein I did not some notorious ill,
> As kill a man, or else devise his death,
> Ravish a maid, or plot the way to do it,
> Accuse some innocent and forswear myself,
> Set deadly enmity between two friends,
> Make poor men's cattle break their necks,
> Set fire on barns and haystacks in the night,
> And bid the owners quench them with their tears.
> Oft have I digg'd up dead men from their graves,
> And set them upright at their dear friends' door,
> Even when their sorrows almost was forgot.
>
> (v, i, 125-137)

The direction is from murder and rape to Hallowe'en pranks; the tendency is that of a clock weight, down. Was Shakespeare sporting with his puppet—giving it a final jerk to prove it merely wood and wool? We shall never be able to answer the question, for we shall never know Shakespeare. But that this is anticlimax, and that this is parody of some sort in the extreme degree, we can be as certain as we are that "Titus Andronicus" is Shakespeare's one unfeeling tragedy.

# THE COMEDY OF ERRORS

"THE COMEDY OF ERRORS" is not Shakespeare's only unfeeling farce. He wrote two others in "The Taming of the Shrew" and "The Merry Wives of Windsor," and a third if "Titus Andronicus" is one. In comedy, says Dr. Johnson, "he seems to repose, or to luxuriate, as in a mode of thinking congenial to his nature." If that is true, it is nevertheless not true of Shakespeare's comedies of situation: plays in which, obedient to the law governing such matters, he confines his interest, or almost confines it, to physical predicament—to things that happen to certain persons not because of who they are but because of what they are. In "The Comedy of Errors" they are not men but twins. The two Antipholuses and the two Dromios exist for no other purpose than to be mutually mistaken. They may groan and seem to go mad in their perplexity, but we only laugh the louder; for it is the figure that gestures, not the man, and our expectation indeed is that the playwright will strain his ingenuity still further in the invention of new tortures, provided new ones are possible. When no others are possible, or when the two hours are up, peace may be restored and the characters may cease to exercise that genius for misunderstanding the obvious which has distinguished them to date. If Shakespeare's spirit reposed in comedy it was not in this kind of comedy. He could write it very well and be hugely funny; but the heart of his interest was elsewhere, and the poet had abdicated.

The poet in "The Comedy of Errors" puffs with unnatural effort, as when for instance he asks us to believe that Aegeon said:

> Though now this grained face of mine be hid
> In sap-consuming winter's drizzled snow,
> And all the conduits of my blood froze up,
> Yet hath my night of life some memory,
> My wasting lamps some fading glimmer left.
>
> (v, i, 311-15)

His rhymes, surviving from an old convention in comedy, rattle like bleached bones. The long verse speeches, whether by Aegeon or by his twin sons, or by Adriana who is wife to one of them and for the most part nothing save the exclamatory wife to be expected in a farce, are stiff and prim and explicit, with no suggestion that their speakers have capacities beyond the needs of asseveration and complaint. Even wit is unnecessary in a play which counts on beatings and beratings to amuse us, and indeed counts rightly. The mental fooling between Antipholus of Syracuse and his Dromio at the beginning of II, ii, is among the dullest things of its kind in Shakespeare. But it does not matter, for to Plautus's idea of twin masters Shakespeare has added the idea of twin servants, and there are riches in the fourfold result which he can mine by manipulation alone. Dromio of Syracuse, to be sure, makes excellent verbal use of his fat kitchen wench: "She is spherical, like a globe; I could find out countries in her." And Antipholus of Ephesus can call names almost as vigorously as Petruchio does in "The Taming of the Shrew":

> Along with them
> They brought one Pinch, a hungry lean-fac'd villain,
> A mere anatomy, a mountebank,
> A threadbare juggler and a fortune-teller,
> A needy, hollow-ey'd, sharp-looking wretch,
> A living dead man.                    (v, i, 237-41)

Yet there is no more need for such eloquence than there is for characters possessing qualities in excess of those required by the situation, or for verisimilitude in the plotted action. "What I should think of this, I cannot tell," says Antipholus of Syracuse (III, ii, 184). What he should think of course is that his twin brother has turned up. He does not so think for the simple reason that he is in a conspiracy with Shakespeare to regale us with the spectacle of his talent for confusion.

The minds of these marionettes run regularly on the supernatural, on magic and witchcraft; but with the difference from "Henry VI" that there is no suggestion of vast state intrigues, and with the still more interesting difference from "A Midsummer Night's Dream" and "Othello" that no special atmosphere is created, whether charming or terrible. "This is the fairy land," whines Dromio of Syracuse (II, ii, 191); "We talk with goblins, owls, and sprites." Dromio is consciously exaggerating; his world, like the world of the play, remains matter-of-fact, however frequent the angry references to jugglers, sorcerers, witches, cheaters, mountebanks, mermaids, wizards, conjurers, and the several fiends of folklore with their drugs and syrups, their nail-parings and pinpoint drops of blood. Cheaters is the word—pretenders to supernatural power, citizens in side streets who prey on the gullible. The play itself is never tinctured; farce must keep its head. So the ludicrous repetition throughout IV, i, of two plain words, "the chain," achieves no effect resembling that achieved by two plain words, "the handkerchief," in a scene to come; and Angelo the goldsmith's remark, "I knew he was not in his perfect wits" (V, i, 42), carries no such burden of meaning as is carried by Lear's "I fear I am not in my perfect mind."

Nor is the business of the shipwreck which has separated Aegeon from one of his sons more than a hint of the shipwrecks which in the last plays will be so beautiful and awful, and so important somehow to the life of Shakespeare's imagination. This catastrophe occurs only as a device to get twins separated, and to start the machinery of farce revolving. Yet it occurs. And Aegeon for all his bad poetry wrings a few drops of pathos from it. So Adriana for one moment, if only for one moment, outgrows her shrewish mold:

> Ah, but I think him better than I say. . . .
> Far from her nest the lapwing cries away.
> My heart prays for him, though my tongue do curse.
>
> (IV, ii, 25-8)

There is a touch in her here of Beatrice, as well as of Shakespeare's silent heroines. And the lyric voice of her sister Luciana has perhaps no place at all in Ephesus, city of slapstick. Such elements, few and feeble though they are, point ahead to the time when Shakespeare will have found the kind of comedy in which his nature can repose, and to the year when he will have another try at twins but will make one of them a girl and give her the name Viola.

# THE TAMING OF THE SHREW

WHEN Petruchio the woman-hater is asked what gale blows him from Verona to Padua he answers airily, being a free and happy fellow with no other care than the need to find himself a wealthy wife:

> Such wind as scatters young men through the world
> To seek their fortunes farther than at home
> Where small experience grows. (I, ii, 50-2)

The hilarious piece of which he is hero might so far, then, be such an excursion into the romantic universe of young Italian adventure as "The Two Gentlemen of Verona" is; for that experiment, of about the same age as "The Shrew," starts also with youthful blades whetting their edges on the wheel of travel.

But Petruchio is hero of a farce, not of a romance. Comedy is made once more from situation: a shrew is to be tamed, a man is found to tame her, and he proceeds to do so by as many devices as can be developed in the time available. The interest of the audience will be in the devices, not in the persons who work them or upon whom they are worked. A certain callousness will be induced to form in the sensibilities of the beholder, so that whereas in another case he would be outraged he will now laugh freely and steadily for two hours. The practitioner in farce, no less than the practitioner in melodrama, must possess the art of insulating his audience's heart so that it cannot be shocked while the machinery hums.

"The Taming of the Shrew," however, has a deep and curious interest such as "The Comedy of Errors" nowhere has. Formally it is as much a farce, and leans as frankly on a doctrine which Shakespeare must have adopted in cold blood, for on the evidence of the other plays it was not his own. This is the doctrine of male superiority, which Luciana had expressed in "The Comedy of Errors" when she reminded Adriana that men "are masters to their females" (II, i, 24), and which Petruchio expresses here not only when he declares of Katherine that

> She is my goods, my chattels; she is my house,
> My household stuff, my field, my barn,
> My horse, my ox, my ass, my any thing     (III, ii, 232-4)

but indeed at all times and by all his actions; nor does Katherine fail at the end to agree. Yet the resulting play, as its popularity attests, is strangely and permanently interesting.

This is because it has hit the relation of the sexes at its livest point. Shakespeare hit the point again, and classically for him, in the story of Beatrice and Benedick; but even now he is master of the theme that lies in the war between love and pride, in the perhaps perversely fascinating spectacle of intellect and will being brought into line with instinct. Love stories are never so engaging as when their principals do not wish to love, and particularly when it is their power that prevents them. For one thing, we are never so sure as then that love is genuine; and for another, there is a peculiar delight in discovering that two persons have mistaken attraction for repulsion, and in listening to the reverse language of raillery which they employ in place of lisps and sighs. The best lovers are witty lovers who bury their perturbation under abuse; at least this is true for comedy, and by all means it is the case where situation is the thing.

Our secret occupation as we watch "The Taming of the Shrew" consists of noting the stages by which both Petruchio and Katherine—both of them, for in spite of everything the business is mutual—surrender to the fact of their affection. Shakespeare has done this not by violating his form, not by forgetting at any point to write farce, and least of all by characterizing his couple. He has left them man and woman, figures for whom we can substitute ourselves, and that is precisely what we do as we commence to understand why Katherine wants so badly to hear Bianca talk of her suitors, even beats her because she will not; as we read reservations into her scorn of Petruchio; as we wait to see her give Petruchio (v, i) his first quiet kiss; and as we assume behind Petruchio's roughness a growing attachment to this woman he is so deliciously—we must confess it—torturing. Shakespeare has done what he has done somewhat as a general takes a city: by sheer strength, in utter confidence, and with the soundest knowledge of our outstanding weakness.

Both the man and the woman are brilliant of tongue. She can call him "a mad-cap ruffian and a swearing Jack," "a frantic fool," "a mad-brain rudesby." But his high spirits carry him as far as genius. His anger, real or pretended, leads him to the limits of language:

> You peasant swain! You whoreson malt-horse drudge!
> (IV, i, 132)
> A whoreson beetle-headed, flap-ear'd knave! (IV, i, 160)

> Why, this was moulded on a porringer. . . .
> Why, 't is a cockle or a walnut-shell,
> A knack, a toy, a trick, a baby's cap. (IV, iii, 64-7)

> Why, thou say'st true; it is a paltry cap,
> A custard-coffin, a bauble, a silken pie. (IV, iii, 81-2)

> What's this? A sleeve? 'T is like a demi-cannon.
> What, up and down, carv'd like an apple-tart?
> Here's snip and nip and cut and slish and slash,
> Like to a censer in a barber's shop. (IV, iii, 88-91)

The language of the play, or at any rate of the play as it concerns Katherine and Petruchio, is everywhere vigorous and vernacular, and healthily grown over with tough local terms.

We hear of a chestnut in a farmer's fire, of boys with bugs, of hazel-twigs and hazel nuts, of kersey boot-hose, of horses shoulder-shotten and begnawn with the bots, of sops thrown in the sexton's face, of apples and oysters, of a bottom of brown thread, of rush-candles, and of parsley in the garden to stuff a rabbit. Petruchio's crowning harangue against the tailor is stuck as full of such terms as a ham with cloves:

> Thou liest, thou thread, thou thimble,
> Thou yard, three-quarters, half-yard, quarter, nail!
> Thou flea, thou nit, thou winter-cricket thou! . . .
> Away, thou rag, thou quantity, thou remnant.
>
> (IV, iii, 107-12)

But the servants also are accomplished in the speech of their region, which it goes without saying is not Italy. And the Induction, wherein Christophero Sly awakes from his sleep to be Bottom in a lord's bedchamber, is as local as an inn-yard, a broken fence, a yawning dog, with its talk of old Sly's son of Burton Heath, Marian Hacket the fat ale-wife of Wincot, Peter Turph, and Henry Pimpernell. The Induction contains several of Shakespeare's later themes—music, the voices of hounds, dreams and delusions, and instructions to players; but significantly enough they are restrained within the bounds of farce, they are enriched with none of the later meaning. The hounds are hunting-dogs, music is a household affair, and dreams are funny.

But the comedy has never strayed from its path, unless the insipid second story of Bianca and her suitors is to be considered an attempt, by Shakespeare or by someone else, to save the whole for romance. It is not saved. A play in which the heroine can be called a devil, a wench, a fiend of hell, a rotten apple, a thing to be boarded, an irksome brawling scold, a wild-cat, and in which we nevertheless take the purest pleasure, has in fact been saved, but saved as farce. How otherwise could we behold so callously the wringing of ears and the knocking of heads which appear to be Petruchio's natural habits—and his servants', and Katherine's, for she ties her sister's hands and strikes at least three persons before she settles down? As for the settling down, there is that last long speech of hers in which she declares the humble duty of a wife in terms which would be painful to us were she a person as Portia and Imogen are persons. Katherine is a shrew. She has been tamed. And the logic of farce is that she should say so.

# THE TWO GENTLEMEN OF VERONA

IN its kind "The Two Gentlemen of Verona" is not nearly as good as "The Taming of the Shrew" is in the kind called farce. But Shakespeare will soon do better in the kind he now discovers, and with one exception, "The Merry Wives of Windsor," he is never to follow any other. "The Two Gentlemen of Verona" is a slight comedy and it minces uncertainly to an implausible conclusion, but it is Shakespeare's own and it sets his course. His problem henceforth is not to keep his fun outside the range of feeling but to keep his feeling within the range of fun; or rather it is to mingle them so that wit and emotion are wedded in an atmosphere which is as grave as it is smiling, as golden as it is bright. This atmosphere, so natural to man's life, so easy to breathe, and so mellow in its hue, is uniquely Shakespeare's, and it will be sufficient for his purposes in comedy; in its amber light he can go anywhere and consider everything, and his people can speak with the richest variety. Its elements are scarcely compounded in "The Two Gentlemen of Verona," which is only a copy of what is to come; but for that very reason they are separately recognizable, they can be witnessed in the process of creation.

Valentine's opening speech announces the tone as he discourses to his fellow-gentleman concerning the advantages of travel. "Such wind as scatters young men through the world" will soon blow both the heroes—rather stiff and humorless figures, newborn in Shakespeare's comic universe—from Verona to Milan, where one of them will forget his beloved Julia and plot to steal the other's Silvia. So far they are at peace, and their voices move lightly through the cadences of a graceful, breeze-haunted music. Valentine's speech is indeed a poem:

> Cease to persuade, my loving Proteus.
> Home-keeping youth have ever homely wits.
> Were 't not affection chains thy tender days
> To the sweet glances of thy honor'd love,
> I rather would entreat thy company
> To see the wonders of the world abroad
> Than, living dully sluggardiz'd at home,
> Wear out thy youth with shapeless idleness.
> But since thou lov'st, love still and thrive therein,
> Even as I would when I to love begin.

The rhyme at the end is amateur, but Valentine has caught the tone which will be heard henceforth in the golden world of gentlemen where Shakespeare's comedy will occur. It is a world whose free and graceful movement finds a symbol for itself in the travel of young men:

> Some to the wars, to try their fortune there;
> Some to discover islands far away;
> Some to the studious universities.           (I, iii, 8-10)

They are awaited somewhere by ladies of fine and disciplined feeling; or they will be followed, as Proteus in the present case is followed by Julia, in brave disguise and be served as pages by the very sweethearts they have lost. The ladies will be accustomed to compliment:

> *Valentine.*                    Sweet lady, entertain him
> To be my fellow-servant to your ladyship. . . .
> *Silvia.*    Servant, you are welcome to a worthless mistress.
> *Proteus.*    I'll die on him that says so but yourself.
> *Silvia.*    That you are welcome?
> *Proteus.*                    That you are worthless.
>                                        (II, iv, 104-15)

In their grace they understand the arts both of bestowing and of receiving praise. And their ideal might be such a man as

Eglamour, whom Silvia invites to be her escort as she follows Valentine:

> Thyself hast lov'd; and I have heard thee say
> No grief did ever come so near thy heart
> As when thy lady and thy true love died. . . .
> I do desire thee, even from a heart
> As full of sorrows as the sea of sands,
> To bear me company.                    (IV, iii, 18-34)

They are not wailing women; their grief is delicate, well-taught, tender, and half-concealed. They are at home in romance: Valentine must climb to Silvia by a corded ladder, Julia must knit up her hair in silken strings with twenty odd-conceited true-love knots (II, vii, 45-6), and there will be outlaws in the dangerous forest—hardly dangerous themselves, once a sweet lady adventures among them. And they live for that love which is both "a mighty lord" (II, iv, 136) and as tenderly capricious as

> The uncertain glory of an April day.    (I, iii, 85)

So do their gentlemen live for love of each other. Friendship is one of the gods here, and he has given laws which Proteus will find it going against the grain to break, so that soliloquies will be necessary before he can comprehend the depth of his default. He has not heard Valentine describe him to the Duke of Milan, but the language would have been familiar:

> I knew him as myself, for from our infancy
> We have convers'd and spent our hours together;
> And though myself have been an idle truant,
> Omitting the sweet benefit of time
> To clothe mine age with angel-like perfection,
> Yet hath Sir Proteus, for that's his name,
> Made use and fair advantage of his days. . . .
> He is complete in feature and in mind
> With all good grace to grace a gentleman.
>                                     (II, iv, 62-74)

It is such a friend that Proteus betrays, and his exclamation at the close, after the reconciliation which no one believes,

> O heaven! Were man
> But constant, he were perfect. That one error
> Fills him with faults,                              (v, iv, 110-2)

covers his untruth to Valentine no less than his abandonment of Julia.

"Heaven-bred poesy," as the Duke puts it, is natural to the mood of this world. And music is so much so that we cannot be surprised to find an excellent sweet song, Who is Silvia, built into the key scene of the play—laced firmly into it with more than simple irony, for Julia, who hears it sung to her rival, does not know that Proteus is pretending to sing it for Thurio. Nor can we fail to note the balances set up here and there—between Julia's coyness (i, ii) and Silvia's (ii, i), between Proteus's concealment of a letter (i, iii) and Valentine's concealment of a ladder (iii, i)—as phrases are balanced in music. And the favorite subjects for quibble are note, burden, sharp, flat, bass, string, and change.

Of quibbles there are many in the play; too many, since they are the only device yet known by Shakespeare for securing the effect of wit and he must overwork them. Valentine and Proteus turn directly in the first scene from talk of travel to an exchange of puns; and the servants, Speed and Launce, are soon at it in their own different fashions. Wit belongs of course in such a world, but this early sample of it is dry and curiously spiritless. It is almost purely verbal. "Your old vice still," says Speed to Launce (iii, i, 283); "mistake the word." Both masters and men, not to speak of Julia with her maid Lucetta, have caught it like the plague. It does not give them the gaiety which their successors in Shakespearian comedy will have, and which will never depend on puns for its expression, though puns will by no means disappear. There is in fact no gaiety in "The Two Gentlemen of Verona" outside of a few scenes dealing with the sensible Launce and his unwanted dog. Launce looks forward not merely to the Launcelot Gobbo whose name he suggests but to a whole line of clowns whose humor is in their hearts and stomachs rather than on their tongues. Speed looks backward to barrenness and will not thrive.

One of the interesting things about "The Two Gentlemen of Verona" is the studies it contains of things to come in Shakespeare. Julia is something like Portia when she discusses suitors with her maid (i, ii), and something like Viola when she discusses herself in disguise (iv, iv). Proteus tells almost as many lies as Bertram does in "All's Well That Ends Well." The Friar Patrick at whose cell Silvia can arrange to meet Eglamour is soon, in "Romeo and Juliet," to change his name to Laurence; and indeed there is already a Friar Laurence here (v, iii, 37). And the forest near Mantua which Valentine finds so much more agreeable than "flourishing peopled towns" is a promise of Arden. But "The Two Gentlemen of Verona" is at best half-grown. Its seriousness is not mingled with its mirth. It has done a great deal in that it has set a scene and conceived an atmosphere. It has done no more.

# LOVE'S LABOUR'S LOST

THE capacities required for the composition of "Love's Labour's Lost" were all but the very highest. They were, to their own loss, purely literary; and this is why, notwithstanding the exquisite skill of the writing, the play is not appreciated. It has no story to tell, or if it has one it tells it artificially. It counts on contemporary occupations with style—occupations now generally forgotten—to keep it interesting; it is Shakespeare's most topical piece. And its purpose, which is literary satire, is one that in the nature of things can never be long popular. That it is brilliant, high-spirited, and verbally masterful does not save it. That its criticism of current affectation and pedantry is so complete as to preserve those vices in their finest form, and to demonstrate their fascination for Shakespeare himself, not the least of whose qualities is a love of language for its own intoxicating sake, does not quite justify it in the human court. And that the texture of its diction and its rhythm is the work of a superb weaver has not seemed to matter with a world which doubtless is right in demanding of poetry that it be other than satin; even the best satin.

The fable is meager, and it is manipulated entirely in the interest of various styles which the persons were created to practice. The four ladies of France who come on a mission to four gentlemen of Navarre pair off with them as simply as dancers take their partners; and indeed the movement of the play is as formal as that of a minuet. The point is that the four gentlemen have sworn to spend three secluded years in a little Academe of their own, studying deep things which daylight and common sense would never reveal to them. They have taken an oath to see no woman, to eat one meal a day, to fast one day a week, and to sleep only three hours of the twenty-four. They have founded a School of Night, and in defiance of every familiar instinct they aim to come as close as men may come to the angelic disposition. The ladies change all that. Love, both among the nobility of the piece and among the lower orders that have assembled their representatives in the shadow of the Academe, brings daylight in. The gentlemen not only fall in love with the ladies but write sonnets to them which by a palpable stage-mechanism they overhear one another reading aloud. Letters are indited and cross-delivered. Masks are put on and off. No action but is maneuvered so as to let us hear the preposterous—and the beautiful—accents of Elizabethan literary pedantry, a pedantry which at its worst was to die like all such things but which at its best was to ripen into poetry. Great periods of poetry begin with an inordinate self-consciousness, and only gradually attain to the natural.

The King of Navarre's opening lines, addressed to the three young lords who are to keep him company in his studies, like most of Shakespeare's opening lines confess the nature of the play to come. They are brocaded with the gilt of a considered style.

> Let fame, that all hunt after in their lives,
> Live regist'red upon our brazen tombs
> And then grace us in the disgrace of death;
> When, spite of cormorant, devouring Time,
> The endeavour of this present breath may buy
> That honour which shall bate his scythe's keen edge
> And make us heirs of all eternity.

But everyone flourishes a style. Boyet, the French lord who will arrive with the Princess and her three ladies, minces his with wit; Biron, the King's sensible colleague who at last will save him for sanity, understands Boyet perfectly:

This fellow picks up wit as pigeons pease,
And utters it again when God doth please.
He is wit's pedler, and retails his wares
At wakes and wassails, meetings, markets, fairs;
And we that sell by gross, the Lord doth know,
Have not the grace to grace it with such show.
This gallant pins the wenches on his sleeve;
Had he been Adam, he had tempted Eve.
'A can carve too, and lisp; why, this is he
That kiss'd his hand away in courtesy.
This is the ape of form, monsieur the nice,
That, when he plays at tables, chides the dice
In honourable terms; nay, he can sing
A mean most meanly; and in ushering
Mend him who can. The ladies call him sweet;
The stairs, as he treads on them, kiss his feet.
This is the flower that smiles on every one,
To show his teeth as white as whalë's bone;
And consciences, that will not die in debt,
Pay him the due of honey-tongu'd Boyet.

(v, ii, 315-334)

Yet Biron's own speech, a masterpiece buried here along with many others, is as mannered as the man it criticizes, and after the same fashion.

The great style of course is that of Don Adriano de Armado, the "refined traveller of Spain"

> That hath a mint of phrases in his brain;
> One who the music of his own vain tongue
> Doth ravish like enchanting harmony.  (i, i, 166-8)

He prowls in the neighborhood of the court, uttering magniloquent nothings in the nicest prose cadences Shakespeare or any Englishman ever managed. There is nothing more delicious than the music of Don Armado; nothing sillier, and nothing nearer genius. We first hear him in a letter informing the King that "the rational hind" Costard has broken the rule of misogyny with the wench Jaquenetta:

Great deputy, the welkin's vicegerent, and sole dominator of Navarre, my soul's earth's god, and body's fostering patron. So it is, besieged with sable-coloured melancholy, I did commend the black oppressing humour to the most wholesome physic of thy health-giving air; and, as I am a gentleman, betook myself to walk. The time when? About the sixth hour; when beasts most graze, birds best peck, and men sit down to that nourishment which is called supper. . . . But to the place where: it standeth north-north-east and by east from the west corner of thy curious-knotted garden. There did I see that low-spirited swain, that base minnow of thy mirth, that unlettered small-knowing soul, that shallow vassal, which, as I remember, hight Costard, sorted and consorted, contrary to thy established proclaimed edict and continent canon, . . . with a child of our grandmother Eve, a female; or, for thy more sweet understanding, a woman.

                                             (I, i, 221-267)

We next behold him with little Moth, his page, from whom he seeks to wring the comfort of knowledge concerning great lovers—Hercules, Samson—of other days; for by an obvious irony he himself has been smitten with Jaquenetta. "Define, define, well-educated infant," he implores the patient Moth. "Sing, boy; my spirit grows heavy in love." Left alone on the stage he can appeal only to the Muses: "Assist me, some extemporal god of rhyme, for I am sure I shall turn sonnet. Devise, wit! write, pen! for I am for whole volumes in folio" (I, ii, 188-91). At the beginning of the third act he is with Moth again:

Warble, child; make passionate my sense of hearing. . . . Go, tenderness of years, take this key, give enlargement to the swain, bring him festinately hither. I must employ him in a letter to my love.

There is the letter (IV, i); there is his ineffable order that Holofernes the Pedant prepare a play for the King and the Princess:

Sir, it is the King's most sweet pleasure and affection to congratulate the Princess at her pavilion in the posteriors of this day, which the rude multitude call the afternoon;

and there is his defense of Hector's name against the irreverent lords who at the play have called him greyhound:

The sweet war-man is dead and rotten; sweet chucks, beat not the bones of the buried. When he breathed, he was a man.

If Shakespeare laughed as he wrote these speeches it was among other things for love of them, and for joy in his power to prance so perfectly in step with so sublime a fool. Thus too in the case of Holofernes the Pedant, who when Nathaniel the Curate recites Biron's sonnet to Rosaline is not satisfied with the elocution:

You find not the apostrophas, and so miss the accent: let me supervise the canzonet. Here are only numbers ratified; but, for the elegancy, facility, and golden cadence of poesy, *caret*. Ovidius Naso was the man, and why, indeed, Naso, but for smelling out the odoriferous flowers of fancy, the jerks of invention.

(IV, ii, 123-8)

This also is matchless; and incidentally it is the best compliment Shakespeare could pay the poet in whose name he had written "Venus and Adonis" and "The Rape of Lucrece."

Biron is in the play not only to save his king for sanity but to register Shakespeare's preference for "barbarism," if that must be the word for it, over books. It is Biron's word. Another would be "nature," and still another "sense." Biron makes characteristic use of an exaggerated term, for he too is sophisticated, and his mind sprints to extremes. "How well he's read, to reason against reading!" exclaims the King at the end of an accomplished harangue which Biron has delivered in rhyme (I, i, 72-93) against the program he has vowed to pursue. He will keep his vow as well as any of the four in spite of his clairvoyance at the beginning; his intelligence protests, but his sportsmanship carries him through to the point where the other three learn by experience the truth of his doctrine that the education of a gentleman consists in studying the eyes of ladies.

They sparkle still the right Promethean fire;
They are the books, the arts, the academes,
That show, contain, and nourish all the world.
                                        (IV, iii, 351-3)

He is a merry mad-cap lord, a sketch for Mercutio and Benedick; and like those comedians he salts his speech with household words. It is consonant with the whole tenor of the play
that Biron's resolution at the end should be to reform his
style.

Taffeta phrases, silken terms precise,
Three-piled hyperboles, spruce affectation,
Figures pedantical; these summer-flies
Have blown me full of maggot ostentation.
I do forswear them, and I here protest,
By this white glove—how white the hand, God knows!—
Henceforth my wooing mind shall be express'd
In russet yeas and honest kersey noes.          (V, ii, 406-13)

Even his recantation, however, is dazzling and elaborate, and
the kersey of his speech is everywhere threaded through with
precise silk, whether he be prating against Eros,

This wimpled, whining, purblind, wayward boy;
This senior-junior, giant-dwarf, Dan Cupid,
                                        (III, i, 181-2)

or mimicking the language of love poets:

a hand, a foot, a face, an eye,
A gait, a state, a brow, a breast, a waist,
A leg, a limb,                          (IV, iii, 184-6)

or cursing out the cause of the failure which his masque encounters:

Some carry-tale, some please-man, some slight zany,
Some mumble-news, some trencher-knight, some Dick . . .
Told our intents before.                (V, ii, 463-7)

Except for his lady Rosaline and in less degree the other
ladies he is the only inhabitant of "Love's Labour's Lost" who

talks like a person of this world; Shakespeare obviously likes him and sees more life in him than the play can use. He will reappear in better plays, and indeed there will be something of him in all of Shakespeare's finest poets, Hotspur and Hamlet included. Rosaline here has some of his sense, and the Princess has enough to supply the moral of the comedy:

> None are so surely caught, when they are catch'd,
> As wit turn'd fool; folly, in wisdom hatch'd,
> Hath wisdom's warrant and the help of school
> And wit's own grace to grace a learned fool.   (v, ii, 69-72)

But that is because they are women, and Shakespeare's women are almost never absurd. Neither in most cases do they achieve the eloquence of his best men. They miss the extremes of idiocy and sublimity. Biron has hovered at both of these limits, never occupying either. When he returns he will have been trimmed like Shakespeare himself of certain literary excesses, certain spruce affectations and figures pedantical. That he like Shakespeare will keep others to the end is only further testimony to the fascination which the writing of "Love's Labour's Lost" must have exercised over its author. The play is literary but it is a delight to any listening ear. It is satire, but it has absorbed the best along with the worst of the manners which it satirizes. It is Shakespeare's most artificial work, but it ends with his most natural song:

> When all aloud the wind doth blow
>    And coughing drowns the parson's saw
> And birds sit brooding in the snow
>    And Marian's nose looks red and raw,
> When roasted crabs hiss in the bowl,
> Then nightly sings the staring owl,
>                    "Tu-whit, tu-who!"—
> A merry note,
> While greasy Joan doth keel the pot.

# ROMEO AND JULIET

WHEN Juliet learns that Romeo has killed Tybalt she cries out that he is a beautiful tyrant, a fiend angelical, a dove-feathered raven, a wolfish lamb, a damned saint, an honorable villain. This echoes Romeo's outcry upon the occasion of Tybalt's first brawl in the streets of Verona: brawling love, loving hate, heavy lightness, serious vanity, chaos of forms, feather of lead, bright smoke, cold fire, sick health, still-waking sleep—Romeo had feasted his tongue upon such opposites, much in the manner of Lucrece when wanton modesty, lifeless life, and cold fire were the only terms that could express her mind's disorder. Of Romeo's lines, says Dr. Johnson, "neither the sense nor the occasion is very evident. He is not yet in love with an enemy, and to love one and hate another is no such uncommon state as can deserve all this toil of antithesis." And of the pathetic strains in "Romeo and Juliet" generally Dr. Johnson adds that they "are always polluted with some unexpected depravations. His persons, however distressed, have a conceit left them in their misery, a miserable conceit."

"Romeo and Juliet," in other words, is still a youthful play; its author, no less than its hero and heroine, is furiously literary. He has written at last a tragedy which is crowded with life, and which will become one of the best-known stories in the world; but it is crowded at the same time with clevernesses, it keeps the odor of ink. Images of poison and the grave are common throughout the dialogue, and they fit the fable. The frame of the author's mind is equally fitted, however, by a literary imagery. There is much about words, books, and reading; as indeed there is in "Hamlet," but with a difference. The servant who delivers Capulet's invitations to the feast cannot distinguish the names on his list, and must have Romeo's help (I, ii). Lady Capulet commands Juliet to

> Read o'er the volume of young Paris' face
> And find delight writ there with beauty's pen; . . .
> This precious book of love, this unbound lover,
> To beautify him, only lacks a cover. (I, iii, 81-8)

Romeo's first kiss to Juliet, she remarks, is given "by the book" (I, v, 112). Love can suggest to Romeo (II, ii, 157-8) the way of schoolboys with their books. Mercutio with his last breath accuses Tybalt of fighting by "the book of arithmetic" (III, i, 106). Juliet, continuing in her rage against Romeo because he has killed her cousin, demands to know:

> Was ever book containing such vile matter
> So fairly bound? (III, ii, 83-4)

And words seem to be tangible things. Romeo wishes his name were written down so that he could tear it (II, ii, 57); when the Nurse tells him how Juliet has cried out upon his name it is to him

> As if that name,
> Shot from the deadly level of a gun,
> Did murder her. (III, iii, 102-4)

And the lovers take eloquent turns (III, ii, iii) at playing variations on "that word 'banished,' " which can "mangle" them and is indeed but "death mis-term'd."

Even the wit of Romeo and his friends—or, as Dr. Johnson puts it, "the airy sprightliness" of their "juvenile elegance"—has a somewhat printed sound. When Romeo, going to the ball, wants to say that the burden of his passion for Rosaline weighs him down and makes him less wanton than his friends he resorts once again to the literary idiom:

> For I am proverb'd with a grandsire phrase. (I, iv, 37)

Not that the wit of these young gentlemen is poor. It is Shakespeare's best thus far, and it is as brisk as early morning; the playful youths are very knowing and proud, and speak always—until the sudden moment when lightness goes out of the play like a lamp—as if there were no language but that of sunrise and spring wind.

Lightness goes out suddenly with the death of Mercutio. Yet everything is sudden in this play. Its speed is as great as that of "Macbeth," though it carries no such weight of tragedy. The impatience of the lovers for each other and the brevity of their love are answered everywhere: by Juliet's complaint at the unwieldly slowness with which the Nurse returns from Romeo, by Capulet's testiness as he rushes the preparations for the wedding, by the celerity of the catastrophe once its fuse has been laid.

It is a tragedy in which the catastrophe is everything and so must be both sudden and surprising. Death is not antici- pated by as much as anticipates the ends of Shakespeare's major tragedies: that is to say, by all that has been said or done. A few premonitions are planted. The Prologue warns us that the lovers are star-cross'd, misadventur'd, and death- mark'd. Romeo's mind misgives him as he arrives at Capulet's feast, and he imagines

> Some consequence yet hanging in the stars. (i, iv, 107)

Juliet's couplet when she learns her lover's name,

> My only love sprung from my only hate!
> Too early seen unknown, and known too late!
> (i, v, 140-1)

and her experience of second sight as Romeo descends from her chamber:

> O God, I have an ill-divining soul!
> Methinks I see thee, now thou art below,
> As one dead in the bottom of a tomb (iii, v, 54-6)

are there to light the way towards a woeful conclusion. And
Friar Laurence's moral is clearly underlined:

> These violent delights have violent ends,
> And in their triumph die, like fire and powder,
> Which as they kiss consume.            (ii, vi, 9-11)

But such things are significantly few, and they are external to
the principal tragic effect, which is that of a lightning flash
against the night.

Night is the medium through which the play is felt and in
which the lovers are most at home—night, together with certain fires that blaze in its depths for contrast and romance.
"Romeo and Juliet" maintains a brilliant shutter-movement
of black and white, of cloud and lightning, of midnight and
morning. We first hear of Romeo as one who cherishes the
torch of his love for Rosaline in "an artificial night" of his
own making; he pens himself in his chamber, "locks fair
daylight out," and is for having the world "black and por-
tentous" (i, i). If day is life, as Friar Laurence says it is, then
life is for Romeo the enemy of love, which can exist in its
purity only by itself, in the little death of a private darkness.
Hidden in that darkness it can shine for the knowing lover
with a brightness unknown to comets, stars, and suns. When
he first sees Juliet he exclaims:

> O, she doth teach the torches to burn bright!
> It seems she hangs upon the cheek of night
> As a rich jewel in an Ethiop's ear.         (i, v, 46-8)

"Blind is his love and best befits the dark," jests Benvolio
(ii, i, 32) as he searches with Mercutio for Romeo in Capulet's garden; but Benvolio does not understand the power that
illuminates his friend's progress. In the next scene, standing
with Romeo under the balcony, we reach the lighted goal.

> It is the east, and Juliet is the sun. . . .
> Two of the fairest stars in all the heaven,
> Having some business, do entreat her eyes

To twinkle in their spheres till they return.
What if her eyes were there, they in her head?
The brightness of her cheek would shame those stars,
As daylight doth a lamp; her eyes in heaven
Would through the airy region stream so bright
That birds would sing and think it were not night.

Juliet and love are Romeo's life, and there is no light but they.
Juliet may be disquieted by the thought of so much haste:

It is too rash, too unadvis'd, too sudden,
Too like the lightning, which doth cease to be
Ere one can say it lightens.

But Romeo can only cry, "O blessed, blessed night!" There
follows a scene in which Friar Laurence salutes and blesses
the morning. Yet his voice does not obliterate our memory of
many good-nights the lovers had called to each other, and it is
soon (III, v) Juliet's turn to bless the night that she and
Romeo have had with each other. She cannot admit that day
is coming. Dawn is some mistake, "some meteor." Day, if it is
indeed here, will be as death. And when the Nurse convinces
her that darkness is done she sighs:

Then, window, let day in, and let life out.

For her too love has become the only light; something that
shines with its own strength and from its own source, and
needs night that it may be known. "O comfort-killing Night,
image of hell!" Lucrece had wailed (764). But night is comfort here, and day—when kinsmen fight, when unwelcome
weddings are celebrated, when families wake up to find their
daughters dead—is the image of distress. "O day! O day! O
day! O hateful day!" howls the Nurse when she finds Juliet
stretched out on her bed. She means a particular day, but she
has described all days for the death-mark'd lovers. It is perhaps their tragedy that they have been moved to detest day,
life, and sun.

At any rate their career derives its brilliance from the contrast we are made to feel between their notion of day and night and the normal thought about such things. Normality is their foe, as it is at last their nemesis; the artificial night of Juliet's feigned death becomes the long night of common death in which no private planets shine. The word normality carries here no moral meaning. It has to do merely with notions about love and life; the lovers' notion being pathetically distinguished from those of other persons who are not in love and so consider themselves realistic or practical. One of the reasons for the fame of "Romeo and Juliet" is that it has so completely and clearly isolated the experience of romantic love. It has let such love speak for itself; and not alone in the celebrated wooing scenes, where the hero and heroine express themselves with a piercing directness, but indirectly also, and possibly with still greater power, in the whole play in so far as the whole play is built to be their foil. Their deep interest for us lies in their being alone in a world which does not understand them; and Shakespeare has devoted much attention to that world.

Its inhabitants talk only of love. The play is saturated with the subject. Yet there is always a wide difference between what the protagonists intend by the term and what is intended by others. The beginning dialogue by Sampson and Gregory, servants, is pornographic on the low level of puns about maidenheads, of horse-humor and hired-man wit. Mercutio will be more indecent (II, i, iv) on the higher level of a gentleman's cynicism. Mercutio does not believe in love, as perhaps the servants clumsily do; he believes only in sex, and his excellent mind has sharpened the distinction to a very dirty point. He drives hard against the sentiment that has softened his friend and rendered him unfit for the society of young men who really know the world. When Romeo with an effort matches one of his witticisms he is delighted:

Now art thou sociable, now art thou Romeo, now art thou
what thou art, by art as well as by nature.          (II, iv, 93-5)

He thinks that Romeo has returned to the world of artful wit, by which he means cynical wit; he does not know that Romeo is still "dead" and "fishified," and that he himself will soon be mortally wounded under the arm of his friend—who, because love has stupefied him, will be capable of speaking the inane line, "I thought all for the best" (III, i, 109). Romeo so far remembers the code of his class as to admit for a moment that love has made him "effeminate." Mercutio would have applauded this, but he has been carried out to become worms' meat and Romeo will have the rest of the play to himself as far as his friends and contemporaries are concerned. There will be no one about him henceforth who can crack sentences like whips or set the hound of his fancy on the magic scent of Queen Mab.

The older generation is another matter. Romeo and Juliet will have them with them to the end, and will be sadly misunderstood by them. The Capulets hold still another view of love. Their interest is in "good" marriages, in sensible choices. They are match-makers, and believe they know best how their daughter should be put to bed. This also is cynicism, though it be without pornography; at least the young heart of Juliet sees it so. Her father finds her sighs and tears merely ridiculous: "Evermore show'ring?" She is "a wretched puling fool, a whining mammet," a silly girl who does not know what is good for her. Capulet is Shakespeare's first portrait in a long gallery of fussy, tetchy, stubborn, unteachable old men: the Duke of York in "Richard II," Polonius, Lafeu, Menenius. He is tart-tongued, breathy, wordy, pungent, and speaks with a naturalness unknown in Shakespeare's plays before this, a naturalness consisting in a perfect harmony between his phrasing and its rhythm:

> How how, how how, chop-logic! What is this?
> "Proud," and "I thank you," and "I thank you not;"
> And yet "not proud." Mistress minion, you,

Thank me no thankings, nor proud me no prouds,
But fettle your fine joints 'gainst Thursday next,
To go with Paris to Saint Peter's Church,
Or I will drag thee on a hurdle thither.  (III, v, 150-6)

We hear his voice in everything he says, as when for instance
the Nurse has told him to go to bed lest he be sick tomorrow
from so much worry about the wedding, and he argues:

No, not a whit! What! I have watch'd ere now
All night for lesser cause, and ne'er been sick.

(IV, iv, 9-10)

His speaking role has great reality, along with an abrasive
force which takes the temper out of Juliet's tongue.

The Nurse, a member of the same generation, and in Juliet's
crisis as much her enemy as either parent is, for she too urges
the marriage with Paris (III, v, 214-27), adds to practicality a
certain prurient interest in love-business, the details of which
she mumbles toothlessly, reminiscently, with the indecency of
age. Her famous speech concerning Juliet's age (I, iii, 12-57),
which still exceeds the speeches of Capulet in the virtue of
dramatic naturalness, runs on so long in spite of Lady Capulet's attempts to stop it because she has become fascinated with
the memory of her husband's broad jest:

*Nurse.*          And since that time it is eleven years;
                For then she could stand high-lone; nay, by the
                    rood,
                She could have run and waddled all about;
                For even the day before, she broke her brow;
                And then my husband—God be with his soul!
                'A was a merry man—took up the child.
                "Yea," quoth he, "dost thou fall upon thy face?
                Thou wilt fall backward when thou hast more
                    wit;
                Wilt thou not, Jule?" and, by my holidame,
                The pretty wretch left crying and said, "Ay."
                To see, now, how a jest shall come about!

> I warrant, an I should live a thousand years,
> I never should forget it. "Wilt thou not, Jule?"
>    quoth he;
> And, pretty fool, it stinted and said, "Ay."

*Lady Capulet.* Enough of this; I pray thee, hold thy peace.

*Nurse.*   Yes, madam; yet I cannot choose but laugh,
> To think it should leave crying and say, "Ay."
> And yet, I warrant, it had upon it brow
> A bump as big as a young cockerel's stone;
> A perilous knock; and it cried bitterly.
> "Yea," quoth my husband, "fall'st upon thy face?
> Thou wilt fall backward when thou comest to
>    age;
> Wilt thou not, Jule?" It stinted and said, "Ay."

The Nurse's delight in the reminiscence is among other things lickerish, which the delight of Romeo and Juliet in their love never is, any more than it is prudent like the Capulets, or pornographic like Mercutio. Their delight is solemn, their behavior holy, and nothing is more natural than that in their first dialogue (I, v) there should be talk of palmers, pilgrims, saints, and prayers.

It is of course another kind of holiness than that which appears in Friar Laurence, who nevertheless takes his own part in the endless conversation which the play weaves about the theme of love. The imagery of his first speech is by no accident erotic:

> I must up-fill this osier cage of ours
> With baleful weeds and precious-juiced flowers.
> The earth, that's nature's mother, is her tomb;
> What is her burying grave, that is her womb;
> And from her womb children of divers kind
> We sucking on her natural bosom find.   (II, iii, 7-12)

The Friar is closer to the lovers in sympathy than any other person of the play. Yet this language is as alien to their mood as that of Capulet or the Nurse; or as Romeo's recent agitation over Rosaline is to his ecstasy with Juliet. The lovers are alone. Their condition is unique. Only by the audience is it understood.

Few other plays, even by Shakespeare, engage the audience so intimately. The hearts of the hearers, surrendered early, are handled with the greatest care until the end, and with the greatest human respect. No distinction of Shakespeare is so hard to define as this distinction of his which consists of knowing the spectator through and through, and of valuing what is there. The author of "Romeo and Juliet" watches us as affectionately as he watches his hero and heroine; no sooner has he hurt our feelings than he has saved them, no sooner are we outraged than we are healed. The author of "King Lear" will work to the same end on a grander scale. Here he works lyrically, through our sentiments, which he keeps in trust. Capulet is an old fool, but we can pity him when the false death of Juliet strikes him dumb at last. As for that false death, our being in on the secret does not prevent us from being touched by it, or from needing the relief which the musicians stand by to give. Five short words at Juliet's bier—"O my love! my wife!"—make up for all of Romeo's young errors. Juliet's appeal after her father has stormed out of the room:

> Is there no pity sitting in the clouds,
> That sees into the bottom of my grief?
>
> (III, v, 198-9)

is not to the outer world, it is to us. The tension of the entire play, while we await the kiss of fire and powder which will consume its most precious persons, is maintained at an endurable point by the simplicity with which sorrow is made lyric. Even the conceits of Romeo and Juliet sound like things that they and they alone would say, for we know their fancies to be on fire, and we have been close to the flame. Tolstoy, wishing to deny Shakespeare's supposed "talent for depicting character," said it was nothing but a knack with the emotions. "However unnatural the positions may be in which he places his characters, however improper to them the language which he makes them speak, however featureless they are, the very play of emotion, its increase, and alteration, and the combination of many contrary feelings, as expressed correctly and powerfully in some of Shakespeare's scenes, and in the play of good actors, evokes even, if only for a time, sympathy with the persons represented." Shakespeare, in other words, was merely a great poet with a correct and powerful understanding of the surrendered heart, the listening mind; it is the audience, whom he spares nothing yet handles gently, that he makes over in his own image. Which of the two things he does, creates characters or creates comprehenders of character, may not ultimately matter. At least it is clear that one who has witnessed "Romeo and Juliet" has been taken apart and put together again; has been strangely yet normally moved; has learned a variety of good things about himself; and has been steadily happy in the knowledge.

# A MIDSUMMER NIGHT'S DREAM

"A MIDSUMMER NIGHT'S DREAM" shines like "Romeo and Juliet" in darkness, but shines merrily. Lysander, one of the two nonentities who are its heroes, complains at the beginning about the brevity of love's course, and sums up his complaint with a line which would not be out of place in "Romeo and Juliet":

> So quick bright things come to confusion. (I, i, 149)

This, however, is at the beginning. Bright things will come to clarity in a playful, sparkling night while fountains gush and spangled starlight betrays the presence in a wood near Athens of magic persons who can girdle the earth in forty minutes and bring any cure for human woe. Nor will the woe to be cured have any power to elicit our anxiety. The four lovers whose situation resembles so closely the situation created in "The Two Gentlemen of Verona" will come nowhere near the seriousness of that predicament; they will remain to the end four automatic creatures whose artificial and pretty fate it is to fall in and out of love like dolls, and like dolls they will go to sleep as soon as they are laid down. There will be no pretense that reason and love keep company, or that because they do not death lurks at the horizon. There is no death in "A Midsummer Night's Dream," and the smiling horizon is immeasurably remote.

Robin Goodfellow ends the extravaganza with an apology to the audience for the "weak and idle theme" with which it has been entertained. And Theseus, in honor of whose marriage with Hippolyta the entire action is occurring, dismisses most of it as a fairy toy, or such an airy nothing as some poet might give a local habitation and a name (v, i, 17). But Robin is wrong about the theme, and Theseus does not describe the kind of poet Shakespeare is. For the world of this play is both veritable and large. It is not the tiny toy-shop that most such spectacles present, with quaint little people scampering on dry little errands, and with small music squeaking somewhere a childish accompaniment. There is room here for mortals no less than for fairies; both classes are at home, both groups move freely in a wide world where indeed they seem sometimes to have exchanged functions with one another. For these fairies do not sleep on flowers. Only Hermia can remember lying upon faint primrose-beds (1, i, 215), and only Bottom in the action as we have it ever dozes on pressed posies (III, i, 162). The fairies themselves—Puck, Titania, Oberon—are too busy for that, and too hard-minded. The vocabulary of Puck is the most vernacular in the play; he talks of beans and crabs, dew-laps and ale, three-foot stools and sneezes (II, i, 42-57). And with the king and queen of fairy-land he has immense spaces to travel. The three of them are citizens of all the universe there is, and as we listen to them the farthest portions of this universe stretch out, distant and glittering, like facets on a gem of infinite size. There is a specific geography, and the heavens are cold and high.

*Oberon.*          Thou rememb'rest
          Since once I sat upon a promontory,
          And heard a mermaid on a dolphin's back
          Uttering such dulcet and harmonious breath
          That the rude sea grew civil at her song,
          And certain stars shot madly from their spheres,
          To hear the sea-maid's music?
*Robin.*                              I remember.
*Oberon.* That very time I saw, but thou couldst not,
          Flying between the cold moon and the earth,
          Cupid all arm'd. A certain aim he took
          At a fair vestal throned by the west.

> And loos'd his love-shaft smartly from his bow,
> As it should pierce a hundred thousand hearts;
> But I might see young Cupid's fiery shaft
> Quench'd in the chaste beams of the watery moon,
> And the imperial votaress passed on,
> In maiden meditation, fancy-free.
> Yet mark'd I where the bolt of Cupid fell.
> It fell upon a little western flower. . . .
> Fetch me that flower, the herb I shew'd thee once. . . .
> Fetch me this herb; and be thou here again
> Ere the leviathan can swim a league.
> *Robin.*    I'll put a girdle round about the earth
> In forty minutes.                                    (II, i, 148-76)

The business may be trivial, but the world is as big and as real as any world we know. The promontory long ago; the rude sea that grew—not smooth, not gentle, not anything pretty or poetical, but (the prosaic word is one of Shakespeare's best) civil; the mermaid that is also a sea-maid; the direction west; and the cold watery moon that rides so high above the earth—these are the signs of its bigness, and they are so clear that we shall respect the prowess implied in Robin's speed, nor shall we fail to be impressed by the news that Oberon has just arrived from the farthest steep of India (II, i, 69).

Dr. Johnson and Hazlitt copied Addison in saying that if there could be persons like these they would act like this. Their tribute was to the naturalness of Shakespeare's supernature. Dryden's tribute to its charm:

> But Shakespeare's magic could not copied be;
> Within that circle none durst walk but he

has an identical source: wonder that such things can be at all, and be so genuine. The explanation is the size and the concreteness of Shakespeare's setting. And the key to the structure of that setting is the watery moon to which Oberon so casually referred.

The poetry of the play is dominated by the words moon

and water. Theseus and Hippolyta carve the moon in our memory with the strong, fresh strokes of their opening dialogue:

> *Theseus.* Now, fair Hippolyta, our nuptial hour
> Draws on apace. Four happy days bring in
> Another moon; but, O, methinks, how slow
> This old moon wanes! She lingers my desires,
> Like to a step-dame or a dowager
> Long withering out a young man's revenue.
> *Hippolyta.* Four days will quickly steep themselves in night;
> Four nights will quickly dream away the time;
> And then the moon, like to a silver bow
> New-bent in heaven, shall behold the night
> Of our solemnities.

This is not the sensuous, softer orb of "Antony and Cleopatra," nor is it the sweet sleeping friend of Lorenzo and Jessica. It is brilliant and brisk, silver-distant, and an occasion for comedy in Theseus's worldly thought. Later on in the same scene he will call it cold and fruitless (73), and Lysander will look forward to

> Tomorrow night, when Phoebe doth behold
> Her silver visage in the watery glass,
> Decking with liquid pearl the bladed grass.
>
> (I, i, 209-11)

Lysander has connected the image of the moon with the image of cool water on which it shines, and hereafter they will be inseparable. "A Midsummer Night's Dream" is drenched with dew when it is not saturated with rain. A film of water spreads over it, enhances and enlarges it miraculously. The fairy whom Robin hails as the second act opens wanders swifter than the moon's sphere through fire and flood. The moon, says Titania, is governess of floods, and in anger at Oberon's brawls has sucked up from the sea contagious fogs, made every river overflow, drowned the fields and rotted the green corn:

> The nine men's morris is fill'd up with mud,
> And the quaint mazes in the wanton green
> For lack of tread are undistinguishable.    (ii, i, 98-100)

Here in the west there has been a deluge, and every object still drips moisture. But even in the east there are waves and seas. The little changeling boy whom Titania will not surrender to Oberon is the son of a votaress on the other side of the earth:

> And, in the spiced Indian air, by night,
> Full often hath she gossip'd by my side,
> And sat with me on Neptune's yellow sands,
> Marking the embarked traders on the flood.
>
>                                        (ii, i, 124-7)

The jewels she promises Bottom will be fetched "from the deep" (iii, i, 161). And Oberon is addicted to treading seaside groves

> Even till the eastern gate, all fiery-red,
> Opening on Neptune with fair blessed beams,
> Turns into yellow gold his salt green streams.
>
>                                        (iii, ii, 391-3)

So by a kind of logic the mortals of the play continue to be washed with copious weeping. The roses in Hermia's cheeks fade fast "for want of rain" (i, i, 130), but rain will come. Demetrius "hails" and "showers" oaths on Helena (i, i, 245), whose eyes are bathed with salt tears (ii, ii, 92-3); and Hermia takes comfort in the tempest of her eyes (i, i, 131).

When the moon weeps, says Titania to Bottom, "weeps every little flower" (iii, i, 204). The flowers of "A Midsummer Night's Dream" are not the warm, sweet, dry ones of Perdita's garden, or even the daytime ones with which Fidele's brothers will strew her forest grave. They are the damp flowers that hide among ferns and drip with dew. A pearl is hung in every cowslip's ear (ii, i, 15); the little western flower which Puck is sent to fetch is rich with juice; and luscious woodbine canopies the bank of wild thyme where Titania sleeps—not on but "in" musk-roses and eglantine. Moon, water, and wet flowers conspire to extend the world of "A Midsummer Night's Dream" until it is as large as all imaginable life. That is why the play is both so natural and so mysterious.

Nor do its regions fail to echo with an ample music. The mermaid on the promontory with her dulcet and harmonious breath sang distantly and long ago, but the world we walk in is filled with present sound.

*Theseus.*     Go, one of you, find out the forester,
                For now our observation is perform'd,
                And since we have the vaward of the day,
                My love shall hear the music of my hounds.
                Uncouple in the western valley, let them go.
                Dispatch, I say, and find the forester.
                We will, fair queen, up to the mountain's top
                And mark the musical confusion
                Of hounds and echo in conjunction.

*Hippolyta.*  I was with Hercules and Cadmus once,
                When in a wood of Crete they bay'd the bear
                With hounds of Sparta. Never did I hear
                Such gallant chiding; for, besides the groves,
                The skies, the fountains, every region near
                Seem'd all one mutual cry. I never heard
                So musical a discord, such sweet thunder.

*Theseus.*     My hounds are bred out of the Spartan kind,
                So flew'd, so sanded, and their heads are hung
                With ears that sweep away the morning dew;
                Crook-knee'd, and dew-lapp'd like Thessalian bulls;
                Slow in pursuit, but match'd in mouth like bells,
                Each under each. A cry more tuneable
                Was never holla'd to, nor cheer'd with horn,
                In Crete, in Sparta, nor in Thessaly.
                Judge when you hear.           (IV, i, 107-31)

Had Shakespeare written nothing else than this he still might be the best of English poets. Most poetry which tries to be music also is less than poetry. This is absolute. The melody which commences with such spirit in Theseus's fifth line has already reached the complexity of counterpoint in his eight and ninth; Hippolyta carries it to a like limit in the line with which she closes; and Theseus, taking it back from her, hugely increases its volume, first by reminding us that the hounds have form and muscle, and then by daring the grand dissonance, the mixed thunder, of bulls and bells. The passage sets a forest ringing, and supplies a play with the music it has deserved.

But Shakespeare is still more a poet because the passage is incidental to his creation. The creation with which he is now busy is not a passage, a single effect; it is a play, and though this one contribution has been mighty there are many others. And none of the others is mightier than bully Bottom's.

Bottom likes music too. "I have a reasonable good ear," he tells Titania. "Let's have the tongs and the bones." So does he take an interest in moonshine, if only among the pages of an almanac. "A calendar, a calendar!" he calls. "Find out moonshine, find out moonshine." When they find the moon, those Athenian mechanics of whom he is king, it has in it what the cold fairy moon cannot be conceived as having, the familiar man of folklore. Bottom and his fellows domesticate the moon, as they domesticate every other element of which Shakespeare has made poetry. And the final effect is parody. Bottom's amazed oration concerning his dream follows hard upon the lovers' discourse concerning dreams and delusions; but it is in prose, and the speaker is utterly literal when he pronounces that it will be called Bottom's dream because it hath no bottom (iv, i, 220). Nor is the story of Pyramus and Thisbe as the mechanics act it anything but a burlesque of "Romeo and Juliet."

> O night, which ever art when day is not! . . .
> And thou, O wall, O sweet, O lovely wall,
> That stand'st between her father's ground and mine!
> Thou wall, O wall, O sweet and lovely wall.    (v, i, 172-7)

Shakespeare has come, even this early, to the farthest limit of comedy. The end of comedy is self-parody, and its wisdom is self-understanding. Never again will he work without a full comprehension of the thing he is working at; of the probability that other and contrary things are of equal importance; of the certainty that his being a poet who can do anything he wants to do is not the only thing to be, or the best possible thing; of the axiom that the whole is greater than the part— the part in his instance being one play among many thinkable plays, or one man, himself, among the multitude that populate a world for whose size and variety he with such giant strides is reaching respect. Bully Bottom and his friends have lived three centuries to good purpose, but to no better purpose at any time than the one they first had—namely, in their sublime innocence, their earthbound, idiot openness and charity of soul, to bring it about that their creator should become not only the finest of poets but the one who makes the fewest claims for poetry.

# RICHARD II

THE Histories of Shakespeare that deal with later reigns than Richard II's will be eloquent with sympathy for the king whom Bolingbroke deposed. Hotspur will rage whenever he remembers "that sweet lovely rose" in whom the canker of another man's ambition grew. When Bolingbroke is dying as Henry IV he will confess to his son

> By what by-paths and indirect crook'd ways
> I met this crown.

And the son as Henry V will do all he can, through prayers, tears, charity, and the building of chantries, to atone for his father's fault. The Bishop of Carlisle, rising in "Richard II" itself to prophesy what things shall follow the triumph of Bolingbroke, speaks with the accent usually reserved by Shakespeare for righteous men:

> Disorder, horror, fear, and mutiny
> Shall here inhabit, and this land be call'd
> The field of Golgotha and dead men's skulls.

(IV, i, 142-4)

There can be no question as to Shakespeare's affection for the hero of his new historical play.

But he has not made a great man of him. He has made a poet, a great minor poet. The author of "Richard II" is perhaps more interested in poetry than he will ever be again. He is still learning to write at a fabulous rate, he is still making the most remarkable discoveries of powers within his pen which he could not have guessed were there before, let alone measured. And the particular power he is now discovering is one that makes him conscious of himself as a poet. It is the power to write the English language musically—with a continuous melody and with unfailing reserves of harmony. His king will be similarly self-conscious; that will explain the sympathy between the author and his creation, as well as provide the author an opportunity to criticize his own excesses in an extension of himself. For Richard will not become a great poet. Merely "musical" poets seldom do. And Shakespeare will understand the limitations of the poetry with which he endows his hero. At the same time he will be as much in love with it as he dares. Nor does any reader of Shakespeare, coming upon this play in the order of its composition, fail to fall in love with the music of its poetry. It is the work of an awakening genius who has fallen in love with the language he writes; who realizes the full possibilities of its idiom and scale; and who lets himself go. The subject of "Richard II" is the reign and deposition of an English king. It is also the beauty of the English language considered as an instrument upon which music can be made.

The play opens with a quarrel between the Dukes of Hereford and Norfolk which only the king can settle, and which in the third scene he settles by banishing both parties. Thomas Mowbray, Duke of Norfolk, is the first to lament the sentence. And what loss does he lament?

> The language I have learn'd these forty years,
> My native English, now I must forgo;
> And now my tongue's use is to me no more
> Than an unstringed viol or a harp,
> Or like a cunning instrument cas'd up,
> Or, being open, put into his hands
> That knows no touch to tune the harmony.
>
> (I, iii, 159-65)

Mowbray's tongue is his most precious organ because with it he can tune the harmonies of English. And "tongue" is the key word, the repeated word, of "Richard II" generally.

The second act opens with John of Gaunt insisting to the Duke of York that something may be accomplished by protests from so old a man as he to the unstaid Richard:

> O, but they say the tongues of dying men
> Enforce attention like deep harmony.
> Where words are scarce, they are seldom spent in vain,
> For they breathe truth that breathe their words in pain.
> He that no more must say is listen'd more
> Than they whom youth and ease have taught to glose.
> More are men's ends mark'd than their lives before.
> The setting sun, and music at the close,
> As the last taste of sweets, is sweetest last,
> Writ in remembrance more than things long past.
>
> (ii, i, 5-14)

The word "tongues" in the first line has released the music of which Gaunt is peculiarly capable, and of which he is soon to supply the grand specimen in his apostrophe to

> This blessed plot, this earth, this realm, this England.
>
> (ii, i, 50)

And when news is brought of his death the phrase for it will be, even in so practical a mouth as that of Northumberland:

> His tongue is now a stringless instrument.
>
> (ii, i, 149)

The word is used everywhere, often to the accompaniment of terms from music. Scroop has a "care-tun'd tongue" (iii, ii, 92); the Queen rebukes the "harsh rude tongue" of the gardener for "sounding" unpleasant news (iii, iv, 74); and Richard's tongue will be the tuning-fork with whose aid he composes the arias of his finest speeches. Meanwhile it attracts images from arts other than music, though only from those that are near allied. Mowbray's soul dances at the tournament which will decide his fate (i, iii, 91); Gaunt begs Bolingbroke, his banished son, to believe that his progress through foreign lands will be

> no more
> Than a delightful measure or a dance.    (I, iii, 290-1)

The tournament, the deposition scene, and most of the meetings between Richard and other men are attended with ritual,
sonorous with ceremony. And by no means the least successful of those passages in which Shakespeare pursues an analogy
between life and the stage is the passage in which York describes the humiliation of Richard as he followed Bolingbroke
through the streets of London:

> As in a theatre, the eyes of men,
> After a well-grac'd actor leaves the stage,
> Are idly bent on him that enters next,
> Thinking his prattle to be tedious;
> Even so, or with much more contempt, men's eyes
> Did scowl on gentle Richard.              (v, ii, 23-28)

The tongues of Mowbray and Gaunt are the symbols of
their tunefulness. But other persons in the play are tuneful.
Indeed everyone is, and sooner or later is given the lead, if
only for a moment, so that he may prove it. The Bishop of
Carlisle, hearing Bolingbroke in the deposition scene swear
that Mowbray too shall be returned to England, says words
that ring like gongs in memory of the dead Duke:

> That honourable day shall ne'er be seen.
> Many a time hath banish'd Norfolk fought
> For Jesu Christ in glorious Christian field,
> Streaming the ensign of the Christian cross
> Against black pagans, Turks, and Saracens;
> And, toil'd with works of war, retir'd himself
> To Italy; and there at Venice gave
> His body to that pleasant country's earth,
> And his pure soul unto his captain Christ,
> Under whose colours he had fought so long.
>                                          (IV, i, 91-100)

Bolingbroke, for the most part a man of few words, meets
Carlisle's magnificence with a plain question: "Why, Bishop,

is Norfolk dead?", as if he were not one who understood poetry. Yet Bolingbroke himself, at least until Richard's muse triumphed over his and made him content with plainness, had been a poet. Northumberland had told him (II, iii, 6) that his "fair discourse" on the rough roads of Gloucestershire was "as sugar"; and his lecture to Richard's captured favorites, Bushy and Green, was mighty in its anger. Nor at the end of the play, in the speech with which upon hearing of Richard's murder he demonstrates the strength of his conscience, does he forget that he has been a poet whose ruling image was blood on grass—or, as he once put it, a "crimson tempest" on "the fresh green lap of fair King Richard's land" (III, iii, 46-7). Now he puts it more soberly, more elliptically, and more powerfully:

> Lords, I protest, my soul is full of woe
> That blood should sprinkle me to make me grow.
>
> (v, vi, 45-6)

The play swarms with poets who practice their several styles and upon occasion copy one another. They are sensitive like their author to the call of a cadence; music that one of them hears from another's tongue is likely to linger in his own words later. The second scene of the play, for instance, is devoted to a dialogue between Gaunt and the Duchess of Gloucester. Their discourse has a political bearing, but there is importance for poetry in the fact that in two passages the Duchess anticipates—so responsive are the movements of this play to one another—the styles of subsequent speakers. One of these is her brother-in-law Gaunt, who when in the next scene he pronounces his famous series of apostrophes to England will remember

> But Thomas, my dear lord, my life, my Gloucester.
>
> (I, ii, 16)

The other is her brother-in-law York, who is not present but the essence of whose worried way with broken phases she catches in the lines:

Lo, this is all:—nay, yet depart not so;
Though this be all, do not so quickly go;
I shall remember more. Bid him—ah, what?—
With all good speed at Plashy visit me.        (i, ii, 63-6)

But the great poet of the play, of course, is Richard. And if
he has to content himself with being a minor poet, that circumstance is consistent with the character of the man and of
the action built around him. The play is organized about a
hero who, more indeed than contenting himself with the role
of minor poet, luxuriates in it. His theme is himself. He
dramatizes his grief. He spends himself in poetry—which is
something he loves more than power and more than any other
person. His self-love is grounded upon an infatuation with the
art he so proudly and self-consciously practices. That is what
"Richard II" is about, and what even its plot expresses. Its
unity therefore is distinct and impressive.

Its first half shows us a king accomplished in the rhetoric
of his office.

Face to face,
And frowning brow to brow, ourselves will hear
The accuser and the accused freely speak.        (i, i, 15-7)

We were not born to sue, but to command.        (i, i, 196)

Not all the water in the rough rude sea
Can wash the balm off from an anointed king;
The breath of worldly men cannot depose
The deputy elected by the Lord.        (iii, ii, 54-7)

His talk is big, his rhythms are tremendous. So we might expect him to put traitors quickly down; or, if a rival appeared
for his throne, we might be certain that mighty measures,
along with mighty phrases, would leave him soon again solitary in unassailable grandeur. What explains his failure to op-
pose Bolingbroke at all, his sudden collapse, as soon as the
threat of deposition becomes real, into a state of sheer elegy,
of pure poetry? The answer is simple. Richard is a poet, not
a king. Surrounded by favorites and deceived by dreams of

his utter safety he can strut in the high style awhile. But an acute ear detects the strut even at the brave beginning; and soon enough there are signs of the precious, conceited musician who hides under the robe. Surely he loves a little too well the words he has chosen for announcing to Mowbray that exile in his case is to be for life:

> The sly, slow hours shall not determinate
> The dateless limit of thy dear exile.  (i, iii, 150-1)

The Duke of York warns Gaunt that the young king will not listen to the wisdom of any old man because his ears are too much in love with the "venom sound" of "lascivious metres" (ii, i, 19). He is too much, York means, the mere poet. York is a foolish old fellow, and may be prejudiced. Yet there is a suspicious excess in the kiss of words bestowed by Richard upon the soil of Wales when he lands from Ireland:

> As a long-parted mother with her child
> Plays fondly with her tears and smiles in meeting,
> So, weeping, smiling, greet I thee, my earth,
> And do thee favours with my royal hands.  (iii, ii, 8-11)

And within a few minutes the secret is entirely out; Richard drops his pretense of being a major poet simultaneously with the surrender of his power, with the crumpling of his front. The break is sudden, and poetically, not to say dramatically, it is brilliant. Richard's last speech in the old style is the best he has made in that style; he never spoke with more appearance of strength than he does now when he hears Scroop say that Wiltshire, Bagot, Bushy, and Green have made peace with Bolingbroke:

> O villains, vipers, damn'd without redemption!
> Dogs, easily won to fawn on any man!
> Snakes, in my heart-blood warm'd, that sting my heart!
> Three Judases, each one thrice worse than Judas!
> Would they make peace? Terrible hell make war
> Upon their spotted souls for this offense!  (iii, ii, 129-34)

But these words are the last hard and heavy ones he uses. For Scroop explains that Richard's friends have made peace with heads, not hands; and to Aumerle's question concerning the whereabouts of York a new kind of answer comes, in a new style which gives us all at once the man we have been waiting for. The new style is exquisite, high-pitched, limpid, lyrical, and boneless; its phrases run sweetly, easily, without the effort of argument or disguise; its music listens to itself, pleased with the high-born whine of a matchless, inimitable melody; and the diction is literary, the imagery is of books, of writing, of story-telling:

> No matter where; of comfort no man speak.
> Let's talk of graves, of worms, and epitaphs;
> Make dust our paper and with rainy eyes
> Write sorrow on the bosom of the earth.
> Let's choose executors and talk of wills;
> And yet not so; for what can we bequeath
> Save our deposed bodies to the ground?
> Our lands, our lives, and all are Bolingbroke's,
> And nothing can we call our own but death,
> And that small model of the barren earth
> Which serves as paste and cover to our bones.
> For God's sake, let us sit upon the ground
> And tell sad stories of the death of kings. . . .
> Cover your heads, and mock not flesh and blood
> With solemn reverence. Throw away respect,
> Tradition, form, and ceremonious duty;
> For you have but mistook me all this while.
> I live with bread like you, feel want,
> Taste grief, need friends: subjected thus,
> How can you say to me I am a king?          (III, ii, 144-77)

All this while Richard had been a poet, not a king; a minor poet, waiting for the cues of sorrow and disaster. Now that he has them he will honor nothing else; he will do nothing but compose fine, tender, heart-breaking lines, nothing but improvise endless variations on the rich, resonant theme of his personal woe.

The name of king? O' God's name, let it go.
I'll give my jewels for a set of beads,
My gorgeous palace for a hermitage,
My gay apparel for an almsman's gown,
My figur'd goblets for a dish of wood,
My sceptre for a palmer's walking-staff,
My subjects for a pair of carved saints,
And my large kingdom for a little grave,
A little little grave, an obscure grave.   (III, iii, 146-54)

The new poet in Richard will develop at a giddy rate, so that in the great deposition scene (IV, i) he will stand full confessed and wail in perfect glory. In this scene, far from concealing his art, he calls attention to it with every gesture, he wantonly loses himself in its mazes. He enters, talking to himself in the role of Christ—a role he fancies now—betrayed by Judas. Upon York's reminding him that he is here to hand over his crown he dramatically seizes one side of the golden object, offers the other side to Bolingbroke, and begins a long poem about buckets in wells. Bolingbroke interrupts him with the prosaic protest:

I thought you had been willing to resign.

Richard's rhyming answer is perhaps his honestest speech:

My crown I am; but still my griefs are mine.
You may my glories and my state depose,
But not my griefs; still am I king of those.

But he is not done. For in his next long speech he must pull out the stops of pity and if possible break other hearts than his own; and after that he must keep the parliament waiting while he wonders what name to call himself, now that he is nothing. Poets must have names to call things, and minor poets must have names to call themselves. The thought of his nothingness moves him to request that a mirror be brought so that he can gaze upon his bankrupt self. It is brought, and it turns out to be a wonderful source of further poetic ideas.

When they are exhausted he dashes it down and breaks it, remarking to Bolingbroke as he does so:

> Mark, silent king, the moral of this sport,
> How soon my sorrow hath destroy'd my face.

The bewildered Bolingbroke, thus far reduced like everyone else to silence and embarrassed awe, makes the mistake of presenting Richard with a metaphor that he can go on with. "The shadow of your sorrow," says the new king, "hath destroy'd the shadow of your face." He has not bothered to search for a fresh image; this one is already stale in Elizabethan poetry; but it is good enough for Richard, who pounces upon it gratefully:

> Say that again.
> The shadow of my sorrow! Ha! let's see.
> 'Tis very true, my grief lies all within;
> And these external manners of laments
> Are merely shadows to the unseen grief
> That swells with silence in the tortur'd soul.
> There lies the substance; and I thank thee, King,
> For thy great bounty, that not only giv'st
> Me cause to wail but teachest me the way
> How to lament the cause.

There is irony in Richard's thanks, but there is also simple truth; he is happy with his sorrow, he is functioning through grief.

The farewell to his Queen gives him a particularly audible cue, and we should note that it is not her sorrow but his that he embroiders with such beautiful harmonies:

> Good sometimes queen, prepare thee hence for France.
> Think I am dead, and that even here thou tak'st,
> As from my death-bed, thy last living leave.
> In winter's tedious nights sit by the fire
> With good old folks and let them tell thee tales
> Of woeful ages long ago betid;
> And ere thou bid good night, to quit their griefs

Tell thou the lamentable tale of me
And send the hearers weeping to their beds.      (v, i, 37-45)

The thought of his own death is delicious pleasure; the allit-
eration in the third line is something of which he is conscious
and sadly proud; the good old folks in France are already
weeping for him as he sings.

But his last scene is his best, returning as it does to all the
themes with which Richard the poet has been most at home.
It begins with him in prison—a productive symbol, a mine of
metaphor.

*& Denmark's a prison*

I have been studying how I may compare
This prison where I live unto the world;
And for because the world is populous
And here is not a creature but myself,
I cannot do it; yet I'll hammer it out.
My brain I'll prove the female to my soul,
My soul the father; and these two beget
A generation of still-breeding thoughts,
And these same thoughts people this little world.

(v, v, 1-9)

The problem is difficult, but since it is a problem in poetry
he has plenty of courage. He continues, and soon he has
solved it; ideas flow in upon him, poetry once more is possible. Then music sounds, since someone outside his cell has
taken pity on him and come to play for his comfort. The
imperfection of the playing suggests the imperfection of his
life; broken time is now his cue:

I wasted time, and now doth Time waste me;

and he carries on until the petulance of his nature turns him
suddenly against the musician, and until a groom enters who
supplies him with the new fancy—it is his last one—of himself as Bolingbroke's horse. Then his murder and the end of
the play; for without Richard's voice in our ears there is no
more to hear.

Richard is Shakespeare's finest poet thus far, and in spite of everything he is a touching person. He is not a great man, nor is the play in consequence a considerable tragedy. But as a performer on the lyre Richard has no match among Shakespeare's many people. And as dramatizer of himself he will be tutor to a long posterity, though none of his pupils—Hamlet is the best known—will be exactly like him. As for his favorite subject, sorrow, there will be Constance in "King John" to explore it even farther than he has explored it—to tread, indeed, the limit which his tact as an artist has prevented him from trampling. Other persons in the play know grief and taste it: Gaunt, the Duchess of Gloucester, the Duchess of York when her son Aumerle is in danger of death as a traitor, and the Queen when she overhears the gardener and cannot refrain from coming forward. But they have nothing like Richard's perfection in poetry. And the Duke of York, fussing like old Capulet over the grievous state of the realm:

> Come, sister,—cousin, I would say,—pray, pardon me
>
> (II, ii, 105)
>
> Tut, tut!
> Grace me no grace, nor uncle me no uncle,   (II, iii, 86-7)

is not so much a sorrower as a worrier; he is perhaps a parody, in the decrepit key, of Richard's full-noted grief. At any rate he is the one clearly comic personage in a play otherwise given over to tragic sentiment. Richard himself would have his comic side if there were a perspective here from which to view it. Shakespeare has the perspective; Bolingbroke, crowned Henry IV, has still one worry, the behavior of his son amongst the taverns of London where Falstaff is king (V, iii, 1-22); and Falstaff will throw a new light on everything. But "Richard II" admits no such light. It sings in its own darkness, listening sweetly to itself.

# THE MERCHANT OF VENICE

WHEN Bassanio declares, early in the comedy of which he is so casually the hero, "To you, Antonio, I owe the most, in money and in love" (i, i, 130-1), he characterizes the world he lives in and the only world he knows. It is once more, and fully now, the gentlemen's world whose tentative capital for Shakespeare had been Verona. The capital moves to Venice; the atmosphere enriches itself until no element is lacking; and a story is found, or rather a complex of stories is assembled, which will be adequate to the golden air breathed on fair days and through soft nights by creatures whose only function is to sound in their lives the clear depths of human grace. In such a world, or at any rate in such inhabitants of it, there is no incompatibility between money and love. Shylock cannot reconcile the two; but Shylock is not of this world, as the quality of his voice, so harshly discordant with the dominant voices of the play, will inform any attentive ear.

In Belmont is a lady richly left, and Bassanio does not hesitate to say that Portia's wealth is necessary to his happiness. But it is necessary only as a condition; that she is fair and good—how much of either he has still to learn—is more than necessary, it is important. She will tell him when he has won her by the right choice of caskets that she wishes herself, for his sake, still richer than she is—not merely in money but in "virtues, beauties, livings, friends" (iii, ii, 158). All of which, sincerely as it is spoken, does not obscure or deny the background for this life of an enormous and happy wealth. The play opens with a conversation between gentlemen whose voices sigh and smile with thoughts of riches. Salarino cannot believe but that Antonio's mind is tossing on the gilded ocean:

> There, where your argosies with portly sail,
> Like signiors and rich burghers on the flood,
> Or, as it were, the pageants of the sea,
> Do overpeer the petty traffickers,
> That curtsy to them, do them reverence,
> As they fly by them with their woven wings. (i, i, 9-14)

He appears to be wrong, but his eloquence has supplied a correct symbol for these folk of whom he is one: for these arrogant yet gentle creatures whose fine clothes stream on the air of Venice and whose golden, glancing talk tosses, curtsies, and plays a constant music among their still uncorrupted thoughts.

Antonio is abstracted and sad for no reason that he knows. Shakespeare's source named a reason, but it has been suppressed in the interest of a mood the play must have. Melancholy in this world must not have in it any over-ripeness as in the case of Jaques, any wildness as in the case of Hamlet, any savagery as in the case of Timon. It must remain a grace, perhaps the distinctive grace of this life which is still young enough for satiety to mean not sourness, not spiritual disease, but a beautiful sadness of that sort which it is the highest pleasure not to explore. Much is said of satiety. Portia and Nerissa begin their scene (i, ii) with talk of weariness and surfeit. But it is charming talk, unclouded by any such "unmannerly sadness" as Portia soon criticizes in her suitor the County Palatine, who suggests "a death's-head with a bone in his mouth." The sadness of her class is a mannerly sadness. Antonio knows with Gratiano that all things

> Are with more spirit chased than enjoy'd.
>
> (ii, vi, 13)

But he has not known it long enough to become other than what Bassanio calls him:

> The dearest friend to me, the kindest man,
> The best-condition'd and unwearied spirit
> In doing courtesies.                    (III, ii, 295-7)

He wearies himself with his want-wit sadness, and thinks he
wearies others; but he is not too tired for courtesies, and
Bassanio's concern for him when news comes to Belmont of
Shylock's insistence on the bond is deep, unspoiled, and serious. Antonio can say

> I am a tainted wether of the flock,
> Meetest for death,                    (IV, i, 114-5)

without causing embarrassment in his hearers or incurring
the charge of self-love. He is in short one of Shakespeare's
gentlemen: one who wears darker clothes than his friends
but knows perfectly how to wear them.

Love is the natural language of these men and women:
love, and its elder brother generosity. Not generosity to Shylock, for he is of another species, and cannot receive what he
will not give. But generosity to all friends, and an unmeasured love. The word love lies like a morsel of down in the
nest of nearly every speech, and the noblest gestures are
made in its name. Portia's surrender to Bassanio of

> This house, these servants, and this same myself
>                                        (III, ii, 172)

is absolute. And so is the gift of Antonio's life to Bassanio,
for there are more kinds of love here than one.

> I think he only loves the world for him,
>                                        (II, viii, 50)

says Salanio, and Antonio counts on Bassanio's silent understanding of the truth. "If your love do not persuade you to
come," he writes to him at Belmont, "let not my letter"
(III, ii, 323-5). Nor is there any rivalry between Antonio and
Portia. It is enough for her that he is her husband's friend:

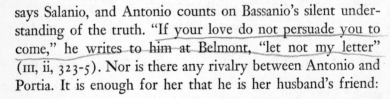

> that this Antonio,
> Being the bosom lover of my lord,
> Must needs be like my lord.          (III, iv, 16-8).

And it is enough for him that she is his friend's beloved:

> Commend me to your honourable wife.
> Tell her the process of Antonio's end;
> Say how I lov'd you, speak me fair in death,
> And, when the tale is told, bid her be judge
> Whether Bassanio had not once a love.   (IV, i, 273-7)

Neither man knows that Portia is listening to this, but the fact that she is, and that "The Merchant of Venice" is after all a comedy, does not invalidate the mood.

The language of love is among other things intellectual. So we are not surprised to encounter abstractions in the graceful discourse of our lords and ladies. They are what make it, indeed, as graceful as it is, with its expert alternation of short and long words, its accomplished and elaborate ease such as Shylock's tongue never knows. It is natural for Portia to credit Antonio with

> a like proportion
> Of lineaments, of manners, and of spirit
> (III, iv, 14-5)

to that of Bassanio, "her governor, her king." It is as natural for her to speak of mercy as a "quality" and an "attribute" as it is for her to reveal upon occasion that nippiness of wit which keeps the conversation of all such people sound and sweet.

> Fie, what a question's that,
> If thou wert near a lewd interpreter!
> (III, iv, 79-80)
> I'll have that doctor for my bedfellow.     (v, i, 233)

The intellect and the wit, and the familiarity with abstractions, have much to do with the effect of music which is so strong and pure throughout "The Merchant of Venice." Not only do the words of the lovers maintain an unbroken, high, golden chime; but actual music is frequently in our ears.

> Let music sound while he doth make his choice;
> Then, if he lose, he makes a swan-like end,
> Fading in music.                              (III, ii, 43-5)

So Portia commands as Bassanio broods before the caskets. And there is no clearer sign that the world is itself again when Shylock goes than the burst of melody, both verbal and performed, with which the fifth act soars upon recovered wings. The sweet wind, the sweet moonlight, the sweet soul of Jessica melt into one singing whole with the sweet touches, the sweet harmony, the sweet power of music.

> I am never merry when I hear sweet music,   (v, i, 69)

sighs Jessica with mannerly sadness. But that is as it should be in the world of Belmont and Venice; and there is of course Portia's wit to civilize the scene.

> He knows me as the blind man knows the cuckoo,
> By the bad voice.                              (v, i, 112-3)

Nor are these people unaware that ultimate music is unheard. "We cannot hear," says Lorenzo, the harmony that is in immortal souls. Much as they love music, they love the melodies of silence more.

> Soft stillness and the night
> Become the touches of sweet harmony,          (v, i, 56-7)

says Lorenzo now, for somewhat the same reason that Bassanio had once found the plainness of a leaden casket moving him more than eloquence (III, ii, 106), and still earlier had fallen in love with Portia because of the "fair speechless messages" he received from her eyes. Music no less than love is absolute in the world of Venice and Belmont.

Nicholas Rowe in 1709 was of the opinion that Shylock's contribution to the play made it a tragedy. "There appears in it such a deadly spirit of revenge, such a savage fierceness and fellness, and such a bloody designation of cruelty and mischief, as cannot agree either with the style or characters of comedy." As time has gone on this has come more and more to seem true. Yet it is but a seeming truth. Shylock is so alien to the atmosphere of the whole, so hostile and in his hostility so forceful, that he threatens to rend the web of magic happiness woven for the others to inhabit. But the web holds, and he is cast out. If the world of the play has not all along been beautiful enough to suggest its own natural safety from such a foe, it becomes so in a fifth act whose felicity of sound permits no memory of ducats and bonds and long knives whetted on the heel. Comedy or not, "The Merchant of Venice" by such means rescues its tone. If this is not comedy, there is no other in the play. The possibilities in Gratiano's loquacity are never developed, and the Gobbos are poor clowns.

The voice of Shylock comes rasping into the play like a file; the edge of it not only cuts but tears, not only slices but saws. He is always repeating phrases, half to himself, as misers do—hoarding them if they are good, unwilling to give them wings so that they may spend themselves generously in the free air of mutual talk.

> Three thousand ducats; well. . . .
> For three months; well. . . .
> Antonio shall become bound; well.        (i, iii, 1-6)

They are short phrases; niggardly, ugly, curt. They are a little hoarse from their hoarding, a little rusty with disuse. And the range of their sound is from the strident to the rough, from the scratchy to the growled.

> The patch is kind enough, but a huge feeder;
> Snail-slow in profit, and he sleeps by day
> More than the wild-cat. Drones hive not with me.
>                                        (ii, v, 46-8)

The names of animals are natural to his tongue, which knows for the most part only concrete things, and crackles with reminders of brute matter. Salarino, musing of shipwrecks in the opening scene, bethinks him straight of dangerous rocks,

> Which, touching but my gentle vessel's side,
> Would scatter all her spices on the stream,
> Enrobe the roaring waters with my silks.    (I, i, 32-4)

Shylock in the third scene rewrites Salarino's passage in his own idiom:

> But ships are but boards, sailors but men; there be land-rats and water-rats, water-thieves and land-thieves, I mean pirates, and then there is the peril of waters, winds, and rocks.
>
> (I, iii, 21-5)

Land-rats and water-rats: the very sound of the words announces their malice, confesses the satisfaction with which their speaker has cursed them as they left his lips. He will go on in the play to remind us of the cur, the goat, the pig, the cat, the ass, the monkey, and the mule.

> *Tubal.* One of them showed me a ring that he had of your daughter for a monkey.
> *Shylock.* Out upon her! Thou torturest me, Tubal. It was my turquoise; I had it of Leah when I was a bachelor. I would not have given it for a wilderness of monkeys.    (III, i, 123-8)

An animal itself is howling, and the emphasis upon "wilderness" is shrill beyond the license of human rhetoric. We may feel pity for the man who remembers Leah, but the spectacle of such pain is not pleasant, the wound is animal, self-inflicted, and self-licked. "I never heard," says Salanio,

> a passion so confus'd,
> So strange, outrageous, and so variable.
> (II, viii, 12-3)

This was when Shylock ran out into the streets and declared the loss of his ducats with his daughter; but he is always strange to the play and outrageous, though in most crises he can cover his agitation with the curt voice of craft, with the insistent sound of a cold hatred.

> I'll have my bond; I will not hear thee speak.
> I'll have my bond; and therefore speak no more. . . .
> I'll have no speaking; I will have my bond.
>
> (III, iii, 12-17)

Nor is he disposed to justify his conduct by a show of reason. If he knows the language of reason he does not use it; if he knows his motives he will not name them.

> So can I give no reason, nor I will not,
> More than a lodg'd hate and a certain loathing
> I bear Antonio.                     (IV, i, 59-61)

It is by no means odd that such a man should detest music. The favored citizens of this world love it so much that they live only for the concord of sweet sounds, and Lorenzo can dismiss any other kind of man as fit for treasons, stratagems, and spoils (v, i, 85). Shylock is another kind of man. Music hurts his ears as it does Malvolio's, and he is as contemptuous of merry-making, which he calls "shallow foppery." A masque in the street brings no comfort of melody; he notes only "the vile squealing of the wry-neck'd fife" (II, v, 30), and holds his ears. So must we hold ours against so hideous a phrase; and withhold, perhaps, our assent from the implication that any musical instrument can be a deformed thing. Or a perverting thing, for there are men, says Shylock in another place, who

> when the bagpipe sings i' the nose,
> Cannot contain their urine.          (IV, i, 49-50)

That is the sort of interest he has in music, in the ridiculous noises which dull and soft-eyed fools with varnished faces can only pretend to believe ennobling. And that is why, since also he is without the concord in his thoughts which love composes, the repetitions of his speech are so lacking in resonance, so sullen in their accent and so blighting in their tone.

Ho, no, no, no, no!                                    (i, iii, 15)

Why, there, there, there, there! A diamond gone, cost me two thousand ducats in Frankfort! The curse never fell upon our nation till now. I never felt it till now. Two thousand ducats in that; and other precious, precious jewels. I would my daughter were dead at my foot, and the jewels in her ear! Would she were hears'd at my foot, and the ducats in her coffin! . . . I thank God, I thank God. Is't true, is't true? . . . I thank thee, good Tubal; good news, good news! Ha, ha! . . . Thou stick'st a dagger in me. I shall never see my gold again. Fourscore ducats at a sitting! Fourscore ducats! . . . I am very glad of it. I'll plague him; I'll torture him. I am glad of it. . . . Nay, that's true, that's very true. Go, Tubal, fee me an officer; bespeak him a fortnight before . . . Go, go, Tubal, and meet me at our synagogue; go, good Tubal; at our synagogue, Tubal.           (III, i, 87-136)

That repetitions like these occur in prose is not what distinguishes them. The prose of Falstaff will contain as many with an entirely different result, with the effect indeed of a great man spending his breath freely. What distinguishes the style of Shylock is in the end, no doubt, one of its author's secrets. But we can hear the difference between him and the brethren of Antonio. And in the quality of that difference we should have no difficulty in recognizing Shylock as the alien element in a world of love and friendship, of nightingales and moonlight sleeping sweetly on a bank.

Where Shakespeare's sympathies lay it has long since been useless to inquire. His gentlemen within the code are as harsh to Shylock as Shylock is to them; however much love they have, they cannot love him. Nor has Shakespeare made the least inch of him lovely. He would seem in fact to have attempted a monster, one whose question whether a Jew hath eyes, hands, organs, dimensions, senses, affections, and passions would reveal its rhetorical form, the answer being no. Yet Shylock is not a monster. He is a man thrust into a world bound not to endure him. In such a world he necessarily looks and sounds ugly. In another universe his voice might have its properties and its uses. Here it can issue as nothing but a snarl, an animal cry sounding outrageously among the flute and recorder voices of persons whose very names, unlike his own, are flowing musical phrases. The contrast between harmony and hate, love and discord, is here complete, and Shakespeare for the time being is content to resolve it in comedy. Even in his tragedies it cannot be more complete.

# KING JOHN

THE old play in two parts which Shakespeare re-wrote as "King John" yielded him perhaps an unexpected result. Such unity as he achieved with his condensation was neither historical nor dramatic; some of the motives were obscured, and the action was left without a single tendency, so that among all of his Histories this one is the least satisfactory as narrative. Its unity is literary. The work of revision has been done line by line rather than scene by scene. Once more Shakespeare is greatly interested in the language he uses, and uses this time to the limit. By taking it to and indeed past the limit he discovers its weakness for any future work. "King John" is his last frontal attack upon the historical, heroic style. In "Henry IV" he will work at the flanks, and though in "Henry V" he will make further forays over open ground he will understand and confess their futility.

The presence in "King John" of a certain famous passage about painting the lily is not accidental but essential, for the theme of the play is excess, and the passage perfectly expresses it. Not only do Pembroke and Salisbury, rebuking John's vanity in having himself twice crowned, put the proposition in terms which themselves are excessive:

> To guard a title that was rich before,
> To gild refined gold, to paint the lily,
> To throw a perfume on the violet,
> To smooth the ice, or add another hue
> Unto the rainbow, or with taper-light
> To seek the beauteous eye of heaven to garnish,
> Is wasteful and ridiculous excess.          (IV, ii, 10-6)

106

They go on gilding their gold through four more speeches, shifting the metaphor to a tale retold, a sail refilled, a piece of work done better than well, a patch repatched. The statement of the fault commits the fault, and indeed the two noblemen continue through the rest of the play as a chorus whose manner, like their matter, is too much. Their lamentations over the body of Arthur are doubtless desired by an audience which at the moment has had all it could stand of meaningless, confused, heaped cruelty; but they are laid on with dripping brushes, each coat before the last is dry:

*Salisbury.*  Sir Richard, what think you? Have you beheld,
Or have you read or heard, or could you think?
Or do you almost think, although you see,
That you do see? Could thought, without this object,
Form such another? This is the very top,
The height, the crest, or crest unto the crest,
Of murder's arms. This is the bloodiest shame,
The wildest savagery, the vilest stroke,
That ever wall-ey'd wrath or staring rage
Presented to the tears of soft remorse.
*Pembroke.*  All murders past do stand excus'd in this;
And this, so sole and so unmatchable,
Shall give a holiness, a purity,
To the yet unbegotten sin of times.  (iv, iii, 41-54)

This is not Shakespeare's mature or final way with metaphor, when with one line—"On horror's head horrors accumulate"— he will be able to do what with many lines he now can but approximate. It is still his first way; carried, though, to a new fineness of excess, to the tallest stem of hyperbole that can stand without breaking.

Elsewhere in "King John" the head of speech grows too heavy and the flower falls. The orations of Lewis, Melun, Prince Henry, the citizen of Angiers, and John himself are likely to be bloated beyond all form; and even the Bastard Faulconbridge, a critic of style if there ever was one, can become a "brabbler." John improves as a poet with his approach towards death. The fustian of his prime gives way in the fourth act to an intensely dramatic dialogue with Hubert when his one personal weakness, his indecisiveness, delays so long the giving of the order for Arthur's murder:

> Come hither, Hubert. O my gentle Hubert . . .
> Give me thy hand. I had a thing to say,
> But I will fit it with some better time. . . .
> I had a thing to say, but let it go. . . .
> I would into thy bosom pour my thoughts.
> But, ah, I will not! yet I love thee well.   (III, iii, 19-54)

And afterwards he plays like an accomplished poet with the theme of fire, which he finds in the tyrant fever that burns him steadily up. Yet his last lines are too accomplished; he succumbs like most of his colleagues in the play to a passion for conceits, to a thirst for the phrase that will end all search for phrases.

> And none of you will bid the Winter come
> To thrust his icy fingers in my maw,
> Nor let my kingdom's rivers take their course
> Through my burn'd bosom, nor entreat the north
> To make his bleak winds kiss my parched lips
> And comfort me with cold. I do not ask you much,
> I beg cold comfort. . . .
> The tackle of my heart is crack'd and burn'd,
> And all the shrouds wherewith my life should sail
> Are turned to one thread, one little hair.
> My heart hath one poor string to stay it by. (v, vii, 36-55)

Prince Henry, the son who will survive him and presumably save England, is nevertheless infected by a like love of style.

> 'T is strange that death should sing.
> I am the cygnet to this pale faint swan,
> Who chants a doleful hymn to his own death,
> And from the organ-pipe of frailty sings
> His soul and body to their lasting rest.       (v, vii, 20-4)

Salisbury reassures the heir:

> Be of good comfort, Prince; for you are born
> To set a form upon that indigest
> Which he hath left so shapeless and so rude.

But we have seen what kind of critic Salisbury is, and it is too late in the play, since this is the last scene, for either poetry or England to be set in form.

The farthest limit, however, the pole of hyperbole, the chill Thule of sigh-blasted excess is reached and passed by Constance. She is the last and most terrible of Shakespeare's wailing women, she is the point to which the line that begins with Lucrece and extends through "Richard III" has been so straightly drawn. Shakespeare is not done in Constance with the theme of grief; it will return with smiles in Viola and with madness in Hamlet, Othello, Lear, and Pericles. But henceforth he will twist its course, he will give it the wry strength it can best employ. Here it comes like the wind, directly, and all but blows the play to pieces. "The Lady's grief," observes Dr. Johnson, "is very affecting," as indeed it is. But his further observation, that "a passion so violent cannot be borne long," fails to take full account of the fact that Constance's passion is borne so long as to become at last intolerable. She is the symbol of "King John's" excess, and is not discarded until she has done her duty many times over.

She first appears before Angiers in a wrangle with Queen Eleanor, herself "an Ate" stirring her weak son John to blood and strife (ii, i, 63). The two women exchange insults—"monstrous slanderer," "monstrous injurer," "Bedlam," "unadvised scold"—but the superiority of Constance's tongue is clearly prophesied in the sarcasm she pours forth like poison when Eleanor makes overtures to Arthur:

> *Eleanor.*         Come to thy grandam, child.
> *Constance.* Do, child, go to it grandam, child;
>         Give grandam kingdom, and it grandam will

> Give it a plum, a cherry, and a fig.
> There's a good grandam.                    (II, i, 159-63)

There is a vicious force in her feeling, an unexplained, un-
tamed intensity which drives her at once into conceits; the
tears of little Arthur are "heaven-moving pearls," are "crystal
beads" with which heaven shall be bribed to do him justice
in spite of Eleanor's power. But such conceits are nothing
compared with those to come—with those, for instance, in
the first scene of Act III, when Constance enters staggering
under the news of Lewis's betrothal to Blanch. The tears in
the eyes of Salisbury, who has conveyed the news, are a
"lamentable rheum," which in turn is a "proud river peering
o'er his bounds"; and the conflict between her will to believe
this latest sorrow and the will to destroy herself becomes an
encounter like that of two desperate men who "in their very
meeting fall and die." If Arthur, who now begs her to be
content, were an ugly boy whom she did not love,

> Full of unpleasing blots and sightless stains,
> Lame, foolish, crooked, swart, prodigious,
> Patch'd with foul moles and eye-offending marks,
>
> (III, i, 45-7)

she could be content. But he is fair, and until of late has
been the favorite of Fortune—who, the strumpet, adulterates
hourly with his uncle John. Then to Salisbury's announcement that she must go with him to the Kings of England and
France she returns a conceit like one of Richard II's. As he
was king of his griefs, so she is queen of hers:

> To me and to the state of my great grief
> Let kings assemble; for my grief's so great
> That no supporter but the huge firm earth
> Can hold it up. Here I and sorrow sit;
> Here is my throne, bid kings come bow to it.
>
> (III, i, 70-4)

She is like Richard, however, in kind only; in degree she
soars beyond him on swift raven wings. And an opportunity

at once occurs for her to prove this. Richard had a talent for catching up the last word or phrase of the speaker before him and making it the text of a new poem, a new wail. In Constance the talent has grown to genius. King Philip of France, entering with his court, assures Blanch that this day of her betrothal will be forever remembered; as each year brings it around again it will be a holiday. Constance, overhearing him, seizes upon the words "this day" and worries them for thirteen lines, repeating them six times in as many contexts. Philip, who never could have dreamed that his phrase would breed so many others, tries to interrupt her; but she tears on, and is diverted only by Austria's attempt to silence her, for now she must turn on Austria and curse him. The entrance of Pandulph supplies her with a still more perfect cue. The papal legate, cursing and excommunicating John, becomes in a trice her tutor in diatribe, sounds in her ears a tuning-fork to which her tongue pays happy homage:

> O, lawful let it be
> That I have room with Rome to curse a while!
> Good father Cardinal, cry thou amen
> To my keen curses; for without my wrong
> There is no tongue has power to curse him right.
>
> (III, i, 179-83)

Her sorrow does not disable her wit; she can play "room" against "Rome," "wrong" against "right." She is drunk not only with grief but with the language of grief; she is infatuated with her ingenuity.

All of this reaches its climax in her last appearance three scenes later. Arthur has been taken prisoner by John, and having learned of the loss offstage she enters to Philip like a stricken ghost, "a grave unto a soul," morbidly refusing all comfort save that of death:

> Death, death. O amiable, lovely death!
> Thou odoriferous stench! sound rottenness!
>
> (III, iv, 25-6)

If death will come to her she will kiss his bones, she will
thrust her eyes in his sockets, she will wear his worms on her
fingers like rings, and she will interpret his grin as a smile
inviting her to be his wife. Pandulph, for a moment off his
guard, gives her the next cue:

> Lady, you utter madness, and not sorrow.

He is correct, but he has committed the error of inspiring
seventeen brilliant lines on madness. She wishes to heaven she
*were* mad. Could the Cardinal teach her how to be so? For
then she could forget her son. Now it is Philip's turn to set
her off. He bids her bind up her tresses, which are loose and
wild. Very well, she will; she will make them prisoners again
because her son is a prisoner, she will create in herself a
symbol of Arthur. For she will never see Arthur again, even
in heaven. Sorrow has so changed him, wherever he is, that
he will be unrecognizable after death. Pandulph comes back
into her hearing with a rebuke for the "too heinous" respect
she holds of grief. Her single cutting line,

> He talks to me that never had a son,

is more than matched by the diagnosis of Philip:

> You are as fond of grief as of your child.

But Philip has offered her the text for her final poem. Grief *is*
her child.

> Grief fills the room up of my absent child,
> Lies in his bed, walks up and down with me,
> Puts on his pretty looks, repeats his words,
> Remembers me of all his gracious parts,
> Stuffs out his vacant garments with his form;
> Then, have I reason to be fond of grief? . . .
> O Lord! my boy, my Arthur, my fair son!
> My life, my joy, my food, my all the world!
>
> (III, iv, 93-104)

No wonder she leaves the men of the play exhausted. They have stood by, speechless and appalled, while her words have filled three acts. They have tried to stop her—Arthur, John, Austria, Philip, Pandulph have in turn labored to extinguish her cries—but every such effort has been in vain. There has been no stopping this wildest of Shakespeare's widows, this queen of all his wailing women, this wonderful and terrible poetess who is so amazingly accomplished in the dialectic of grief. Lewis is no more exhausted than the others, but his two dispirited lines,

> Life is as tedious as a twice-told tale
> Vexing the dull ear of a drowsy man,

puts the case for all. And perhaps for Shakespeare, who now sends Constance out of the play forever, and sends with her the burden of a theme he could carry no further except as Hamlet and Ophelia, conceived in another spirit of playwriting, will help him carry it. He is done with the long, full rhetoric of sorrow, with the drama of declamation and sad set speeches.

The conceits of Constance and the stuffiness of the prevailing style would keep the air of "King John" unbreathable were it not for the breeze that blows ever fresh and strong from Philip Faulconbridge, the Bastard. No character in Shakespeare thus far has been more delightfully and unaccountably himself. He seems to exist for no other reason than that existence pleases him. His personality is hugely in excess of the demands made on him by the plot, or by any other personality. He is, in other words, one of Shakespeare's first evidences that he can create life without formula and without effort—life that overruns the play designed to contain it, capering off on by-paths under its own happy power.

The Bastard, as befits in part the legend concerning men of his "natural" kind, comes bursting into the first scene with

all of the aboriginal vigor which is to race in him throughout the play. His speech is peppered with vernacular terms,
which he can no more do without than he can repress the
impudence that is the outward sign of his courage. If his
brother can prove him a bastard,

> 'a pops me out
> At least from fair five hundred pounds a year.
>
> (I, i, 68-9)

His talk, here and elsewhere, is of eel-skins, riding-rods,
three-farthings, Sir Nob, the Absey book, Joan, George, and
Peter, the toothpick, the toasting-iron, mine hostess' door,
buckets in wells, chests, needles, trunks, thimbles, and stable
planks. Time is a clock-setter, a bald sexton; death "mouses"
the flesh of men; the war with France is "tug and scamble";
and if Hubert has been the cause of Arthur's death

> the smallest thread
> That ever spider twisted from her womb
> Will serve to strangle thee; a rush will be a beam
> To hang thee on; or wouldst thou drown thyself,
> Put but a little water in a spoon,
> And it shall be as all the ocean,
> Enough to stifle such a villain up.     (IV, iii, 127-33)

Unconscious of the poetry that works like yeast in every
line he utters, the Bastard thinks he despises poets. And he
does, and rightly, despise those mannered fellows who plan
and carve their phrases for effect. He is Shakespeare's critic
of the rant he has been writing, he is the force with whose
aid Shakespeare stamps himself free from fustian, from the
limitations of a too formal heroic verse. Shakespeare no less
than Faulconbridge delighted in this outburst against the citizen of Angiers on the score of his style:

> Here's a stay
> That shakes the rotten carcass of old Death
> Out of his rags! Here's a large mouth, indeed,
> That spits forth death and mountains, rocks and seas,

Talks as familiarly of roaring lions
As maids of thirteen do of puppy-dogs!
What cannoneer begot this lusty blood?
He speaks plain cannon fire, and smoke, and bounce;
He gives the bastinado with his tongue:
Our ears are cudgell'd; not a word of his
But buffets better than a fist of France.
Zounds! I was never so bethump'd with words
Since I first call'd my brother's father dad.    (II, i, 455-67)

That is as natural as it is excessive. With such a speech Shakespeare is forever free of the poetical, forever past his apprentice days in an art which cannot thrive till it forgets itself—even, as the Bastard's poetry does, spurns itself. Shakespeare is to return to the attack in Hotspur, who will lead it for him still more brilliantly, and indeed will finish it so that it need never be undertaken in English again. But that is only to say that Hotspur will be the full creature for whom Faulconbridge is still no more than a sketch. Charming as the Bastard's strength may be, it is unchanneled. The cynicism of his speech about commodity (II, i, 561-98), the surprise of his insolence when he twits Austria with repetitions of Constance's line,

And hang a calf's-skin on those recreant limbs,    (III, i,)

the heartiness of his wrath when Arthur dies, the simplicity of his trust in John, the valor of his tongue at all times, and of course the God's gift of his contempt for the poetical in poetry—these, attractive as they are in series, do not compose into a man whose every syllable makes him better understood than he was before. Hotspur will be such a man, and there will be many others. Meanwhile life has been created. And its abundance even here is unique in literature.

# HENRY IV

NO play of Shakespeare's is better than "Henry IV." Certain subsequent ones may show him more settled in the maturity which he here attains almost at a single bound, but nothing that he wrote is more crowded with life or happier in its imitation of human talk. The pen that moves across these pages is perfectly free of itself. The host of persons assembled for our pleasure can say anything for their author he wants to say. The poetry of Hotspur and the prose of Falstaff have never been surpassed in their respective categories; the History as a dramatic form ripens here to a point past which no further growth is possible; and in Falstaff alone there is sufficient evidence of Shakespeare's mastery in the art of understanding style, and through style of creating men.

The vast dimensions of the comic parts should not be permitted to obscure the merit of the rest. History is enlarged here to make room for taverns and trollops and potations of sack, and the heroic drama is modified by gigantic mockery, by the roared voice of truth; but the result is more rather than less reality, just as a cathedral, instead of being demolished by merriment among its aisles, stands more august. The King of the play is more remote from the audience than any of Shakespeare's kings have been; he is more formal, and speaks with a full organ tone which as Bolingbroke he never used; but that is as it should be in a work which has so much distance to fill between laughter and law, between the alehouse and the throne. Henry wears his robes regally, and his sighs because they weigh him down are dignified and sono-

116

rous. One of his cares is that domestic rebellion keeps him
from Jerusalem, where he was sworn

> To chase these pagans in those holy fields
> Over whose acres walk'd those blessed feet
> Which fourteen hundred years ago were nail'd
> For our advantage on the bitter cross.        (1-1, i, 24-7)

He knows how to send his voice through four such lines as
that, which in their lack of pause are incantation rather than
speech; though in the second play, when age and illness and
despair of his son have somewhat shattered his tone, he
deepens his style (III, i; IV, v) to something like the complexity and variety of Shakespeare's dramatic verse at its best.

Another and the chief of his cares is the behavior of his
son who will be Henry V, and who as early as the fifth act
of "Richard II" was causing concern by the amount of time
he spent with Falstaff's dissolute crew. The King preaches
more than one sermon to the Prince, and if one were free to
choose a companion for Hal one would certainly prefer the
fat knight with the great belly doublet; for the sermons are
heavy with state and conscious of the speaker's exalted virtue. But one is not free to choose. The King is after all the
King, high away from puns and drunkenness. And Hal himself, though he will play with Falstaff through ten long acts,
has secretly chosen his father all the while.

> I know you all, and will a while uphold
> The unyok'd humour of your idleness;
> Yet herein will I imitate the sun,
> Who doth permit the base contagious clouds
> To smother up his beauty from the world,
> That when he please again to be himself
> Being wanted, he may be more wonder'd at.
>                                    (1-1, ii, 218-24)

If this is priggish, and it surely is, we must remember how
conscious Shakespeare's princes always are of their careers,
and we must remember that the uppermost drift of "Henry

IV" is steadily in the direction of Hal's regeneration as Henry V. Falstaff is an interlude in his life: a circumstance from which Falstaff in fact derives much of his power. Falstaff like any other man must have his background, and it had best be a background that moves in time; if he is to be an unkempt knight, there must be banks of knights beyond him in fair dress, in full flower.

Shakespeare never permits us to forget Hal's sober side. Before Shrewsbury he confesses to his father that he has been a truant to chivalry (1-v, i, 94). And Warwick assures the King that

> The Prince but studies his companions
> Like a strange tongue, wherein, to gain the language,
> 'T is needful that the most immodest word
> Be look'd upon and learn'd; which once attain'd,
> Your Highness knows, comes to no further use
> But to be known and hated. So, like gross terms,
> The Prince will in the perfectness of time
> Cast off his followers.            (2-IV, iv, 68-75)

Humorless as Warwick is, and much as he shocks us who have learned Falstaff's language at the Prince's side, we must recognize here the young man who had killed Hotspur in battle and who will come to such swift maturity in the scene with his dying father's crown (2-IV, v); who will commend the Chief Justice because he had imprisoned a Prince of Wales (2-v, ii); who will mock the expectation of the world and live henceforth a life of formal majesty (2-v, ii); and who at the very end will turn from Falstaff as from an old man he has never seen. This is the young man upon whom Vernon has lavished the brightest vocabulary of solemn praise; on one occasion describing to Hotspur the appearance of Hal and his comrades as they set out for Shrewsbury:

> All furnish'd, all in arms;
> All plum'd like estridges that with the wind
> Bated, like eagles having lately bath'd;

Glittering in golden coats, like images;
As full of spirit as the month of May,
And gorgeous as the sun at midsummer;
Wanton as youthful goats, wild as young bulls.
I saw young Harry, with his beaver on,
His cuisses on his thighs, gallantly arm'd,
Rise from the ground like feathered Mercury,
And vaulted with such ease into his seat,
As if an angel dropp'd down from the clouds;

(1-IV, i, 97-108)

and on another occasion crediting the Prince with every attribute of a knightly soul:

I never in my life
Did hear a challenge urg'd more modestly,
Unless a brother should a brother dare
To gentle exercise and proof of arms.
He gave you all the duties of a man,
Trimm'd up your praises with a princely tongue,
Spoke your deservings like a chronicle,
Making you ever better than his praise
By still dispraising praise valued with you;
And, which became him like a prince indeed,
He made a blushing cital of himself,
And chid his truant youth with such a grace
As if he mast'red there a double spirit
Of teaching and of learning instantly.
There did he pause; but let me tell the world,
If he outlive the envy of this day,
England did never owe so sweet a hope,
So much misconstrued in his wantonness.

(1-V, ii, 52-69)

We shall not end by liking Hal better than the Hotspur whom he challenges and kills, or by preferring the new king of England to the sometime prince of London's stews. The life of "Henry IV," indeed, is not in the handsome boy who will be Henry V. But he is the foil to that life, the brocaded curtain against which we watch it moving; he is the mold it is trying to break, the form of which it is the foe. If he could be broken the life would spill itself meaninglessly; whereas nothing is meaningless in "Henry IV," and least of all this pair of passages in which the first gentleman of England is so splendidly described.

Not that Hotspur is less the gentleman than Harry, but that he is more the person, the created speaking man. The King, comparing him with the Prince, pours on him the most courteous terms of praise; he is the theme of Honour's tongue, sweet Fortune's minion and her pride, the very straightest plant amongst the grove (1-1, i, 81-3). And Lady Percy, Hotspur's wife, speaks of him after his death as Ophelia speaks of the Hamlet she once knew; he was a miracle of men,

> and by his light
> Did all the chivalry of England move
> To do brave acts. He was indeed the glass
> Wherein the noble youth did dress themselves. . . .
> In diet, in affections of delight,
> In military rules, humours of blood,
> He was the mark and glass, copy and book,
> That fashion'd others.                    (2-II, iii, 19-32)

But in the same speech Lady Percy lets us know something about her husband which we never know of Harry, and which Shakespeare henceforth will take the pains to publish in the case of any man who immensely interests him. Hotspur had a voice, a particular voice; one so specific in its qualities as to sound now in his widow's ears a bit abnormal. He talked "low and tardily." "Speaking thick" was the only blemish nature had given him. There was in other words a certain roughness in his throat. It went with the tartness of his tongue and with the rashness of his courage, the quick, busy directness of his purpose. It was this in him, along with his astonishing and unconventional vocabulary, that Lady Percy imitated when she called him "mad-headed ape" and "weasel," and threatened to break his little finger if he withheld his plans from her (1-11, iii). She never learned to swear as well as her master (1-111, i), but she could tell him to lie still, ye thief, as he dropped into her lap like Hamlet into the lap of Ophelia; and it can scarcely be doubted that he lived for her in his voice, as indeed he still lives for any reader of the play.

Northumberland, his father, calls him once "a wasp-stung and impatient fool." He is a high horse with dancing steel for muscles, an uncontrollable charger with gadflies ever at both flanks. It is not ambition that goads him, or any ordinary pride; it is rather a sense of his own superb mettle, a feeling of his strength, a toxin that attacks him because his energy is excessive and finds no outlet in life as most men live it. His scorn for most men takes the form of detesting their pretense; they are but apes of greatness, humbugs who profess the power he has without needing to profess it. He on the contrary, and with a certain perversity, insists furiously that he is but an ordinary fellow; there is nothing that he hates, or thinks he hates, more than the extraordinary. He even fancies that he is a silent fellow, a soldier of few words; "for I profess not talking" (1-v, ii, 92). Yet Northumberland can chide him for his "woman's mood,"

> Tying thine ear to no tongue but thine own.
> (1-1, iii, 238)

And the truth is that he talks all the time. He is one of Shakespeare's most copious poets, as well as one of his best.

His earliest appearance in Shakespeare was during the rebellion in "Richard II," when, entering to his father without a nod for Bolingbroke who stood by, he was asked whether he had forgotten the noble Duke. His answer was in some indefinable way impertinent, as if the contempt he was to feel for Bolingbroke as Henry IV already simmered in his blood.

> No, my good lord, for that is not forgot
> Which ne'er I did remember. To my knowledge,
> I never in my life did look on him.            (ii, iii, 37-9)

If there was impertinence in this it was overlooked, and the
courtesy he followed with was impeccable. But now in
"Henry IV" he is asked by the King why he has not delivered certain prisoners for whom a messenger has asked him,
and although in a great speech of forty-one lines (i-i, iii,
29-69) he puts the reason off on the affectations of the messenger, and upon

> my impatience
> To be so pest'red with a popinjay,

we learn as soon as the King leaves that the King himself had
been the reason. Hotspur's elders labor to stop his tirade;
they interrupt and rebuke him as many as seven times; but
he flows on, spilling his scorn in flawlessly natural lines of
blank verse which he seems not to recognize as verse. And
incidentally we discover the quality of his feeling towards
Bolingbroke on that occasion of their first meeting.

> I'll keep them all!
> By God, he shall not have a Scot of them;
> No, if a Scot would save his soul, he shall not!
> I'll keep them, by this hand. . . .
> Nay, I will; that's flat.
> He said he would not ransom Mortimer;
> Forbad my tongue to speak of Mortimer;
> But I will find him when he lies asleep,
> And in his ear I'll holla "Mortimer!"
> Nay,
> I'll have a starling shall be taught to speak
> Nothing but "Mortimer," and give it him,
> To keep his anger still in motion. . . .
> All studies here I solemnly defy,
> Save how to gall and pinch this Bolingbroke;
> And that same sword-and-buckler Prince of Wales,
> But that I think his father loves him not
> And would be glad he met with some mischance,

I would have him poison'd with a pot of ale. . . .
Why, look you, I am whipp'd and scourg'd with rods,
Nettled and stung with pismires, when I hear
Of this vile politician, Bolingbroke.
In Richard's time,—what do you call the place?—
A plague upon it, it is in Gloucestershire;
'T was where the madcap duke his uncle kept,
His uncle York; where I first bow'd my knee
Unto this king of smiles, this Bolingbroke,—
'Sblood!—
When you and he came back from Ravenspurgh.
(1-1, iii, 213-48)

Northumberland relieves his son's agony; it was at Berkley
Castle.

You say true.
Why, what a candy deal of courtesy
This fawning greyhound then did proffer me!
Look, "when his infant fortune came to age,"
And "gentle Harry Percy," and "kind cousin;"
O, the devil take such cozeners!—God forgive me!
Good uncle, tell your tale; for I have done.

His uncle Worcester cannot believe the last remark, and with
ponderous irony invites him to go on till he is really done.

I have done, i' faith.

And for the time being he is done. But in the play it is not
long until he has started again. The occasion is the rebels'
conference at Bangor (1-III, i), and just as he had forgotten
the name of Berkley Castle he now has forgotten, or thinks
he has forgotten, a map that is necessary to the conference.
When they find it for him he settles down to the business of
the day; soon, however, to be nettled and stung by what he
considers the pompous self-deception of Glendower, the tall
Welshman with the deep voice who believes that he is not
in the roll of common men, for at his birth the frame and
huge foundation of the earth shak'd like a coward, and the
heavens were all on fire because this son of Merlin had come

to tread the tedious ways of art, of deep experiments. Hotspur hops about like a wasp on a hot griddle. He cannot bear such talk, and of course cannot be still. If the earth shook at Glendower's birth it must have had a kind of colic; the reason, his perverseness insists, was common and prosaic. For there is no such thing as poetry, this magnificent poet declares. His uncle Worcester had once, somewhat in the language of Theseus in "A Midsummer Night's Dream," accused him of apprehending "a world of figures" instead of the plain form of truth (1-1, iii, 209-10), but he had let that pass. Now when Glendower, roused to wrath, denies him the virtue of framing ditties lovely well as he himself has done, Hotspur explodes and cries:

> Marry,
> And I am glad of it with all my heart.
> I had rather be a kitten and cry mew
> Than one of these same metre ballad-mongers.
> I had rather hear a brazen canstick turn'd,
> Or a dry wheel grate on the axle-tree;
> And that would set my teeth nothing on edge,
> Nothing so much as mincing poetry.
> 'T is like the forc'd gait of a shuffling nag.
>
> (1-III, i, 127-35)

And after Glendower has left, a speech which commences as an apology mounts quickly to the peak of wrath again:

> I cannot choose. Sometime he angers me
> With telling me of the moldwarp and the ant,
> Of the dreamer Merlin and his prophecies,
> And of a dragon and a finless fish,
> A clip-wing'd griffin and a moulten raven,
> A couching lion and a ramping cat,
> And such a deal of skimble-skamble stuff
> As puts me from my faith. I tell you what:
> He held me last night at least nine hours
> In reckoning up the several devils' names
> That were his lackeys. I cried "hum," and "well, go to,"
> But mark'd him not a word. O, he is as tedious

As a tired horse, a railing wife;
Worse than a smoky house. I had rather live
With cheese and garlic in a windmill, far,
Than feed on cates and have him talk to me
In any summer-house in Christendom.     (1-III, i, 148-64)

"I tell you what: he held me last night at least nine hours."
That is blank verse, but it is also speech, and it is as difficult
to scan as a casual remark. In Hotspur Shakespeare has
learned at last to make poetry as natural as the human voice—
as natural, furthermore, as Falstaff's prose, or as the whole
conduct of the incomparable action which is "Henry IV."

He must have been fond of his creation: of this high-
strung youth who was so far above liking the art he mastered, who could be a fine poet without knowing that he
was, who indeed made his poetry out of a hot love for nothing except reality and hard sense. For the paradox of Hotspur is the paradox of Shakespeare; the best poet least pam-
pers and preens his talent, and in public at any rate would
rather abuse it than take off its edge by boasting of its power
to cut. Shakespeare lets Hotspur be proud of his plainness—
"By God, I cannot flatter" (1-IV, i, 6)—but never of his
poetry. He lets Worcester criticize his nephew for

Defect of manners, want of government,
Pride, haughtiness, opinion, and disdain,
                                   (1-III, i, 184-5)

but he will lavish two scenes of the second play upon the
memory of a man whose death in the first play he must have
regretted as much as the audience did. One of these scenes
(II, iii) is that in which Lady Percy tells us how Hotspur
had been the glass of England's fashion and charges Northumberland with his death. The charge is merited, for Northumberland's pretense of illness had been the cause of Hotspur's going unsupported into battle with Prince Hal. The
other scene is the opening scene, with its elaborate business
of Rumour's false news to Northumberland that his son has

won the battle. Dr. Johnson dismissed this business as "wholly useless," but he was wholly wrong. The new play pauses at the start to fix the memory of Hotspur in our minds, to render his death still more unthinkable than it had been, to honor him after his sorry mischance. Shakespeare cannot let him go without such obsequies, and without the suitable spectacle of Northumberland's frenzy once the truth has been made clear to him:

> Now let not Nature's hand
> Keep the wild flood confin'd! Let order die!
> And let this world no longer be a stage
> To feed contention in a ling'ring act;
> But let one spirit of the first-born Cain
> Reign in all bosoms, that, each heart being set
> On bloody courses, the rude scene may end,
> And darkness be the burier of the dead! (2-1, i, 153-60)

The father's turmoil of mind is more than an expression of his conscience; it is an adequate tribute to the finest figure Shakespeare has been able to carve for the serious portion of his History. For Hotspur was very serious. He was almost, indeed, insanely serious. He did not know that he was amusing. He did not understand himself—could not have named his virtues, would never have admitted his limitations. As handsome as Hamlet, and apparently as intelligent, he was not in fact intelligent at all. He was pure illusion, pure act, pure tragedy, just as Falstaff at the opposite pole of "Henry IV" is pure light, pure contemplation, pure comedy.

Falstaff understands everything and so is never serious. If he is even more amusing to himself than he is to others, that is because the truth about himself is something very obvious which he has never taken the trouble to define. His intelligence can define anything, but his wisdom tells him that the effort is not worth while. We do not know him in our words. We know him in his—which are never to the point, for they glance off his center and lead us away along tan-

gents of laughter. His enormous bulk spreads through
"Henry IV" until it threatens to leave no room for other
men and other deeds. But his mind is still larger. It is at home
everywhere, and it is never darkened with self-thought. Falstaff thinks only of others, and of the pleasure he can take in
imitating them. He is a universal mimic; his genius is of that
sort which understands through parody, and which cannot
be understood except at one or more removes. He is so much
himself because he is never himself; he has so much power
because he has more than that maximum which for ordinary
men is the condition of their identity's becoming stated. His
is not stated because there is no need of proving that he has
force; we feel this force constantly, in parody after parody
of men he pretends to be. The parodist, the artist, is more
real than most men whom we know. But we cannot fix him
in a phrase, or claim more for ourselves than that we have
been undeniably in his living presence.

There is a fine thread of personal idiom worked through
the text of Falstaff's talk. His private voice rings out in such
sentences as these:

Indeed, you come near me now, Hal.            (1-1, ii, 14)

No; I'll give thee thy due, thou hast paid all there.
                                             (1-1, ii, 59-60)

Indeed, I am not John of Gaunt, your grandfather; but yet no
coward, Hal.                                 (1-II, ii, 70-1)

I'll never wear hair on my face more.        (1-II, iv, 153)

Ah, no more of that, Hal, an thou lovest me!  (1-II, iv, 312-3)

Peace, good Doll! do not speak like a death's-head. Do not
bid me remember mine end.                    (2-II, iv, 254-5)

His native speech is casual yet pure, natural yet distinguished,
easy and yet expertly wrenched out of line with the conventions of syntax; impossible to define, yet audibly his very

own. We hear it, however, but seldom. Most of the time it is buried under heaps of talk delivered from a hundred assumed personalities, a hundred fictitious identities.

He is limited as a mimic only by the facts of his physique; being old and fat, he is short of breath and so must be brief of phrase.

Tut, tut; good enough to toss; food for powder, food for powder; they'll fill a pit as well as better. Tush, man, mortal men, mortal men.                    (1-IV, ii, 71-3)

How now, lad! is the wind in that door, i' faith? Must we all march?                    (1-III, iii, 102-3)

How now! whose mare's dead? What's the matter?
                    (2-II, i, 46-7)

But it will be seen at once—or heard—that he has made the most of this limitation. Artist that he is, he has accepted its challenge and employed it in effects that express his genius with a notable and economical directness. If he must gasp he will make each further gasp an echo of its fellow—an echo, but with ineffable additions. His speech then is not merely brief; it is repetitive, it rolls back on itself, it picks up its theme and tosses it to us again, with rich improvements.

Why, Hal, 't is my vocation, Hal. 'T is no sin for a man to labour in his vocation.                    (1-I, ii, 116-7)

If the rascal have not given me medicines to make me love him, I'll be hang'd. It could not be else; I have drunk medicines.
                    (1-II, ii, 18-20)

A plague of all cowards, I say, and a vengeance too! marry, and amen! Give me a cup of sack, boy. . . . A plague of all cowards! Give me a cup of sack, rogue. Is there no virtue extant?
                    (1-II, iv, 127-32)

If I fought not with fifty of them, I am a bunch of radish. If there were not two or three and fifty upon poor old Jack, than am I no two-legg'd creature.                    (1-II, iv, 205-8)

What, shall we be merry? Shall we have a play extempore?
                                        (1-II, iv, 308-9)

Bardolph, am I not fallen away vilely since this last action?
Do I not bate? Do I not dwindle? Why, my skin hangs about
me like an old lady's loose gown; I am withered like an old
apple-john.                              (1-III, iii, 1-4)

I am not only witty in myself, but the cause that wit is in
other men. I do here walk before thee like a sow that hath over-
whelm'd all her litter but one. If the Prince put thee into my
service for any other reason than to set me off, why then I have
no judgement. Thou whoreson mandrake, thou art fitter to be
worn in my cap than to wait at my heels. I was never mann'd
with an agate till now.                  (2-I, ii, 10-9)

What, a young knave, and begging! Is there not wars? Is there
not employment? Doth not the King lack subjects? Do not the
rebels need soldiers?                    (2-I, ii, 84-7)

If the cook help to make the gluttony, you help to make the
diseases, Doll. We catch of you, Doll, we catch of you. Grant
that, my poor virtue, grant that.       (2-II, iv, 48-51)

Do you think me a swallow, an arrow, or a bullet? Have I, in
my poor and old motion, the expedition of thought?
                                        (2-IV, iii, 35-7)

And, once more, its burden, its high business, is parody: imitation not always of another man who is standing by, if it is
ever that, but of some man Falstaff suddenly, without warning, decides to be. Upon occasion it is the man—the bluff,
successful soldier—he had been trained in his youth to be and
has never become, though he knows the manner perfectly.
"Tush, man, mortal men, mortal men"—there speaks the busy
ghost of Sir John Falstaff, who rises again in "Whose mare's
dead? What's the matter?" But there are many manners,
many men. "Do not bid me remember mine end"—that is
dolorously delivered, with a long face that remembers psalms.
"I have drunk medicines," "Is there no virtue extant?", "I

am withered like an old apple-john"—in such sighs we hear
a feigned self-pity, a fooling with the music of elegy, which
becomes classic in "A plague of sighing and grief! it blows a
man up like a bladder" (1-II, iv, 364-5). In "We catch of
you, Doll, we catch of you" there is a tickling levity, a
chuckle and a poke in the ribs.

The essence of Falstaff is that he is a comic actor, most of
whose roles are assumed without announcement. In at least
two cases he forewarns us: when he proposes to the Prince
that they take turns playing the King (1-II, iv), and when
he orders his page to help him play deaf before the Lord
Chief Justice (2-I, ii).

My good lord! God give your lordship good time of day. I
am glad to see your lordship abroad. I heard say your lordship
was sick; I hope your lordship goes abroad by advice.

That is deliberate acting, as is the mournful gesture later on:

Well, I cannot last ever; but it was alway yet the trick of our
English nation, if they have a good thing, to make it too common.

And the mummery of Falstaff and the Prince as Henry IV
provides some of the best stuff in all the play; the Prince, incidentally, showing both there and elsewhere that he has
been Falstaff's aptest pupil in the school of style, for he can
take off both his old master—"How now, wool-sack! what
mutter you?" (1-II, iv, 149)—and his young rival in honor
Hotspur (1-II, iv, 110-25). But Falstaff's stage acting, first-
rate as it is, falls short of the natural acting he is incessantly
busy with, whether the fiction of the moment be that he is
a soldier with secret responsibilities or whether it be that he
is a gay old blade of the town come to chuck the hostess
under the chin and set Doll Tearsheet on his knee. Under
pressure of the necessity to imitate his environment he can
even break into verse, as when the Hostess's theatrical excite-

ment over the little play of Henry IV and his son suggests to him that he treads a tragic stage:

> For God's sake, lords, convey my tristful queen;
> For tears do stop the flood-gates of her eyes;
>
> (1-II, iv, 434-5)

and as when, having so great a desire to hear what news the magnificent Pistol brings of Hal and the kingship, he knows he must fall in with the rascal's style if he is ever to get anything out of him:

> O base Assyrian knight, what is thy news?
> Let King Cophetua know the truth thereof.
>
> (2-v, iii, 105-6)

Of course he gets what he wanted; the style works like magic:

> Sir John, thy tender lambkin now is king;
> Harry the Fifth's the man. I speak the truth.
> When Pistol lies, do this, and fig me like
> The bragging Spaniard. (2-v, iii, 122-5)

And it would have been a pity if somewhere in "Henry IV" Falstaff had not added Pistol to his list of roles. For there is nothing more absurd and glorious in Shakespeare than the old-tragedy verse of Ancient Pistol:

> Fear we broadsides? No, let the fiend give fire.
>
> (2-II, iv, 196)

> There roar'd the sea, and trumpet-clangor sounds.
>
> (2-v, v, 42)

The ripest piece of Falstaff's miming is reserved, however, for a series of scenes toward the close of the second play, when Sir John, recruiting soldiers in Gloucestershire, happens upon an old friend of his London youth, the now doddering Justice Shallow. Shallow has lost all the juices that Falstaff has kept. He is thin and dry, and drones reminiscences in an old man's witless tenor.

Come on, come on, come on, sir; give me your hand, sir, give me your hand, sir. An early stirrer, by the rood! And how doth my good cousin Silence?                                    (2-III, ii, 1-4)

Certain, 't is certain; very sure, very sure. Death, as the Psalmist saith, is certain to all; all shall die.          (2-III, ii, 40-2)

I will not excuse you; you shall not be excus'd; excuses shall not be admitted; there is no excuse shall serve; you shall not be excus'd. Why, Davy! . . . Davy, Davy, Davy, Davy, let me see, Davy; let me see, Davy; let me see. Yea, marry, William cook, bid him come hither. Sir John, you shall not be excus'd.

                                                    (2-v, i, 5-13)

His unit of utterance is as brief as Falstaff's, and the Lord knows he repeats himself; but if any evidence were needed of the muscle in his big friend's style it could be found at once in the contrast Shallow provides. For his repetitions are relaxed, nerveless, foolish—the work of weakness, not of a still joyful strength; just as those of the Hostess are the signs of a fluttering rather than a doing mind:

I have borne, and borne, and borne, and have been fubb'd off, and fubb'd off, and fubb'd off, from this day to that day, that it is a shame to be thought on.                              (2-II, i, 35-9)

If he swagger, let him not come here; no, by my faith. I must live among my neighbours; I'll no swaggerers. I am in good name and fame with the very best. Shut the door; there comes no swaggerers here. I have not liv'd all this while, to have swaggering now. Shut the door, I pray you.          (2-II, iv, 79-85)

Falstaff, whose memory of Shallow is doubtless less perfect than he says it is, takes in the truth at a glance; sees that this old forked radish, this pitiful cheese-paring of a man, lives only in the remembrance of his youth; and nobly decides—for even though he may think to have fun with Shallow later, and cash in on him as a butt for whom the Prince will pay, there is something noble in the instantaneous decision—

to fall in with his way of speech, to grant him just what he desires.

*Shallow.* O, Sir John, do you remember since we lay all night in the windmill in Saint George's field?

*Falstaff.* No more of that, good Master Shallow, no more of that.

*Shallow.* Ha! 't was a merry night. And is Jane Nightwork alive?

*Falstaff.* She lives, Master Shallow.

*Shallow.* She never could away with me.

*Falstaff.* Never, never; she would always say she could not abide Master Shallow.

*Shallow.* By the mass, I could anger her to the heart. She was then a bona-roba. Doth she hold her own well?

*Falstaff.* Old, old, Master Shallow.

*Shallow.* Nay, she must be old; she cannot choose but be old; certain she's old; and had Robin Nightwork by old Nightwork before I came to Clement's Inn.

*Silence.* That's fifty-five year ago.

*Shallow.* Ha, cousin Silence, that thou hadst seen that that this knight and I have seen! Ha, Sir John, said I well?

*Falstaff.* We have heard the chimes at midnight, Master Shallow. (2-III, ii, 206-29)

The last and best of these sentences sums up all that Shallow could hope to say in twenty quavering years, and does it so briefly that the breath of any hearer must be taken; and expresses its speaker so completely that he can never be absent from our consciousness henceforth. We may not know the man who says this, but we know that a man says it, and we know him better than we do most members of his race. And we have not failed to note the magnanimity which after all has been from the beginning the groundwork of his humor: a magnanimity which will sound once more when, listening to the simple, bemused merriment of Silence as he sings his little songs, he generously puts in the remark:

I did not think Master Silence had been a man of this mettle.

(2-v, iii, 40)

And Silence responds:

Who? I? I have been merry twice and once ere now.

The wit of Falstaff's answers when charges of cowardice, treachery, and lying are truly urged against him is the wit of a man who knows that other men are waiting to hear what he will pretend, who he will become, how he will get out of it. "Answer, thou dead elm, answer," "Come," says Poins, "your reason, Jack, your reason." Poins is thirsty for another of Jack's good reasons. He must be patient a while, for Falstaff to make time insists that though reasons were as plenty as blackberries he will give none on compulsion; but in good season it comes: "Why, hear you, my masters. Was it for me to kill the heir-apparent? Should I turn upon the true prince?" (1-11, iv, 295-7). Something like that was what Poins and the true Prince wanted, though they could not have predicted it, being no Falstaffs. Like any remark by a great man, it is at the same time surprising and in character; the form of such a man grows clearer with everything he utters, and his dimensions increase. We could not have known that he would say it; and afterwards we cannot imagine him saying anything else or better, though the next thing will be better. "Thy love is worth a million; thou ow'st me thy love" (1-111, iii, 155-6). That is better; and so is "I disprais'd him before the wicked, that the wicked might not fall in love with him; in which doing, I have done the part of a careful friend and a true subject, and thy father is to give me thanks for it" (2-11, iv, 346-50). That the King does not thank him is not surprising. Falstaff has not expected it.

What now of his vices, and why is it that they have not the sound of vices? None of them is an end in itself—that is their secret, just as Falstaff's character is his mystery. He does not live to drink or steal or lie or foin o' nights. He even does not live in order that he may be the cause of wit in other men. We do not in fact know why he lives. This great boulder is balanced lightly on the earth, and can be tipped with the lightest touch. He cannot be overturned. He knows too much, and he understands too well the art of delivering with every lie he tells an honest weight of profound and personal revelation.

# THE MERRY WIVES OF WINDSOR

THE Falstaff of "Henry IV" is missing from "The Merry Wives of Windsor," which is said to have been written for a queen who wanted to see the fat knight in love. The trouble is just there; he is in love with the merry wives—or with the plot to make them think he is— rather than with truth and existence, rather than with the merry lives he had been living when Shakespeare caught him in his comic prime. His ambition for Mistress Ford and Mistress Page, together with the delusions which it requires, fills all his mind; he has a single end in view, and believes he can attain it. He does not lose his belief until the last act, though to every other person in the play he has been a fool from the first. The old man who once had missed nothing now misses everything; he has toppled from his balance, he is unintelligent. Hitherto he had made a large world merry by playing the butt; here he makes a small one sad by being the butt of coarse-grained men and women who drag and buffet him about until the business grows as boring as a practical joke. His dignity was never touched in "Henry IV"; rather it increased with every exposure, for what exposed itself was his understanding. In "The Merry Wives" he has none to lose, being no longer a man of mind but a tub of meat to be bounced downstairs and thrown in the muddy river. Even the dull senses of Sir Hugh Evans can smell in him a man of middle-earth. And it is not until a few minutes from the final line that Falstaff sees he has been grossly over-reached. Then he utters the incredible sentence:

I do begin to perceive that I am made an ass.     (v, v, 125)

136

"I do begin to perceive." His perception had once been without beginning or end; or if there was a beginning it ran
nimbly before that of the quickest eyes about him. No wonder he has to beg off at the close with three equally incredible
words:

I am dejected. (v, v, 171)

So will any audience be which remembers the chimes at
midnight, Master Shallow.

Only the husk of Falstaff's voice is here. Shakespeare has
written the part with great talent but without love. The long
speeches, descriptive in most cases of mishaps by hamper and
flood, are certainly very able, and a phrase in one of them,
"I have a kind of alacrity in sinking" (iii, v, 12), almost restores the man we knew. Nor has he dropped the habit of
spilling his speech in short repeated units: "I warrant thee,
nobody hears; mine own people, mine own people" (ii, ii,
51-2). The labor of composition, however, is often apparent
in passages where Falstaff forces his wit. "No quips now,
Pistol! Indeed, I am in the waist two yards about; but I am
now about no waste, I am about thrift"—the pun is poor, and
furthermore Falstaff used to get on without puns, just as he
used to manage an effect of verbal felicity without having to
lug in monstrous circumlocutions like "pullet-sperm in my
brewage" for "eggs in my sack" (iii, v, 32-3). Perhaps his
best remark is a reference to the Welshman Evans as "one
who makes fritters of English." But that is because he retains
something of his old interest in language; though it should be
pointed out in passing that Falstaff would have been entertained by the fritters of a vastly better Welshman than Evans
if he had lived to hear Fluellen in "Henry V." So for that
matter with Pistol and Bardolph, who do not survive in
"Henry V" with all of their old vigor, but who are happier
there, along with the laconic Nym, than these poor pieces of
them are in "The Merry Wives." Their betrayal of the fat

jester whom once they feared and adored (ɪ, iii) is doubtless the clearest sign of their degradation—not in moral character, for they had none, but in that dramatic character
which preserved them in their prime from the indignity of
a descent to conventional comic devices. In their prime they
lived for no other reason than that they were alive, and loved
to come swaggering out of the darkness into lighted taverns.
Here they exist simply to keep a comic machinery turning,
as Mistress Quickly exists solely in the profession of go-
between and tale-bearer. As for Master Shallow, we have
one or two remnants of the well-starved justice: "Come, coz;
come, coz; we stay for you. A word with you, coz; marry,
this, coz" (ɪ, i, 2ɪ3-4); and "Bodykins, Master Page, . . . we
have some salt of our youth in us; we are the sons of women,
Master Page" (ɪɪ, iii, 46-5ɪ). But the full music of his fool-
ishness is missing too.

The one satisfactory person of the comedy is, perhaps
naturally enough, a new one. Mine host of the Garter Inn
comes bellowing into the dialogue with something like the
primeval force his fellows formerly had. He wields a mad,
winy (or is it beery) eloquence. He is a man of few words
but he uses them over and over, mounting through repetitions of them to a preposterous peak of self-induced excitement. As his custom is in such cases, Shakespeare has hit upon
a single word that will do the trick, and will seem to do it
without any further effort on his part. The word is "bully."

*Falstaff*. Mine host of the Garter!
*Host*. What says my bully-rook? Speak scholarly and wisely.
*Falstaff*. Truly, mine host, I must turn away some of my fol-
lowers.
*Host*. Discard, bully Hercules; cashier. Let them wag. Trot,
trot.
*Falstaff*. I sit at ten pounds a week.
*Host*. Thou 'rt an emperor, Caesar, Keisar, and Pheezar. I will

entertain Bardolph; he shall draw, he shall tap. Said I well, bully Hector?

*Falstaff.* Do so, good mine host.

*Host.* I have spoke; let him follow. Let me see thee froth and lime. I am at a word; follow.                    (I, iii, 1-15)

The dialogue is clearly mine host's, not Falstaff's. It is he that carries it away, for he is mad about words, he goes into ecstasies of epithet, he boils over into a foam of phrases.

Is he dead, my Ethiopian? Is he dead; my Francisco? Ha, bully! What says my Aesculapius? my Galen? my heart of elder? Ha! is he dead, bully stale? Is he dead?     (II, iii, 27-31)

Let him die; but first sheathe thy impatience, throw cold water on thy choler, go about the fields with me through Frogmore. I will bring thee where Mistress Anne Page is, at a farm-house a-feasting; and thou shalt woo her.           (II, iii, 87-92)

Peace, I say! hear mine host of the Garter. Am I politic? Am I subtle? Am I a Machiavel? Shall I lose my doctor? No; he gives me the potions and the motions. Shall I lose my parson, my priest, my Sir Hugh? No; he gives me the proverbs and the noverbs. Give me thy hand, terrestrial; so. Give me thy hand, celestial; so. Boys of art, I have deceiv'd you both.   (III, i, 102-9)

What say you to young Master Fenton? He capers, he dances, he has eyes of youth, he writes verses, he speaks holiday, he smells April and May. He will carry 't, he will carry 't; 't is in his buttons; he will carry 't.                  (III, ii, 67-71)

"Trust me," ventures Shallow, "a mad host." Completely and most comically mad he is; and the only fresh thing in "The Merry Wives."

Master Fenton has eyes of youth and speaks in verses of the sweet Anne Page whom the action ushers into his arms at the end. But they are meager verses, like those in which she simpers her reciprocated love. It is not a comedy in which poetry would be expected, any more than comedy itself. After "The Comedy of Errors" it is Shakespeare's most heartless farce. And this is too bad, since it is his only citizen play, his one local and contemporary piece. In another mood he might have made much of Ford and Page, and of their wives who to our loss are here so coarse-grained, so monotonous and broad-hipped in their comic dialect.

*Mrs. Ford.* "Boarding," call you it? I'll be sure to keep him above deck.

*Mrs. Page.* So will I. If he come under my hatches, I'll never to sea again.                              (II, i, 93-6)

With craft and talent Shakespeare has supplied what the convention and a queen demanded. But his genius is not here, or his love.

"IN his comick scenes," said Dr. Johnson, "he seems to produce without labour what no labour can improve. . . . His tragedy seems to be skill, his comedy to be instinct." Whatever applicability this may have to the tragedies of Shakespeare's prime, and it appears to have none at all, its truth is perhaps self-evident with respect to the three comedies he wrote during the last year or so of the sixteenth century. And it provides a convenient starting-point for any discussion of "Much Ado About Nothing," whose comedy of Benedick and Beatrice is so flexible, so instinctive, and whose tragedy of Claudio and Hero is so strangely stiff. If the last epithet is deserved there would seem to have been no skill employed in the painful tale of Leonato's daughter. Nor in its own terms can much be said for the sober plot which somewhat duskily weaves its web across the heart of an otherwise bright play. But in the strategy of the play as a whole much skill was used. A difficult problem had been posed, and it was more than satisfactorily solved. This does not mean that the Hero story would be convincing by itself or that the Beatrice story is substantial out of its context. It means that the two must be considered together; that Shakespeare did in fact consider them together, and did with ingenuity maintain them in a relation of mutual support. The problem was dual: how to prevent the main action, and indeed the only action, from turning the play into a tragedy or a near-tragedy; and how to bestow enough body upon the comic theme to make it matter either in itself or in its function as preventive. The result of Shakespeare's labor, most of which he concealed, is that Hero and Claudio never come close enough to us for pity or terror to be felt, and that Beatrice and Benedick, created as an insulating medium between tragedy and us, become finally so important as to bear all away upon their comic backs. But it is the seriousness of the central situation that sheds upon Benedick and Beatrice so much importance. As the play stands, neither pair of lovers can do without the other. Both skill and instinct are maneuvering every scene.

"Much Ado" begins and ends with Beatrice and Benedick, whose prose thus describes the circumference of Shakespeare's comic circle. The first interesting thing of which we hear is the "merry war" between the two; "they never meet," Leonato explains to Don Pedro's messenger whom Beatrice has so much bewildered, "but there's a skirmish of wit between them" (I, i, 63-4). Beatrice with her fine strong voice and her masculine humor has come in haste to hear the news of Benedick and others, but chiefly of Benedick; and in advance of his arrival she has baited his name. In a few minutes he comes swinging on and they are at it:

*Beatrice.* I wonder that you will still be talking, Signior Benedick. Nobody marks you.
*Benedick.* What, my dear Lady Disdain! are you yet living?
(I, i, 117-20)

Even so early a tone is set for the play which the somber doings of Hero and Claudio will find it difficult to destroy. A wall of brass-bright words begins to be erected, a wall which terror perhaps will never pierce. There is to be much talk for the sake of talk, and our experience of the theater leads us therefore to expect pure comedy. But a conflicting note is struck at once, for the villain of such tragedy as we shall have has arrived with Benedick; he is Don John, and his first speech is a cold one. "I am not of many words" (I, i, 159). Is the communication ominous? We do not know yet, for our attention is immediately turned to the wager between

Benedick and his friends. Benedick is one of those spirited bachelors who ride high over love but who for that very reason can fall with wonderful suddenness into its arms. Don Pedro and Claudio, predicting his fall, prod him into swearing that if it happens they can hang him in a bottle like a cat (i, i, 259). Surely now there is nothing but comic stuff ahead; Benedick, who already has admitted that Beatrice is beautiful except for her fury (193-5), fools nobody, and least of all ourselves. We know what will happen. We settle ourselves to see whether it is to be amusingly worked out.

Here again, however, intrudes the cold, muffled voice of Don John. "Let me be that I am" (i, iii, 38), he mutters. That is the accent of an unalterable villain. Furthermore, he is cynical about marriage, for a man who would wed is one "that betroths himself to unquietness" (i, iii, 50). Yet we have just heard Benedick deny that he is one to "sigh away Sundays," and we are soon to hear Beatrice thank God because he sends her no husband (ii, i, 28-30); her hope of heaven is of a place where she can sit with the bachelors and be as merry as the day is long. Don John's hatred of love, however serious it may be, is stupidly stated and sounds harmless in the envelope of banter into which Shakespeare has slipped it. The plot nevertheless is thickening, and a complication potentially as grave as that of "Othello," and indeed analogous to it, commences to declare itself. Don Pedro, wooing Hero for Claudio at a masked ball, acts his part so cleverly that Don John can make Claudio jealous at the spectacle; and when nothing comes of this, for the lovers straighten the matter out and are at once betrothed, there is the further threat to their happiness of the window-plot which Don John and Borachio now disclose.

This is a serious threat, but before it is felt as real or dangerous a lighter fiction is hatched by the high-hearted persons of the play. It is in fact a pair of fictions, and Don Pedro, who wooed Hero so gaily for his friend, is at the

bottom of both. Benedick and Beatrice are to be induced to
fall in love with each other—or, since they already are in
love, to confess that they are—by overhearing certain con-
versations prepared for the purpose. Each is to hear that the
other is afflicted with love but is too proud to say so, being
too sure that a confession would be scorned; each of them
suffers in silence from the other's unthinking cruelty. Benedick and Beatrice, in other words, are to be turned into
lovers by hearing themselves talked about—a common occurrence in the world, but they are not common. The ruse is
sure to succeed, we want to see it succeed, and the play
pauses while we do. There is no attempt on Shakespeare's
part to complicate the business with plausible delays. The
one charming scene follows hard upon the other; the lovers
are converted schematically in turn; and a brisk vocabulary
of sporting terms brightens and speeds this portion of the
play. Benedick had likened Claudio, jealous of Don Pedro,
to a poor hurt fowl creeping into sedges (II, i, 208-9), but
he himself is now a fish on a hook (II, iii, 113), a fowl to be
stalked (II, iii, 94); and Beatrice is a golden fish to be angled
for (III, i, 26-7), a bird to be limed (III, i, 104), a lapwing
who runs close by the ground to hear the ladies' conference
(III, i, 24-5), a coy wild haggard of the rock (III, i, 35-6).
The tone of comedy would seem then to be firmly set, not
only by the prattle but by the kind of brittle action that
belongs to comedy everywhere.

And it is very firmly set. "Much Ado" henceforth will be
nothing if not comic. But its texture will be unique. For
Benedick and Beatrice do not meet to confess their love until
the threat to their friends' love has been made good; until
the catastrophe of Claudio's denunciation has struck like
lightning in the church; and until Hero is understood by him
to be dead. Nothing of melodrama is remitted here, except
that the villainy of Don John is narrated, not witnessed; and
the words of Claudio about his rotten orange (IV, i, 33) are

for the moment shocking. The disaster is swift and real enough for us to feel a difference in Benedick and Beatrice when they come together just after it to reap the harvest of their twin deceptions. For their relation has deepened under the strain; and once more there is something that prevents them from making love simply. The briefest declarations are followed by a sharp command from Beatrice:

> *Benedick.* I protest I love you.
> *Beatrice.* Why, then, God forgive me!
> *Benedick.* What offense, sweet Beatrice?
> *Beatrice.* . . . I was about to protest I loved you.
> *Benedick.* And do it with all thy heart.
> *Beatrice.* I love you with so much of my heart that none is left to protest.
> *Benedick.* Come, bid me do anything for thee.
> *Beatrice.* Kill Claudio.

This introduces the sequence of events which leads up to Benedick's challenge of Claudio, and which lightens in tone to the point where the challenge is farcical—as farcical as old Antonio's whipping out his sword against Claudio (v, i). In itself, however, the dialogue is as rich in dramatic meaning as any in Shakespeare; the serious and the silly meet here in a marriage which the whole play thus far has conspired to arrange, and which the rest of it will subtly solemnize. Henceforth the persons central to the action will grow more and more like puppets, and the puppets of the comic byplay will grow more and more like persons. Hero will exist only as one who plays dead, and Claudio merely as one who mourns over an empty tomb. Benedick and Beatrice, even though they will never find time to make love simply, have all the future in their hands until Benedick shall send the audience home with "Strike up, pipers." Meanwhile the abused lady whose shadow falls on their dialogue and colors it to a brave tension will have done much for them; Hero it is who, whether she knows it or not, has given them their lofty position among Shakespeare's most interesting lovers.

Meanwhile as well there have been Dogberry, Verges, and the Watch. If nothing else had directed the audience how to feel, and whether to feel deeply, the ineffable presence of these simpletons would have done so. Only a comedy could contain such harmless and irrelevant officials, such senseless and fit men for constables of a solemn watch. Their dunder-headedness remains indefinable; their nature is as resistant to analysis as that of the somehow sublime Bottom; and yet their destiny on any stage would be as clear as day. Their minds are muddy but their course is charted. They will blunder about in their tedious and stubborn "vigitance" till they have made all well. Fools like that cannot fail. What the wisdoms of gentlemen would never discover they bring to light, moping about with their hiccups and their lanterns, and stumbling into the grace of our loud laughter. Benedick and Beatrice draw a clear circle of wit about the play to keep its tragedy in place. Dogberry and his fellows are a coarse tallow candle burning near the center, keeping the comic peace.

Talk is the business of "Much Ado." Most of its merit is therefore in its prose, compared with which the verse is generally insignificant. An exception is the dialogue of Hero and Ursula while Beatrice listens like a lapwing close by the ground. The dialogue would be an exception if it contained no more than the one good line,

> Disdain and scorn ride sparkling in her eyes.
>
> (III, i, 51)

But it is crowded with good lines, as befits the sudden concentration of our interest in a scene where for once—and we shall find that it is only once—Beatrice stands exposed as the romantic young woman she is. Elsewhere she wears for protection the impenetrable veil of wit. That may make her still more romantic, but prose is the medium through which we should discover that this is so, for the economy of prose is irony's most faithful servant, and epigrams take best effect in something that sounds like conversation. Beatrice can scarcely be imagined in love with a man who is a poet all the time. Benedick never is. Finding himself in love he tries to show it in rhyme, but he can think of nothing better than "baby" to go with "lady," "horn" with "scorn," and "fool" with "school." "Very ominous endings," he concludes. "No, I was not born under a rhyming planet, nor I cannot woo in festival terms" (v, ii, 40-1). He is of course not far distant from Hotspur, who with him helps to say for Shakespeare that verse, at any rate for the time being, seems limited as a channel when the full tide of life comes pouring through.

The prose of Benedick and Beatrice is a brilliant brocade of artifice. But its counterpoint of antithesis and epithet is natural to two such desperate defenders of pride against the leveling guns of love, of personality against passion. It is a logical language for persons who seldom say what they mean, and who, since they love nothing better than talk, must talk always for effect. It is the inevitable idiom for lovers who would deny their love.

O, she misus'd me past the endurance of a block! An oak but with one green leaf on it would have answered her. My very visor began to assume life and scold with her. She told me, not thinking I had been myself, that I was the Prince's jester, that I was duller than a great thaw; huddling jest upon jest with such impossible conveyance upon me that I stood like a man at a mark, with a whole army shooting at me. She speaks poniards, and every word stabs. If her breath were as terrible as her terminations, there were no living near her; she would infect to the north star. . . . Will your Grace command me any service to the world's end? I will go on the slightest errand now to the Antipodes that you can devise to send me on; I will fetch you a toothpicker now from the furthest inch of Asia, bring you the length of Prester John's foot, fetch you a hair off the great Cham's beard, do you any embassage to the Pigmies, rather than hold three words' conference with this harpy.    (II, i, 246-79)

Benedick is a virtuoso in hyperbole, and is so much at home in the language of lies that he can make prose music, just for the fun of it, out of long words juxtaposed with short, out of rare silken terms thrust suddenly among russet yeas and noes. "With such impossible conveyance," "as terrible as her terminations," "do you any embassage"—this is the accent of Hamlet as he holds Rosencrantz and Guildenstern at the far end of his tongue, and it is the accent indeed of any gentleman in Shakespeare when his mind races ahead of his discourse. Benedick can be plain enough when he is alone, though even then he enjoys his voice and smiles at his brevity. "No, the world must be peopled. When I said I would die a bachelor, I did not think I should live till I were married" (ii, iii, 250-3).

Beatrice is "my Lady Tongue," and no better than Benedick can manage the art of keeping still. Don Pedro hits off her lover's loquacity when he remarks that "he hath a heart as sound as a bell and his tongue is the clapper, for what his heart thinks his tongue speaks" (iii, ii, 12-4). But it is usually Beatrice who make the accusation, just as it is Benedick from whom we hear that Beatrice talks honest men to death. Both are right. Beatrice is so much in love with words that she can even be impatient with the silence of others. "Speak, count, 't is your cue," she cries to Claudio when he stands tongue-tied before Hero at the betrothal. And "Speak, cousin," she cries in turn to Hero; "or, if you cannot, stop his mouth with a kiss" (ii, i, 321-22). We shall remember this in the last scene when Benedick, listening to the fabulous lie she tells of having yielded to him only to save him from a consumption, all but ends the play with "Peace! I will stop your mouth," and kisses her soundly.

There is poetry in her repartee:

*Don Pedro.* In faith, lady, you have a merry heart.
*Beatrice.* Yea, my lord; I thank it, poor fool, it keeps on the

windy side of care. . . . I was born to speak all mirth and no matter. . . .

   *Don Pedro.* Out o' question, you were born in a merry hour.

   *Beatrice.* No, sure, my lord, my mother cried; but then there was a star danc'd, and under that was I born.    (II, i, 325-50)

And there is sometimes a dash of indecency:

   *Don Pedro.* You have put him down, lady, you have put him down.

   *Beatrice.* So I would not he should do me, my lord, lest I should prove the mother of fools.    (II, i, 292-5)

"Neither his gentlemen nor his ladies," thought Dr. Johnson, "have much delicacy," and Shakespeare indeed made Benedick still franker. Their indelicacy sorts perfectly, as a matter of fact, with the suddenness of their poetry. Both are signs of their beautiful, unlimited power—a power whose existence we need to know in order that we may measure a love that must live without any other expression than the inverted one of raillery. There is never, perhaps, any doubt about this love. Beatrice in the first scene resents Benedick's new friend Claudio—"O Lord, he will hang upon him like a disease" (I, i, 86). And she is woefully let down when, going among the women for the first time after she has overheard their conference, she hints that she is in love and Margaret teases her by pretending to misunderstand (III, iv). The wit of Benedick and his Lady Tongue is wonderful but it is after all transparent. It is almost never absent. Even when he humbles himself to say:

   Thou and I are too wise to woo peaceably,    (v, ii, 73)

she cannot let him rest without asking him how he knows *he* is wise. But we see through such wit as through a prism, and the love we behold is all the more convincing because of the refraction. If there is nothing more attractive in comedy than a picture of two brilliant persons in love against their will, then we shall like "Much Ado About Nothing" as much better than "The Taming of the Shrew" as it is a better play by a maturer playwright. And if this playwright, being Shakespeare, is near the height of his powers we shall expect in his hero and heroine that kind of excellence which sets a standard. So for all time it does—with Mirabell and Millamant waiting a century off to measure themselves and miss it by no finest hair of their white wigs.

# AS YOU LIKE IT

THE airiness of "As You Like It" is as much the work of thought as the reward of feeling. The comedy seems to balance like a bubble on a point of thin space; yet space in its neighborhood has not worn thin, and the bubble is as tough as eternity, it does not break. This, doubtless, is because the sentiments of its author were at the moment in a state of rare equilibrium, and because his nerves were happy in an unconscious health. Also, however, it is because his mind was tuned to its task. "As You Like It" is so charming a comedy that in order to enjoy it we need not think about it at all. But if we do think about it we become aware of intellectual operations noiselessly and expertly performed. We see an idea anatomized until there is nothing left of it save its original mystery. We watch an attitude as it is taken completely apart and put completely together again. And all of this is done without visible effort. Shakespeare's understanding of his subject increases until the subject is exhausted, until there is no more to understand; and still there are no signs of labor or fatigue. Shakespeare has been denied an intellect. But whatever it took to write "As You Like It" was among other things mental, and the exact like of it, as well as the exact degree, has never been seen in literature again.

"As You Like It" is a criticism of the pastoral sentiment, an examination of certain familiar ideas concerning the simple life and the golden age. It is not satire; its examination is conducted without prejudice. For once in the world a proposition is approached from all of its sides, and from top and bottom. The proposition is perhaps multiple: the country is

more natural than the court, shepherds live lives of enviable
innocence and simplicity, the vices that devour the heart of
civilized man will drop from him as soon as he walks under
a greenwood tree, perversion and malice cannot survive in
the open air, the shade of beech trees is the only true Acad-
emy, one impulse from the vernal wood will teach us more
than all the sages can. Yet it is single too, and pastoral literature has monotonously intoned it. Shakespeare relieves the
monotony by statement which is also understanding, by
criticism which is half laughter and half love—or, since his
laughter is what it is, all love. The result is something very
curious. When Rosalind has made her last curtsy and the
comedy is done, the pastoral sentiment is without a leg to
stand on, yet it stands; and not only stands but dances. The
idea of the simple life has been smiled off the earth and yet
here it still is, smiling back at us from every bough of Arden.
The Forest of Arden has been demonstrated not to exist, yet
none of its trees has fallen; rather the entire plantation waves
forever, and the sun upon it will not cease. The doctrine of
the golden age has been as much created as destroyed. We
know there is nothing in it, and we know that everything is
in it. We perceive how silly it is and why we shall never be
able to do without it. We comprehend the long failure of
cynicism to undo sentiment. Here there is neither sentiment
nor cynicism; there is understanding. An idea is left hanging
in free air, without contamination or support. That is the
place for ideas, as Shakespeare the comic poet seems to have
known without being told.

"Where will the old Duke live?" asks Orlando's villainous
brother of the still more villainous wrestler Charles. The unscrupulous bruiser answers in terms that may surprise us by
their prettiness:

They say he is already in the forest of Arden, and a many
merry men with him; and there they live like the old Robin
Hood of England. They say many young gentlemen flock to

him every day, and fleet the time carelessly, as they did in the
golden world.                                    (I, i, 120-25)

That is the text to be annotated, the idea to be analyzed in
the comedy to come. But analysis has already taken place, a
cross-glance has already been shot by one whose mind will
go on to draw lines in every direction athwart the theme.
Shakespeare's first operation consists of putting such a speech
into such a mouth, and letting it be ground between great
molars there, unsympathetically. We get the doctrine, but
we get it crooked, as comedy prefers: through the most unlikely medium, and the most unconscious. The first act is for
the most part mechanically introductory to what follows; its
business is to push everybody off to Arden, and Shakespeare
writes it without much interest, since his sole interest is
Arden. Rosalind is introduced, and of course it is important
that we should find her from the first a gallant and witty
girl, as we do. But she too is being saved for the forest.
Charles's speech is the one memorable thing we have heard
before we plunge into the depths of Arden at the beginning
of the second act. But it is distinctly memorable, and it modi-
fies the music which plays for us in the old Duke's mind.

> Now, my co-mates and brothers in exile,
> Hath not old custom made this life more sweet
> Than that of painted pomp? Are not these woods
> More free from peril than the envious court? . . .
> Sweet are the uses of adversity,
> Which, like the toad, ugly and venomous,
> Wears yet a precious jewel in his head;
> And this our life, exempt from public haunt,
> Finds tongues in trees, books in the running brooks,
> Sermons in stones, and good in every thing.   (II, i, 1-17)

There is the text once more, translated into so quiet and so
sweet a style that we may be tempted to believe it is the
author speaking. But he was speaking as well in Charles; or
rather he speaks in both—in their relation, which is only one

of many relations the play will explore. The simple text will receive further statement through four pleasant acts. Good old Adam reminds Orlando of "the antique world" which was so much purer than "the fashion of these times" (ii, iii, 57-9). Shepherds appear named <u>Corin</u> and Silvius, and one of them goes sighing through the forest for love of his Phebe. A member of the Duke's retinue in exile knows how to be philosophical about everything; the humorous sadness of Jaques promises to ripen into wisdom now that ingratitude is forgotten and ambition can be shunned. We look to him for the sermons that so far have remained silent in their stones.

> Give me leave
> To speak my mind, and I will through and through
> Cleanse the foul body of the infected world,
> If they will patiently receive my medicine. (ii, vii, 58-61)

So radical a boast in such emancipated terms, delivered by one who sees through the mummery of manners and considers compliment to be but the encounter of two dog-apes (ii, v, 26-7), leads us to expect that in Jaques if in no one else the doctrine of the Duke will yield edifying fruit. Glimpses of a paradisal landscape are not withheld—boughs mossed with age, antique oaks whose roots peep out at brawling brooks, and purlieus of the forest where stand sheepcotes fenced about with olive trees. And Shakespeare by no means stops short of miraculous conversions under the influence of this place. It seems to work. Oliver's transformation tastes sweetly to him, making him the thing he is; he will live and die a shepherd. The base Duke Frederick scarcely sets foot in the forest before an old religious man, harmonious with the wild wood, turns him not only from his hatred for the old Duke but from the world. The text is given every opportunity to state itself, and nowhere does the comedy overtly contradict it.

All the while, however, it is being subtly undermined and

sapped of its simplicity. Touchstone shreds it with the needle of his dialectic, with the razor of his parody. Silvius's cry of "Phebe, Phebe, Phebe" reminds him of his country love:

I remember, when I was in love I broke my sword upon a stone, and bid him take that for coming a-night to Jane Smile; and I remember the kissing of her batlet and the cow's dugs that her pretty chopt hands had milk'd; and I remember the wooing of a peascod instead of her; from whom I took two cods and, giving her them again, said with weeping tears, "Wear these for my sake."                    (II, iv, 46-53)

Encountering Corin in the forest and receiving from him the pastoral gospel—that courts are corrupt and manners unnatural—he juggles it till he has proved that courtiers are indistinguishable from shepherds, for tar on the hands of the one class is equivalent to civet on the hands of the other, and both substances are lowly born. When Corin takes refuge in the immemorial claim of the countryman that he lives and lets live, his only pride being to watch his ewes graze and his lambs suck, Touchstone trips him up by translating what he has said into the cynical language of cities:

That is another simple sin in you, to bring the ewes and the rams together, and to offer to get your living by the copulation of cattle; to be bawd to a bell-wether, and to betray a she-lamb of a twelvemonth to a crooked-pated, old, cuckoldy ram, out of all reasonable match.                    (III, ii, 81-7)

Rosalind enters reading one of the poems Orlando has written for her on the bark of a tree. It is a bad poem, and she knows it; but Touchstone knows it well enough to have a parody ready (III, ii). He has no patience with country love, yet because he is where he is he cultivates the one wench available—ill-favored Audrey, whom the gods have not made poetical, and on whom literary puns are lost. He makes one nevertheless, on Ovid and the goats; and presses in at last among the country copulatives to be wedded with his poor virgin. He is without illusion; so much so that he will not claim he can do without it. His dryness touches the pastoral text throughout, and alters it; the detachment of his wit gives everything perspective, including himself. He is intellect afield; contemptuous of what he sees so far from home, but making the thin best of what is there. Not much is there when his withering, somewhat bored glance has circled the horizon.

Nor do we miss the sour look in Jaques's eyes as he roams this paradise. The exiled gentlemen are tyrants to the deer (II, i, 61) even as their usurpers are to them.

> He pierceth through
> The body of the country, city, court,
> Yea, and of this our life.          (II, i, 58-60)

The songs which thread the play so prettily are little better than noise to him, and he parodies one of them without mercy (II, v). Orlando does not impress him by the innocence and eagerness of his love; he is a young fool who mars trees with verses (III, ii). The huddle of marriages at the end is "another flood, and these couples are coming to the ark." He is not dry like Touchstone, for there is in him the juice of discontent; but he also takes down the temperature of romance, he sophisticates the pastoral text with grimaces of understanding.

But nothing is more characteristic of the comedy than the fact that its heroine is the most searching critic of its theme. Rosalind's laughter is neither dry nor wry; it is high and clear, it has a silver sound, and the sun dances among its fiery, impalpable particles. Her disguise as a man does not explain the quality of this laughter. There are as many kinds of men as of women, and a different girl would have become a different boy; one, for instance, who moped and sighed and languished in the purlieus of romance. Rosalind has no difficulty with the language of scoffing youth. To such a fellow the poems of Orlando are tedious homilies of love. "I was never so berhym'd since Pythagoras' time, that I was an Irish rat, which I can hardly remember" (III, ii, 186-8). Her vocabulary is as tart and vernacular as that of Mercutio, Faulconbridge, or Hotspur. The skirts of the forest are for her the "fringe upon a petticoat," love is a madness deserving the dark house and the whip, if Orlando will accept her as his physician she will wash his liver "as clean as a sound sheep's heart," Phebe has no more beauty than without candle may go dark to bed, when lovers lack words they should kiss as orators in the same predicament spit, she will be as jealous over Orlando as a Barbary cock-pigeon over his hen, her affection hath an unknown bottom like the bay of Portugal, love hath made Silvius a tame snake. Language like this is not learned by putting on man's apparel, nor is there any sign that it goes against Rosalind's grain to jest about incontinence, your neighbor's bed, and the inevitable horns; there is a rank reality in her speech, as in the speech of Shakespeare's best women always. And she would appear to be without any understanding whatever of the rare states to which lovers can be reduced. Her account of Oliver and Celia is that they

no sooner met but they look'd; no sooner look'd but they lov'd; no sooner lov'd but they sigh'd; no sooner sigh'd but they ask'd one another the reason; no sooner knew the reason but they sought the remedy; and in these degrees have they made a pair of stairs to marriage which they will climb incontinent, or else be incontinent before marriage. They are in the very wrath of love and they will together. Clubs cannot part them.

(v, ii, 35-45)

The tone is unsympathetic, logically enough for a young woman whose diatribe against the doctrine of the broken heart has become classic:

The poor world is almost six thousand years old, and in all this time there was not any man died in his own person, videlicet, in a love-cause. Troilus had his brains dash'd out with a Grecian club; yet he did what he could to die before, and he is one of the patterns of love. Leander, he would have liv'd many a fair year though Hero had turn'd nun, if it had not been for a hot mid-summer night; for, good youth, he went but forth to wash him in the Hellespont and being taken with the cramp was drown'd; and the foolish chroniclers of that age found it was— Hero of Sestos. But these are all lies. Men have died from time to time and worms have eaten them, but not for love.

(IV, i, 93-108)

The realism is uproarious, as the prose is artful and the wit is incessant. "You shall never take her without her answer," she warns Orlando of the true Rosalind, "unless you take her without her tongue." Her gaiety runs like quicksilver, and is as hard to head off. She is of great value for that reason to her author, who can so easily use her as a commentator on his play when it grows absurd—as, being a pastoral play, it must. He can use her, for instance, to silence Phebe, Silvius, Orlando, and even herself when the four of them have carried too far the liturgy of one another's names. "Pray you," she says, "no more of this; 't is like the howling of Irish wolves against the moon" (v, ii, 118-9).

All this is true. Yet it is also true that Rosalind loves Orlando without limit, and that she is the happiest of many happy persons in Arden. Her criticism of love and cuckooland is unremitting, yet she has not annihilated them. Rather she has preserved them by removing the flaws of their softness. That is the duty of criticism—a simple duty for a girl with sound imagination and a healthy heart. As Arden emerges from the fires of "As You Like It" a perfected symbol of the golden age, so Rosalind steps forth not burned but brightened, a perfected symbol of the romantic heroine. Romance has been tested in her until we know it cannot shatter; laughter has made it sure of itself. There is only one thing sillier than being in love, and that is thinking it is silly to be in love. Rosalind skips through both errors to wisdom.

She, not Jaques, is the philosopher of the play. Hers is the only mind that never rests; his bogs down in the mire of melancholy, in the slough of self-love. He is too fond of believing he is wise to be as wise as he sounds, either in the set speech he makes about man's seven ages (ii, vii) or in the insults he considers himself privileged at all times to deliver. His distrust of manners turns out to be the disaffection of a boor. His melancholy, like his wit, is an end in itself, a dyspeptic indulgence, an exercise of vanity that serves none of wisdom's purposes. "Motley's the only wear," he decides (ii, vi, 34), but when he is dressed in it he has no place to go. "I can suck melancholy out of a song as a weasel sucks eggs," he tells Amiens (ii, v, 12-3), and the figure is better than he knows. He slithers through Arden, in love with his own sad eyes. "Will you sit down with me?" he asks Orlando, "and we two will rail against our mistress the world, and all our misery." Orlando's answer is priggish, but it is nearer to the meaning of the play. "I will chide no breather in the world but myself, against whom I know most faults" (iii, ii, 297-8). Jaques is a fat and greasy citizen of the world of easy words. He is a fine poet at this stage of Shakespeare's career, but he will degenerate into Thersites and Apemantus. Rosalind it is who knows his weakness best.

*Jaques.* I have neither the scholar's melancholy, which is emulation; nor the musician's, which is fantastical; nor the courtier's, which is proud; nor the soldier's, which is ambitious; nor the lawyer's, which is politic; nor the lady's, which is nice; nor the lover's, which is all these; but it is a melancholy of mine own, compounded of many simples, extracted from many objects; and indeed the sundry contemplation of my travels, in which my often rumination wraps me in a most humourous sadness—
*Rosalind.* A traveller! By my faith, you have great reason to

be sad. I fear you have sold your own lands to see other men's; then, to have seen much, and to have nothing, is to have rich eyes and poor hands.

*Jaques.* Yes, I have gained my experience.

*Rosalind.* And your experience makes you sad. I had rather have a fool to make me merry than experience to make me sad; and to travel for it too! (IV, i, 10-29)

Jaques has seen much and can say anything, but he has nothing. Experience has made him sad. The more experience Rosalind has the merrier she grows. She too is a traveler, but she has not sold her own lands. She has taken her integrity with her to Arden, tucked under her three-cornered cap. It is proper that the limitations of Jaques should be stated by her, for if in him we have the pastoral sentiment criticized we have in her the only intelligence capable of judging the criticism. She judges with more than intelligence—with, for instance, instinct and love—but that again is proper to the comedy of Shakespeare's prime.

# TWELFTH NIGHT

IF so absorbing a masterpiece as "Twelfth Night" permits the reader to keep any other play in his mind
while he reads, that play is "The Merchant of
Venice." Once again Shakespeare has built a world out of
music and melancholy, and once again this world is threatened by an alien voice. The opposition of Malvolio to Orsino and his class parallels the opposition of Shylock to Antonio and his friends. The parallel is not precise, and the
contrast is more subtly contrived; Shakespeare holds the balance in a more delicate hand, so that the ejection of Malvolio
is perhaps less painful to our sense of justice than the punish-
ments heaped upon Shylock until he is crushed under their
weight. But the parallel exists, and nothing provides a nicer
opportunity for studying the way in which Shakespeare, returning to a congenial theme, could ripen and enrich it.

Orsino's opening speech is not merely accompanied by
music; it discusses music, and it is music in itself. Furthermore, a suggestion of surfeit or satiety occurs as early as the
second line: this suggestion, so consonant with Orsino's melancholy tone, to be developed throughout a speech of considerable complexity. For at more than one point "Twelfth
Night" foreshadows the concentration and even the difficulty
which will be found in the poetry of the later plays.

> If music be the food of love, play on!
> Give me excess of it, that, surfeiting,
> The appetite may sicken, and so die.
> That strain again! It had a dying fall.
> O, it came o'er my ear like the sweet sound
> That breathes upon a bank of violets

> Stealing and giving odour. Enough! no more!
> 'T is not so sweet now as it was before.
> O spirit of love, how quick and fresh art thou,
> That, notwithstanding thy capacity
> Receiveth as the sea, nought enters there,
> Of what validity and pitch soe'er,
> But falls into abatement and low price
> Even in a minute! So full of shapes is fancy
> That it alone is high fantastical.

The music of "The Merchant of Venice" is freer than this, more youthful and less tangled with ideas of sickness; and the bank of violets has aged beyond the simple sweetness of Lorenzo's bank whereon the moonlight slept. Orsino's love for Olivia turns in upon him and torments him. He is as mannerly in his sadness as Antonio was, but he knows, or thinks he knows, the origin of his state. He may not wholly know; his melancholy is in part a fine convention of his class, like the preference he feels for olden days and the gentle idiom of an outmoded music.

> Give me some music. Now,—good morrow, friends,—
> Now, good Cesario, but that piece of song,
> That old and antique song we heard last night.
> Methought it did relieve my passion much,
> More than light airs and recollected terms
> Of these most brisk and giddy-paced times. . . .
> O, fellow, come, the song we had last night.
> Mark it, Cesario, it is old and plain.
> The spinsters and the knitters in the sun
> And the free maids that weave their thread with bones
> Do use to chant it. It is silly sooth,
> And dallies with the innocence of love,
> Like the old age.                    (II, iv, 1-6; 43-9)

Orsino is indeed an exquisitely finished portrait of his type. His is the luxury of a "secret soul" (I, iv, 14), and it is natural that he should so easily understand the young gentleman who is Viola in disguise, and who lets concealment, like a worm i' the bud, feed on her damask cheek (II, iv, 114-5).

Viola's variety of melancholy is green and yellow. Olivia's is "sad and civil" (III, iv, 5-6). But all of them are graced with sadness. It is the mark of their citizenship in a world which knows a little less than the world of "The Merchant of Venice" did what to do with its treasure of wealth and beauty, and whose spoken language has deepened its tone, complicated its syntax, learned how to listen to itself. This is the way Orsino argues himself into believing that Olivia will love him when she is done mourning her dead brother:

> O, she that hath a heart of that fine frame
> To pay this debt of love but to a brother,
> How will she love when the rich golden shaft
> Hath kill'd the flock of all affections else
> That live in her; when liver, brain, and heart,
> These sovereign thrones, are all suppli'd, and fill'd
> Her sweet perfections with one self king! (I, i, 33-9)

And here is Olivia remembering how Cesario (Viola) had spoken in her presence:

> "What is your parentage?"
> "Above my fortunes, yet my state is well.
> I am a gentleman." I'll be sworn thou art.
> Thy tongue, thy face, thy limbs, actions, and spirit
> Do give thee five-fold blazon. Not too fast! Soft, soft!
> Unless the master were the man. How now!
> Even so quickly may one catch the plague?
> Methinks I feel this youth's perfections
> With an invisible and subtle stealth
> To creep in at mine eyes. Well, let it be. (I, v, 308-17)

The involutions of such discourse are entirely natural to both speakers. For their caste is the noblest in Illyria. One of them is a lady and the other is a gentleman.

Sir Toby Belch is a gentleman too, or at any rate he belongs. He is an old relation and retainer in the somewhat cluttered household of Olivia. "The Merchant of Venice" never took us so deep into domestic details. The household

of Olivia is old-world, it is Merry England. At its center sits
the lady Olivia, but there is room for every other kind of
person here for whom a changing age has still not made existence impossible. There is the clown Feste and the clever
servant Fabian; and there is the still cleverer servant Maria,
whose extreme smallness is rendered clear to us, in the perverse language of a good-natured people, by such terms as
"giant" and "Penthesilea," though she is also a "wren" and
a "little villain." Chiefly, however, there is Sir Toby. He is
gluttonous and drunken, and must be kept out of sight as
much as possible; but Olivia would no more turn him away
than she would refuse to hear an excellent old song sung to
the lute. For one thing there is no place for Sir Toby to go.
He is as old-fashioned as Falstaff, and as functionless in the
modern world. "Am not I consanguineous? Am I not of her
blood?" (ii, iii, 82-3). He even talks like Falstaff, puffingly
and explosively, as he reminds Maria that he is Olivia's uncle.
And for another thing he belongs. Old households harbor
such old men. They are nuisances to be endured because
they are symbols of enduringness, signs of the family's great
age. Sir Toby has another parasite on him—Sir Andrew
Aguecheek, whose foolish devotion to Olivia he makes use
of to keep himself in money. For of course he has no money;
and Sir Andrew has a little. It is a crowded household,
swarming with gross life behind high walls of custom. When
Sir Andrew says he is of the opinion that life consists of eat-
ing and drinking, Sir Toby applauds him roundly: "Thou'rt
a scholar; let us therefore eat and drink" (ii, iii, 13-4). The
fat old fellow's second appearance in the play (i, v, 129-30)
brings him on belching—"a plague o' these pickle-herring!"
And he is ever as full of wine as he is loud with song. "How
now, sot!" "Shall we make the welkin dance indeed? Shall
we rouse the night-owl in a catch that will draw three souls
out of one weaver? Shall we do that?" (ii, iii, 58-61).

It is to Sir Toby that Malvolio is most alien. "Dost thou think, because thou art virtuous, there shall be no more cakes and ale?" This most famous sentence in the play is more than Sir Toby disposing of his niece's steward; it is the old world resisting the new, it is the life of hiccups and melancholy trying to ignore latter-day puritanism and efficiency. On the occasion when it is spoken there is danger for Sir Toby in the fact that Olivia is moody with her new love for Cesario; she has lost patience with her kinsman's misdemeanors, and may send him off. But Malvolio is the last man on earth to come with the message. "Tell us something of him," says Sir Toby to Maria.

> *Maria.* Marry, sir, sometimes he is a kind of puritan.
> *Sir Andrew.* O, if I thought that, I'd beat him like a dog!
> *Sir Toby.* What, for being a puritan? Thy exquisite reason, dear knight?
> *Sir Andrew.* I have no exquisite reason for 't, but I have reason good enough. (II, iii, 151-8)

So has Sir Toby, though neither of them is articulate enough to say what it is. Doubtless they have never thought it out. They only know that the sight of Malvolio, like the sound of his voice, threatens death to their existence. His own existence somehow challenges their right to be freely what they are. He is of a new order—ambitious, self-contained, cold and intelligent, and dreadfully likely to prevail. That is why Sir Toby and his retinue hate him. Feste at the end provides too simple an explanation. The humiliation of Malvolio, he says, was his personal revenge upon one who had discounted him to his mistress as "a barren rascal," a jester unworthy of his hire. But the others had been as active as Feste, and they had had no such motive. "The devil a puritan that he is," Maria insists, "or anything constantly, but a time-pleaser; an affection'd ass" (II, iii, 159-60). Puritan or not, Malvolio has offended them as a class. They could have forgiven his being a climber, his having affection for himself, if he had been any other kind of man than the cool kind he is.

The earliest protest against his disposition is made in fact by Olivia herself, on the occasion when Feste has been amusing her with samples of his wit and Malvolio, asked for his opinion of the stuff, cuts in with this commentary:

I marvel your ladyship takes delight in such a barren rascal. I saw him put down the other day with an ordinary fool that has no more brain than a stone. Look you now, he's out of his guard already. Unless you laugh and minister occasion to him, he is gagg'd. I protest, I take these wise men, that crow so at these set kind of fools, no better than the fools' zanies.

(I, v, 88-96)

He has appeared to be judging the kind of fool Feste is, and his success within that kind; but Olivia sees through to the root of the matter, which is that he does not like jesting at all.

O, you are sick of self-love, Malvolio, and taste with a distemper'd appetite. To be generous, guiltless, and of free disposition, is to take those things for bird-bolts that you deem cannon-bullets. There is no slander in an allow'd fool, though he do nothing but rail; nor no railing in a known discreet man, though he do nothing but reprove.

She gives him, in brief, a lesson in the manners of her breed. If he supposes Feste's jibes at her to have been slanderous, that is because he does not understand how little time her people spend in thinking of themselves; if they are free and generous, and know the code, they will laugh at things which to an outsider must sound outrageous. Malvolio may have a sense of humor, but it is not the kind that goes with her code.

Olivia does not bother with him again until he comes, cross-gartered and smiling, to make her think him mad. Meanwhile the roysterers within her gates carry the criticism on. And Malvolio is given a voice which perfectly explains the criticism. The fatal difference between his nature and

that of the drunken singers in Olivia's cellar rings out as
clearly as if notes had been struck on a warning bell. To
begin with there is the fact that Malvolio hates music; as
Shylock had declared the harmonies of a carnival to be wry-
necked and squealing, so he denounces the strains of "O
mistress mine, where are you roaming?" as "the gabble of
tinkers" (ii, iii, 95). And then there is the icy, tight-lipped
fashion of his speech, a fashion that contrasts with the
thoughtless, bawling, open-throated style of Sir Toby as frost
contrasts with foam, and with the grave, rich style of Orsino
or Olivia as steel contrasts with gold. In his niggard's nature
he has developed a mannerism which he forces to do all the
work of his thought. It is economical and efficient, and it
attests his trained intelligence, but it cuts offensively into the
hearing of his foes.

Do ye make an alehouse of my lady's house, that ye squeak
out your coziers' catches *without any mitigation or remorse of
voice?*                                             (ii, iii, 96-8)

And then *to have the humour of state;* and *after a demure
travel of regard,* . . . to ask for my kinsman Toby. . . . Seven
of my people, *with an obedient start,* make out for him. . . . I
extend my hand to him thus, *quenching my familiar smile with
an austere regard of control.*                      (ii, v, 58-74)

I am no more mad than you are. Make the trial of it *in any
constant question.*                                 (iv, ii, 51-3)

And tell me, *in the modesty of honour.*            (v, i, 343)

And, acting this *in an obedient hope.*             (v, i, 348)

The syntax is brilliantly condensed, but the tone is conde-
scending; a man speaks who thinks of himself as master and
frowns the while, tapping the floor till it tinkles like iron
and winding up his watch as if it kept time for a universe of
"lighter people" (v, i, 347). No wonder his enemies loathe
him. "O, for a stone-bow, to hit him in the eye!" (ii, v, 51-2).

And no wonder, since their ears are clever, that they mimic his precious manner when they compose the note he is to read as a love-letter from Olivia:

Let thy tongue tang *arguments of state;* put thyself *into the trick of singularity*.                              (II, v, 163-4)

They have not failed to notice his lordly way with the little word "of," or the practice of his hand as he plucks the string of any other preposition, or the miracle by which he can give an effect of terseness to polysyllables. And they have studied his vocabulary as though it were an index of terms never to be used again. "I might say 'element,'" Feste observes, "but the word is overworn" (III, i, 65-6). The word is Malvolio's, though we are not aware of this till later. "You are idle shallow things; I am not of your element" (III, iv, 136-7), he draws himself straighter and higher than ever and announces as gables announce icicles.

"He hath been most notoriously abus'd" (v, i, 387). Olivia's line rights Malvolio's wrong, but her household will never grant him the last justice of love. Where there is such difference there cannot be love. That is what "Twelfth Night" is most interested in saying, and saying with an impartiality which precludes sentiment. The balance between Malvolio and his enemies is delicate; they are attractive, as all loose livers are, yet there is an integrity in his tightness, a loftiness other than the misguided one, which we cannot but respect. Modern audiences have bestowed more sympathy upon Malvolio than Shakespeare perhaps intended, so that the balance is now not what it was. It can scarcely be overthrown, however, whatever changes the whirligig of time brings in. The foundation for comedy here is too firm for that, the counterpoint of effects is too sanely arranged. This world of music and mannerly sadness is not sentimentally conceived. Even within its gates the violin voice of Orsino is corrected by the bawling bass of Sir Toby, and the elegant neuroses of the nobility are parodied on servants' tongues. "Now, the melancholy god protect thee," calls Feste after Orsino, mocking him. And Fabian, told of the plot against Malvolio, can rub his hands and say: "If I lose a scruple of this sport, let me be boil'd to death with melancholy" (II, v, 2-4). A balance of tones is maintained, indeed, everywhere in "Twelfth Night." Nature and artifice, sanity and sentiment, are so equally at home here that they can with the greatest difficulty be distinguished from one another; nor in our delight are we disposed to try.

All the while, of course, a story of twins is being told, and three cases of love at first sight (Viola and Orsino, Olivia and Viola, Sebastian and Olivia) are being dove-tailed into a pattern of romance. Shakespeare's interest in Viola cannot be doubted.

> My father had a daughter lov'd a man,
> As it might be, perhaps, were I a woman,
> I should your lordship.                     (II, iv, 110-2)

Nor can that of the audience, for she is Julia grown to greatness. But other portions of the pattern deserve and are given only such attention as is necessary. The confusion of the twins and the farce of the fencing-match are not what the comedy is essentially about, any more than the marriage of Olivia and Sebastian is—and the perfunctoriness of Shakespeare's feeling with respect to that marriage is clearly confessed in the kind of verse he gives the priest to speak (v, i, 159-66). Even Viola, much as we like her, stands a little to one side of the center. The center is Malvolio. The drama is between his mind and the music of old manners.

# HENRY V

SHAKESPEARE in "Henry IV" had still been able to pour all of his thought and feeling into the heroic drama without demolishing its form. His respect for English history as a subject, his tendency to conceive kings in tragic terms, his interest in exalted dialogue as a medium through which important actions could be advanced—these, corrected by comedy which flooded the whole with the wisdom of a warm and proper light, may have reached their natural limit, but that limit was not transgressed. "Henry IV," in other words, both was and is a successful play; it answers the questions it raises, it satisfies every instinct of the spectator, it is remembered as fabulously rich and at the same time simply ordered. "Henry V" is no such play. It has its splendors and its secondary attractions, but the forces in it are not unified. The reason probably is that for Shakespeare they had ceased to be genuine forces. He marshals for his task a host of substitute powers, but the effect is often hollow. The style strains itself to bursting, the hero is stretched until he struts on tiptoe and is still strutting at the last insignificant exit, and war is emptied of its tragic content. The form of the historical drama had been the tragic form; its dress is borrowed here, but only borrowed. The heroic idea splinters into a thousand starry fragments, fine as fragments but lighted from no single source.

Everywhere efforts are made to be striking, and they succeed. But the success is local. "Henry V" does not succeed as a whole because its author lacks adequate dramatic matter; or because, veering so suddenly away from tragedy, he is unable to free himself from the accidents of its form; or because, with "Julius Caesar" and "Hamlet" on his horizon, he finds himself less interested than before in heroes who are men of action and yet is not at the moment provided with a dramatic language for saying so. Whatever the cause, we discover that we are being entertained from the top of his mind. There is much there to glitter and please us, but what pleases us has less body than what once did so and soon will do so with still greater abundance again.

The prologues are the first sign of Shakespeare's imperfect dramatic faith. Their verse is wonderful but it has to be, for it is doing the work which the play ought to be doing, it is a substitute for scene and action. "O for a Muse of fire," the poet's apology begins. The prologues are everywhere apologetic; they are saying that no stage, this one or any other, is big enough or wealthy enough to present the "huge and proper life" of Henry's wars; this cockpit cannot hold the vasty fields of France, there will be no veritable horses in any scene, the ship-boys on the masts and the camp-fires at Agincourt will simply have to be imagined. Which it is the business of the play to make them be, as Shakespeare has known and will know again. The author of "Romeo and Juliet" had not been sorry because his stage was a piece of London rather than the whole of Verona, and the storm in "King Lear" will begin without benefit of description. The description here is always very fine, as for example at the opening of the fourth act:

> Now entertain conjecture of a time
> When creeping murmur and the poring dark
> Fills the wide vessel of the universe.
> From camp to camp through the foul womb of night
> The hum of either army stilly sounds,
> That the fix'd sentinels almost receive
> The secret whispers of each other's watch;
> Fire answers fire, and through their paly flames
> Each battle sees the other's umber'd face;
> Steed threatens steed, in high and boastful neighs

> Piercing the night's dull ear; and from the tents
> The armourers, accomplishing the knights,
> With busy hammers closing rivets up,
> Give dreadful note of preparation.

But it is still description, and it is being asked to do what description can never do—turn spectacle into plot, tableau into tragedy.

The second sign of genius at loose ends is a radical and indeed an astounding inflation in the style. Passages of boasting and exhortation are in place, but even the best of them, whether from the French or from the English side, have a forced, shrill, windy sound, as if their author were pumping his muse for dear life in the hope that mere speed and plangency might take the place of matter. For a few lines like

> Familiar in his mouth as household words     (IV, iii, 52)

> The singing masons building roofs of gold     (I, ii, 198)

> I see you stand like greyhounds in the slips,
> Straining upon the start          (III, i, 31-2)

there are hundreds like

> The native mightiness and fate of him     (II, iv, 64)

> With ample and brim fullness of his force     (I, ii, 150)

> That caves and womby vaultages of France
> Shall chide your trespass and return your mock.
>                             (II, iv, 124-5)

Mightiness and fate, ample and brim, caves and vaultages, trespass and mock—such couplings attest the poet's desperation, the rhetorician's extremity. They spring up everywhere, like birds from undergrowth: sweet and honey'd, open haunts and popularity, thrive and ripen, crown and seat, right and title, right and conscience, kings and monarchs, means and might, aim and butt, large and ample, taken and impounded, frank and uncurbed, success and conquest, desert and merit, weight and worthiness, duty and zeal, savage and inhuman,

botch and bungle, garnish'd and deck'd, assembled and col-
lected, sinister and awkward, culled and choice-drawn, o'er-
hang and jutty, waste and desolation, cool and temperate,
flexure and low bending, signal and ostent, vainness and self-
glorious pride. Shakespeare has perpetrated them before, as
when in "Henry VI" he coupled ominous and fearful, trouble and disturb, substance and authority, and absurd and
reasonless. But never has he perpetrated them with such
thoughtless frequency. Nor has he at this point developed
the compound epithet into that interesting mannerism—the
only mannerism he ever submitted to—which is to be so no-
ticeable in his next half-dozen plays, including "Hamlet."
The device he is to use will involve more than the pairing of
adjectives or nouns; one part of speech will assume the duties
of another, and a certain very sudden concentration of meaning will result. There is, to be sure, one approximation to the
device in "Henry V"—"the quick forge and working-house
of thought" (Prologue, v, 23). But our attention is nowhere
else held and filled by such lines as these in "Hamlet":

> In the dead waste and middle of the night
>
> The perfume and suppliance of a minute
>
> Unto the voice and yielding of that body
>
> And in the morn and liquid dew of youth
>
> The slings and arrows of outrageous fortune
>
> Which is not tomb enough and continent;

or these in "Troilus and Cressida":

> The sinew and the forehand of our host
>
> For the great swing and rudeness of his poise
>
> The unity and married calm of states
>
> Than in the pride and salt scorn of her eyes;

or these in "Measure for Measure":

Whether it be the fault and glimpse of newness

Now puts the drowsy and neglected act

There is a prone and speechless dialect.

In such lines there is not merely the freshness and the emphasis which an expert distortion of conventional meanings
can give; there is a muscled cadence, an abrupt forward stride
or plunge of sound. All this is lacking for the most part in the
style of "Henry V," which is fatty rather than full, relaxed
instead of restrung.

The third sign is a direct and puerile appeal to the pa-
triotism of the audience, a dependence upon sentiments outside the play that can be counted on, once they are tapped,
to pour in and repair the deficiencies of the action. Unable
to achieve a dramatic unity out of the materials before him,
Shakespeare must grow lyrical about the unity of England;
politics must substitute for poetry. He cannot take England
for granted as the scene of conflicts whose greatness will
imply its greatness. It must be great itself, and the play says
so—unconvincingly. There are no conflicts. The traitors
Scroop, Cambridge, and Grey are happy to lose their heads
for England (ii, ii), and the battles in France, even though
the enemy's host is huge and starvation takes its toll, are
bound to be won by such fine English fellows as we have
here. If the French have boasted beforehand, the irony of
their doing so was obvious from the start. But it was patri-
otism, shared as a secret between the author and his audience,
that made it obvious. It was not drama.

And a fourth sign is the note of gaiety that takes the place
here of high passion. The treasure sent to Henry by the
Dauphin is discovered at the end of the first act to be tennis-
balls: an insult which the young king returns in a speech
about matching rackets and playing sets—his idiom for bloody
war. When the treachery of Scroop, Cambridge, and Grey
is detected on the eve of his departure for France he stages

their discomfiture somewhat as games are undertaken, and with a certain sporting relish watches their faces as they read their dooms. The conversation of the French leaders as they wait for the sun to rise on Agincourt is nervous as thorough-breds are nervous, or champion athletes impatient for a tour-nament to commence; their camp is a locker room, littered with attitudes no less than uniforms (III, vii). The deaths of York and Suffolk the next day are images of how young knights should die. They kiss each other's gashes, wearing their red blood like roses in the field, and spending their last breath in terms so fine that Exeter, reporting to the King, is overcome by "the pretty and sweet manner of it" (IV, vi, 28). And of course there are the scenes where Katharine makes fritters of English, waiting to be wooed (III, iv) and wooed at last (v, ii) by Henry Plantagenet, "king of good fellows." "The truth is," said Dr. Johnson, "that the poet's matter failed him in the fifth act, and he was glad to fill it up with whatever he could get; and not even Shakespeare can write well without a proper subject. It is a vain endeavour for the most skilful hand to cultivate barrenness, or to paint upon vacuity." That is harsh, but its essence cannot be ignored. The high spirits in which the scenes are written have their attraction, but they are no substitute for intensity.

Nor do they give us the king we thought we had. "I speak to thee plain soldier," boasts Henry in homespun vein. "I am glad thou canst speak no better English; for, if thou couldst, thou wouldst find me such a plain king that thou wouldst think I had sold my farm to buy my crown. I know no ways to mince it in love, but directly to say, 'I love you.' . . . These fellows of infinite tongue, that can rhyme themselves into ladies' favours, they do always reason themselves out again. . . . By mine honour, in true English, I love thee, Kate" (v, ii). "I know not," breaks in Dr. Johnson's voice once more, "why Shakespeare now gives the king nearly such a character as he made him formerly ridicule in Percy.

This military grossness and unskillfulness in all the softer arts does not suit very well with the gaieties of his youth, with the general knowledge ascribed to him at his accession, or with the contemptuous message sent him by the Dauphin, who represents him as fitter for the ball room than the field, and tells him that he is not 'to revel into dutchies,' or win provinces 'with a nimble galliard.' " Shakespeare has forgotten the glittering young god whom Vernon described in "Henry IV"—plumed like an estridge or like an eagle lately bathed, shining like an image in his golden coat, as full of spirit as the month of May, wanton as a youthful goat, a feathered Mercury, an angel dropped down from the clouds. The figure whom he has groomed to be the ideal English king, all plumes and smiles and decorated courage, collapses here into a mere good fellow, a hearty undergraduate with enormous initials on his chest. The reason must be that Shakespeare has little interest in the ideal English king. He has done what rhetoric could do to give us a young heart whole in honor, but his imagination has already sped forward to Brutus and Hamlet: to a kind of hero who is no less honorable than Henry but who will tread on thorns as he takes the path of duty—itself unclear, and crossed by other paths of no man's making. Henry is Shakespeare's last attempt at the great man who is also simple. Henceforth he will show greatness as either perplexing or perplexed; and Hamlet will be both.

Meanwhile his imagination undermines the very eminence on which Henry struts. For the King and his nobles the war may be a handsome game, but an undercurrent of realism reminds us of the "poor souls" for whom it is no such thing. We hear of widows' tears and orphans' cries, of dead men's blood and pining maidens' groans (II, iv, 104-7). Such horrors had been touched on in earlier Histories; now they are given a scene to themselves (IV, i). While the French leaders chaff one another through the night before Agincourt the English common soldiers have their hour. Men with names

as plain as John Bates and Michael Williams walk up and
down the dark field thinking of legs and arms and heads
chopped off in battle, of faint cries for surgeons, of men in
misery because of their children who will be rawly left.
Henry, moving among them in the disguise of clothes like
theirs, asks them to remember that the King's cause is just
and his quarrel honorable. "That's more than we know,"
comes back the disturbing cool voice of Michael Williams.
Henry answers with much fair prose, and the episode ends
with a wager—sportsmanship again—which in turn leads to
an amusing recognition scene (IV, viii). But the honest voice
of Williams still has the edge on Henry's patronizing tone:

*Williams.* Your Majesty came not like yourself. You appear'd
to me but as a common man; witness the night, your garments,
your lowliness; and what your Highness suffer'd under that
shape, I beseech you take it for your own fault and not
mine. . . .

   *King Henry.* Here, uncle Exeter, fill this glove with crowns,
       And give it to this fellow. Keep it, fellow;
       And wear it for an honour in thy cap
       Till I do challenge it.       (IV, viii, 53-64)

Henry has not learned that Williams knows. He is still the
plumed king, prancing on oratory and waving wagers as he
goes. That he finally has no place to go is the result of Shakespeare's failure to establish any relation between a hero and
his experience. Henry has not absorbed the vision either of
Williams or of Shakespeare. This shrinks him in his armor,
and it leaves the vision hanging.

    The humor of the play, rich as it sometimes is, suffers like-
wise from a lack of vital function. The celebrated scene (II,
iii) in which the Hostess describes Falstaff's death shuts the
door forever on "Henry IV" and its gigantic comedy. Pistol
and Bardolph continue in their respective styles, and continue cleverly; the first scene of the second act, which finds

them still in London, may be indeed the best one ever written for them—and for Nym in his pompous brevity.

I cannot tell. Things must be as they may. Men may sleep, and they may have their throats about them at that time; and some say knives have edges. It must be as it may.

Pistol was never excited to funnier effect.

> O hound of Crete, think'st thou my spouse to get?
> No! to the spital go,
> And from the powdering-tub of infamy
> Fetch forth the lazar kite of Cressid's kind,
> Doll Tearsheet she by name, and her espouse.
> I have, and I will hold, the quondam Quickly
> For the only she; and—*pauca*, there's enough.
> Go to.

Yet this leads on to little in France beyond a series of rather mechanically arranged encounters in which the high talk of heroes is echoed by the rough cries of rascals. "To the breach, to the breach!" yells Bardolph after Henry, and that is parody. But Henry has already parodied himself; the device is not needed, any more than the rascals are. Shakespeare seems to admit as much when he permits lectures to be delivered against their moral characters, first by the boy who serves them (III, ii, 28-57) and next by the sober Gower (III, vi, 70-85), and when he arranges bad ends for them as thieves, cutpurses, and bawds.

There is a clearer function for Fluellen, the fussy Welsh pedant who is for fighting wars out of books. Always fretting and out of breath, he mourns "the disciplines of the wars," the pristine wars of the Romans, now in these latter days lost with all other learning. There was not this tiddle taddle and pibble pabble in Pompey's camp. The law of arms was once well known, and men—strong, silent men such as he fancies himself to be—observed it without prawls and prabbles. He has no shrewdness; he mistakes Pistol for a brave man because he talks bravely, and there is his classic comparison of Henry with Alexander because one lived in Monmouth and the other in Macedon and each city had a river and there were salmons in both. He has only his schoolmaster's eloquence; it breaks out on him like a rash, and is the one style here that surpasses the King's in fullness.

*Fluellen.* It is not well done, mark you now, to take the tales out of my mouth, ere it is made and finished. I speak but in the figures and comparisons of it. As Alexander kill'd his friend Cleitus, being in his ales and his cups; so also Harry Monmouth, being in his right wits and his good judgements, turn'd away the fat knight with the great belly doublet. He was full of jests, and gipes, and knaveries, and mocks; I have forgot his name.
*Gower.* Sir John Falstaff.
*Fluellen.* That is he.                    (IV, vii, 43-55)

Fluellen reminds us of Falstaff. That is a function, but he has another. It is to let the war theme finally down. Agincourt is won not only by a tennis-player but by a school-teacher. Saint Crispin's day is to be remembered as much in the pibble pabble of a pedant as in the golden throatings of a hollow god. Fluellen is one of Shakespeare's most humorous men, and one of his best used.

# JULIUS CAESAR

SHAKESPEARE idealized Plutarch's Brutus, but not in the direction of his own Henry V. The Roman conspirator has become an exemplary gentleman, and the chief sign of this is his set of scruples. His imagination is indeed so selfless, and his consideration of other men so full and kind, as almost to smother his powers and render him inactive. He is not very much like Hamlet, whose inaction, if inaction it is, has its paradoxical dynamics. But he is a sober step in that direction—too sober for the kind of success his creator, with a nimble bound back into the northern scene, is next to achieve.

If Brutus is less interesting than Hamlet, if his internal complications diminish rather than exhibit his dramatic force, the principal reason may be that Shakespeare has kept himself too conscious of a remote Roman grandeur in the scene. In Plutarch he seems always to have recognized an artist whom it would be rash to change, but his respect for the biographer was in the present case perhaps too solemn. The accommodation of his style to an ancient and alien atmosphere is amazingly complete, and there is in "Julius Caesar" a perfection of form which even he will never surpass. But the accommodation is something of a tour de force, and the perfection is of that sort which limits rather than releases poetry. "Julius Caesar" is more rhetoric than poetry, just as its persons are more orators than men. They all have something of the statue in them, for they express their author's idea of antiquity rather than his knowledge of life. They have the clarity and simplicity of worked marble, and are the easiest of Shakespeare's people to understand if one expects everything from speeches, and if one is innocent of the distinction between men and public men. The characters of "Julius Caesar" are public men. Even Antony and Caesar are. But Shakespeare's deepest interest is in the private man. And though he tries to find that man in Brutus he does not do so, because he has already submitted Brutus, like everybody else in the play, to the smoothing and simplifying process of a certain style. This style is in its way wonderful, but the hero who follows Brutus will accomplish infinitely greater wonders in no style at all, or at any rate in none that can be named; unless its name is Shakespeare's English.

"Julius Caesar" is least notable among Shakespeare's better plays for the distinctions of its speech. All of its persons tend to talk alike; their training has been forensic and therefore uniform, so that they can say anything with both efficiency and ease. With Marullus's first speech in the opening scene the play swings into its style: a style which will make it appear that nobody experiences the least difficulty in saying what he thinks. The phrasing is invariably flawless from the oral point of view; the breathing is right; no thought is too long for order or too short for roundness. Everything is brilliantly and surely said; the effects are underlined, the i's are firmly dotted. Speeches have tangible outlines, like plastic objects, and the drift from one of them to another has never to be guessed, for it is clearly stated.

The characters are accomplished in all the practical arts of statement. Not merely in the Forum is Brutus an orator—"I pause for a reply" (III, ii, 37)—but in his private tent, quarreling with Cassius. Dryden admired the famous quarrel scene (IV, iii) because it was "masculine," and his admiration was sound; yet the epithet implies a limitation of effect. The thump and rap of the repartee remind us once more that public men are training their tongues against each other; the dialogue, for all its power, could do with some relief by way of things half said or never said. Brutus and Cassius say it all

—with knowledge, too, of how it will be taken. Along with the rest here they are artists in declamation.

Rhetorical questions abound in "Julius Caesar."

> Wherefore rejoice? What conquest brings he home?
> What tributaries follow him to Rome
> To grace in captive bonds his chariot-wheels? . . .
> And do you now put on your best attire?
> And do you now cull out a holiday?
> And do you now strew flowers in his way
> That comes in triumph over Pompey's blood? (I, i, 37-56)

There they are piled in parallel formation, and this is frequently the case. Antony knows best the trick of letting them forth singly, with the force of simple assertion:

> Did this in Caesar seem ambitious?    (III, ii, 95)

> You will compel me, then, to read the will?
>     (III, ii, 161)

Portia, the public wife of a public man, goes so far as to answer one of hers:

> Is Brutus sick? . . .
>         No, my Brutus;
> You have some sick offence within your mind.
>     (II, i, 261-8)

But all in their various ways know how to ask them, and how not to pause for a reply unless the pause too will be effective.

So are they tutored in the music of monosyllables. No play of Shakespeare's has so many, so superbly used. The seasoned orator strings short words together as often as he can—for an effect of artlessness, of sincerity that only speaks right on, and also because there is a secret pleasure in demonstrating the discipline of his tongue. It takes skill to deliver monosyllables in an agreeable and natural rhythm, and a rhetorician likes nothing better than problems of skill. In "Julius Caesar" there may be in one place as many as thirty monosyllables together.

And when the fit was on him, I did mark
How he did shake—'t is true, this god did shake.

(ɪ, ii, 120-1)

When went there by an age, since the great flood,
But it was fam'd with more than with one man?
When could they say, till now, that talk'd of Rome . . .

(ɪ, ii, 152-4)

I will come home to you; or, if you will,
Come home to me, and I will wait for you.
I will do so; till then, think of the world.   (ɪ, ii, 309-11)

What's to do?
A piece of work that will make sick men whole.
But are not some whole that we must make sick?

(ɪɪ, i, 326-8)

Let me know some cause,
Lest I be laugh'd at when I tell them so.
The cause is in my will; I will not come.   (ɪɪ, ii, 69-71)

If thou dost bend and pray and fawn for him,
I spurn thee like a cur out of my way.   (ɪɪɪ, i, 45-6)

'T is good you know not that you are his heirs;
For, if you should, O, what would come of it!   (ɪɪɪ, ii, 150-1)

I pray you, sirs, lie in my tent and sleep;
It may be I shall raise you by and by. . . .
I will not have it so: lie down, good sirs. . . .
I know young bloods look for a time of rest. . . .
I will not hold thee long. If I do live,
I will be good to thee.   -   (ɪv, iii, 246-66)

They may occur in orations or they may crop out in discourse; they may be triumphs by the orator Antony—

But, as you know me all, a plain blunt man
That love my friend;

But here I am to speak what I do know;
And I must pause till it come back to me—

or they may be the last words of a dying man:

> I kill'd not thee with half so good a will.

They may serve any purpose at the moment. But the purpose they serve at all times is to pour into the ear an unimpeded stream of eloquence, a smooth current of artful sound. And once again it is to be noted that monosyllables are no one speaker's monopoly. The craft is native to them all.

So is the loftier craft of framing superlatives, of condensing infinite compliment into a finite phrase. Antony, being the best orator, does best at this:

> With the most noble blood of all this world (III, i, 156)

> The choice and master spirits of this age     (III, i, 163)

> Thou art the ruins of the noblest man
> That ever lived in the tide of times      (III, i, 256-7)

> This was the noblest Roman of them all.      (v, v, 68)

But the second best of Brutus is impressive:

> That struck the foremost man of all this world
> (IV, iii, 22)
> The last of all the Romans, fare thee well!
> It is impossible that ever Rome
> Should breed thy fellow.          (v, iii, 99-101)

And again the gift is common to the cast.

Their voices are not differentiated then. Nor are their states of mind. Brutus anticipates Hamlet, Othello, Lear, and Macbeth when he soliloquizes concerning the disorder in his soul:

> Between the acting of a dreadful thing
> And the first motion, all the interim is
> Like a phantasma or a hideous dream.
> The Genius and the mortal instruments
> Are then in council; and the state of a man,
> Like to a little kingdom, suffers then
> The nature of an insurrection.      (II, i, 63-9)

This is fine, like everything else in "Julius Caesar," but it is rotund and political, and it was relatively easy for Brutus to say; nor is it impossible to imagine another man's saying it. It is not, like comparable speeches in the tragedies ahead, cut to the individual, and cut with so keen a knife that the individual is dissected in the process and seems to bleed his words. Brutus addresses us through a wrapping of rhetoric, of public speech. And this wrapping is around the imageries of blood and sleep which are so prominent in the play—so prominent, and yet, if one remembers "Macbeth," so remote from contact with us. The blood that smears the entire surface of "Macbeth" is physical; we see, feel, and smell it. Not so with Caesar's blood; it is "noble" and "costly" because Caesar was the foremost man of all the world, but it remains a metaphor, a political metaphor, distant from the experience of our senses. It may be significant that it can pour from Caesar's statue as well as from his body (ii, ii, 76-9), and that when he falls at the base of Pompey's statue it too runs red. There is as much real blood in "Julius Caesar" as there is in stone. And Brutus, once more ancestor to Macbeth, cannot sleep. At home before the assassination, in his tent on the eve of battle, and facing death in his last hour, his lids are heavy, his bones want rest. Yet the fact is not ghastly as in the case of one who will murder Sleep itself, and whose resulting exhaustion will visit itself upon the audience. The fatigue of Brutus is the noble tiredness of a great man, and we respect it; but our pity for the sufferer is not tinged with fear. This is the noblest Roman of them all, and even in distress he keeps his distance.

In such an atmosphere Caesar has little chance to be himself, yet Shakespeare has permitted him to make the most of it. Caesar is not a noble Roman, not one of Plutarch's men. He is that rarity in the play, an Elizabethan personality; he is one of Shakespeare's men. While he lasts he reveals himself in his irregularity, not in his symmetry, in picturesqueness rather than in pose. His monosyllables—for he speaks them too—tell us that he is deficient in one of the senses:

> Come on my right hand, for this ear is deaf;  (I, ii, 213)

that he changes his mind suddenly, with no reason given:

> He is a dreamer; let us leave him. Pass;          (I, ii, 24)

> The cause is in my will; I will not come;       (II, ii, 71)

and that he is inordinately vain:

> But there's but one in all doth hold his place.
> So in the world; . . . and that I am he.    (III, i, 65-70)

His enemies tell us that he has the falling sickness (I, ii, 256), that he is gullible to flattery (II, i, 207-8), that he is superstitious grown of late and loves to be regaled with wondrous tales of unicorns, bears, lions, and elephants (II, i, 195-206). He appears, indeed, only in his singularity; and he appears but briefly before he falls at the hands of men so completely unlike him that the difference alone might pass as motive for their hatred. Their hatred is of a man not noble, a man who has not suppressed himself. And for a similar reason they distrust Antony, who revels long o' nights (II, ii, 116) and whose orator's tongue flicks unfairly with the serpent speed of irony. They cannot cope with his irony; it is a thing to which solemn men feel superior, and so, since they are not only solemn but innocent, it is a thrust they cannot parry. It is what destroys them, along with much mischance and the heaped mountain of their blunders. They never know him as we do; they do not hear him, for example, prick down the character of Lepidus with epigrams as merciless as bullets (IV, i). They never know the force that is coiled behind his charm. Nor do we know it as we shall in "Antony and Cleopatra." But it is here, if only briefly as in the case of the eccentric Caesar.

The blunders of Brutus and Cassius, but particularly of Brutus, are many and pathetic. If they do not achieve the dignity of tragic error, of heroic fault, the trouble is with the men who make them; their virtues are not positive

enough. This is less true of Cassius, who misconstrues everything at Philippi and so brings on the catastrophe (v, iii, 84).
Throughout the play he has been the sharper figure. Caesar
defines him in negative terms—"he hears no music" and
"loves no plays" as Antony does, and "seldom he smiles"
(i, ii, 203-5)—and yet it is from the same source that we
learn something we never forget: "a lean and hungry look
. . . such men are dangerous." His voice is lean and hungry
too, as his mind is rank and practical; when Brutus sees Antony after the assassination he thinks of nothing but assuring him of his "kind love, good thoughts, and reverence,"
whereas Cassius is only waiting till he can ask:

> But what compact mean you to have with us?  (iii, i, 215)

Brutus has no patience with the poet who sneaks in at Philippi:

> What should the wars do with these jigging fools?

But Cassius rasps out an angrier rebuke:

> Ha, ha! how vilely doth this cynic rhyme!    (iv, iii, 133)

He is the angrier of the two when they quarrel, and therefore he is dramatically the more interesting. He has more
flaws than Brutus, who indeed has none except the dramatic
one of an impenetrable and inexpressible nobility.

The mistakes of Brutus are the mistakes of a man whose
nobility muffles his intelligence. His conquest of himself has
extended to his wit; his excellence is not inconsistent with a
certain lethargy of mind. He knows this well enough:

> I am not gamesome; I do lack some part
> Of that quick spirit that is in Antony.    (i, ii, 28-9)

His honesty is absolute and disarming, so that he will not
wait as Cassius does for Caesar to compare him unfavorably
with the one brilliant person of the play. But honesty in him

is humorless and edgeless; it rings a little dully in our ears, and even a little smugly:

> There is no terror, Cassius, in your threats,
> For I am arm'd so strong in honesty
> That they pass by me as the idle wind,
> Which I respect not.                    (IV, iii, 66-9)

He would not call this boasting; he would call it the truth, as indeed it is; but the fact that it is, and that he is the speaker, tells us everything about him. Neither would he admit that his behavior to Messala when Messala brings him the news of Portia's death is a piece of acting.

> *Brutus.*   Now, as you are a Roman, tell me true.
> *Messala.*  Then like a Roman bear the truth I tell:
>             For certain she is dead, and by strange manner.
> *Brutus.*   Why, farewell, Portia. We must die, Messala.
>             With meditating that she must die once,
>             I have the patience to endure it now.
> *Messala.*  Even so great men great losses should endure.
> *Cassius.*  I have as much of this in art as you,
>             But yet my nature could not bear it so.
> *Brutus.*   Well, to our work alive. What do you think
>             Of marching to Philippi presently? (IV, iii, 187-97)

He would call it a demonstration of how Stoic gentlemen should conduct themselves. And in truth it is. Brutus already knows of Portia's death, for we have heard him telling Cassius of it. Cassius then is assisting him in the act, and Messala is being impressed as he should be. It is not vanity. It is virtue, it is true manhood demonstrating itself for the benefit of others. But to say as much is again to say that Brutus is humorlessly good. If his duty is to know himself, his performance fails. Nobility has numbed him until he cannot see himself for his principles. When his principles are expressing themselves they are beautiful in their clarity; his consideration for the tired boy Lucius is exquisite (IV, iii), and his last compliment to mankind should have been deserved:

My heart doth joy that yet in all my life
I found no man but he was true to me.    (v, v, 34-5)

But when he speaks to himself he knows not who is there; he addresses a strange audience, and fumbles. The reasoning with which he convinces himself that Caesar should be murdered is woefully inadequate.

So Caesar may;
Then, lest he may, prevent.          (II, i, 27-8)

The soliloquy of which these pitiful phrases are a part is riddled with rank fallacy. The fine man is a coarse thinker, the saint of self-denial has little self left to deny.

Shakespeare has done all that could be done with such a man, but what could be done was limited. The hero is heavy in the poet's hands; his reticence prevents intimacy, so that his blunders—as a conspirator with respect to Antony and as a general with respect to the time for attack—are difficult to excuse, they do not arouse in us any instinct to insist that to fail as such a man fails is to be glorious after all. Even the gentleness which will not let him desire Antony's death is in the last analysis confused. He is not mad, or haunted, or inspired, or perplexed in the extreme. He is simply confused. And the grounds of confusion in a man so negative are not to be known. Neither perhaps are they to be known in a man like Hamlet who uncovers something in himself with every word he utters. Yet we know the man—so well that his very attempts to evade us bring him closer. Hamlet may seldom mean what he says; and Shakespeare will never commit the error of exposing him in thought as he exposes Brutus; but we shall be instantly aware of what he means, at any rate to us, and we shall not fail to measure the disturbance in a too much changed mind.

# HAMLET

IT has been said of Hamlet that something in his genius renders him superior to decision and incapable of act, and it has been pointed out that he dominates the busiest of all known plays. Both views are right. His antic disposition has been analyzed as a symptom of abnormality and as a device for seeming mad. Neither theory is without support. He has been called the best of men and the worst of men. One judgment is as just as the other. Opinions have differed as to whether his deepest attention is engaged by the murder of his father, the marriage of his mother, the villainy of his uncle the King, the senility of Polonius, the apparent perfidy of Ophelia, the reliability of Horatio, the meddling of Rosencrantz and Guildenstern, or the manliness of Fortinbras. Any of them will do. Scarcely anything can be said that will be untrue of this brilliant and abounding young man the first crisis in whose life is also, to our loss, the last.

It has been said of the play "Hamlet" that its best scene is the one in which Horatio first sees the ghost, or the one in which he tells Hamlet of it, or the one in which Hamlet himself sees it and swears his friends to secrecy, or the one in which Polonius bids farewell to his son and warns his daughter away from the prince, or the one in which Ophelia reports Hamlet's disorder, or the one in which Polonius explains it to the King and Queen, or the one in which Hamlet, entering with a book, seems to Polonius to support the explanation, or the one in which Hamlet discovers the intentions of Rosencrantz and Guildenstern and discourses to them of his misanthropy, or the one in which he greets the

players and conceives a use to which they can be put, or the
one in which Ophelia is loosed to him while the King and
Polonius listen as spies, or the one in which he addresses the
players on the subject of their art, or the one in which the
play he has planned breaks down the King's composure, or
the one with the recorders, or the one in which Hamlet cannot kill the King because he is praying, or the one in his
mother's closet when Polonius is stabbed and the ghost walks
again, or the one in which he makes merry over Polonius's
supper of worms, or the one in which he watches Fortinbras
march against Poland, or the one in which Ophelia sings mad
songs and rouses her brother to revenge, or the one in which,
while Laertes plots with the King, the Queen reports
Ophelia's death, or the one in the graveyard, or the one with
Osric, or the one at the end which leaves only Horatio and
Fortinbras alive. Any of them will do. For all of the scenes
in "Hamlet" are good, and relatively to the play as a whole
each one in its turn is best.

The two absolutes are related. Neither the hero nor his
play can be taken apart. The joints are invisible. The character of Hamlet would appear to be no character at all because a name cannot be found for it, or—which is the same
thing—because too many can be found. Yet no reader or beholder of the play has ever doubted that Hamlet was one
man, or doubted that he knew him better than most men. He
is so singular in each particular, to paraphrase Florizel's account of Perdita, that all his acts are kings. He is alive to the
last syllable, and where there is so much life there is no blank
space for labels. So likewise with the tragedy of which he is
the heart and brain if not the whole moving body. There is
no best scene in "Hamlet" because it is not made up of scenes;
it is one situation and one action, and though like any whole
it is composed of parts there is no part whose tissue can be
separated from the rest without the sound of tearing. "Hamlet" is a highly organized animal, sensitive and thoroughbred,

each of whose sinews overlaps another, each of whose tendons tightens some extremity, and all of whose blood-stream is necessary to the unique, quick life which even the quietest movement expresses.

An attempt to enter the play through any scene of the conventional division will leave us still outside it—aware once more of its unspeakable vitality, but rewarded with no other sight than that of divers muscles rippling under skin. The thing has been put together, but either there are no joints or there are so many that the creature is all curves. Take, for instance, the section of the play which is called Act II, Scene ii. The number of its incidents is not the measure of its fullness, nor is the sum total of the things it tells us about Hamlet the final sum of our experience. The linkage of the incidents, the way they glide into one another without our being warned, is more important than their number; and our experience is not confined to the present Hamlet, or to what is happening around him now. The scene twitches remote corners of a dramatic web whose size we for the moment do not see; we gather that the whole play is implicit here, though we cannot be specific as to what is coming.

Rosencrantz and Guildenstern, two old friends of Hamlet, have arrived at court to keep him company; to draw him on to pleasures in the midst of which, as now the King makes clear, he may disclose the nature of his affliction. The King admits no other explanation than a father's death, and lets it be understood, the Queen concurring, that the motive behind this lawful espionage is a desire to cure the prince's condition. As Rosencrantz and Guildenstern are led away to find Hamlet and begin their work, Polonius enters to announce that the ambassadors from Norway have returned and to assure the King and Queen that he has found the cause of Hamlet's lunacy. They are eager to hear the cause, but first they must receive the ambassadors, who bring word that old Norway has forbidden Fortinbras to continue the advance on Den-

mark which has so much troubled the King; and that Fortinbras, marching now against Poland, requests the right to
cross Denmark so that he may gain his objective. The King,
promising to consider the request at another time, dismisses
the ambassadors and turns to Polonius, who with more art
than matter, and with promises of brevity which his amusing
tediousness belies, develops the theory that Hamlet is mad
because Ophelia has repulsed him. The Queen has believed
that her overhasty marriage was the cause, but agrees that
Polonius's explanation is very likely. The King asks for better proof, whereupon Polonius remarks that Hamlet is in the
habit of walking here in the lobby and that Ophelia can be
set in his way while the King and her father watch behind
an arras. As the King consents, Hamlet, who may have overheard the conclusion of the dialogue, enters reading a book.
Polonius asks the King and Queen to be left alone with him,
and argues from the nature of the insults he stays to receive
that Hamlet is indeed afflicted with love-melancholy; though
Hamlet's only state would appear to be boredom with old
fools and anxiety for his own safety—"except my life, my
life" (221). As Polonius goes out, bewildered yet all the
more convinced that he is right and that a meeting between
Hamlet and his daughter must take place, Rosencrantz and
Guildenstern pass him and are greeted by Hamlet, who plays
a game of wit with them until their guard is down and he can
ask them bluntly why they have come to Elsinore. They hesitate and temporize, but he forces them to confess that they
have been sent for by the King and Queen. At once he tells
them he will make everything clear: he has of late lost all
his mirth, so that the earth and the great sky above it are to
him but foul and pestilent, and man—the beauty of the world,
the paragon of animals, the creature nearest the angels and
most like a god—delights not him. He has spoken his best
prose for the benefit of two fools upon whom he wishes to
make a certain impression. But he has been betrayed into the

eloquence of truth, and so he breaks off with the abrupt addition that woman delights him neither, though by their smiling they seem to say so. Their only thought, they assure him, is of the poor entertainment such a prince would be able to offer the players who have just come to Elsinore. He is very much interested in the news that players have come, and as a trumpet announces their approach he summons high spirits to inform Rosencrantz and Guildenstern that the King and Queen are deceived: he is but mad north-north-west. In still higher spirits he jests at Polonius who has entered in advance of the players, and when they enter at last he greets them excitedly, pressing one of them to recite Aeneas's speech about Priam's slaughter. The player complies, but is so overcome by the speech that he weeps and cannot go on. Hamlet, dismissing the rest of the troupe to Polonius's care, holds this one member until he consents to play "The Murder of Gonzago" tomorrow night and to learn some dozen or sixteen lines which will be inserted in the text. Then Hamlet, commanding him to follow Polonius and mock him not, and sending away Rosencrantz and Guildenstern with assurances of their welcome to Elsinore, is left alone for the soliloquy which ends the scene. In a mere dream of passion, a fiction, this player here has wept for Hecuba. What would he do had he the motive and the cue for passion that Hamlet has? Is Hamlet a coward that so far he has done nothing to avenge his father's murder? The question enrages him and he falls to cursing the King. But that is nothing. He must act. He still must be indirect, for the spirit he has seen may have been the devil and not his father. So—now he has it—he will act to gain the knowledge he needs. He will put on a play that will make the King blench if he is guilty. And if he but blench, Hamlet will know his course. The play's the thing.

Such a synopsis is circumstantial and would seem to be complete. But it leaves almost everything out. It does not suggest the quality of Rosencrantz and Guildenstern—the combination in them of the sinister and the commonplace—and it does not begin to explore the processes of Hamlet as he discourses with them, or to explain the full meaning for himself of the great speech about earth and man. It does not record the suspicions we may have as we listen to the King's expressed motive for spying on Hamlet; for we can guess that he is lying, but we do not know just what he fears, nor do we know how deeply the Queen is disturbed. It does not render our still unripened sense of a stern and remote significance in the military movements of Fortinbras, whom we perceive we are not being permitted to forget but whose importance as a symbol is to manifest itself much later. It does not balance Polonius on that subtle point of space which he occupies throughout three acts, moving us to consider him simultaneously as ridiculous and pathetic, consequential and a nuisance, the father of Ophelia and the victim with her of the prince's newborn savagery; it does not indicate that his diagnosis can be credited as correct, and it certainly does not examine the whole question of Hamlet's feeling towards the man who was to have been his father-in-law—"and look you mock him not." It does not register our conviction that Hamlet's interest in the players is general as well as particular; he has thought much about the theater, and it may be that he is more at home with actors than with other people. It does not describe the beautiful courtesy, even if it be tempered by mockery, with which he welcomes Rosencrantz and Guildenstern to Elsinore. It fails, in brief, to follow the innumerable nerves which connect this part of the play with every other part, and which converge in the vital organ of the closing soliloquy as extensions of the same nerves converge to produce other soliloquies, other organs, in other areas.

No synopsis of "Hamlet," whole or part, can hope to succeed. The play is its own synopsis, and nothing shorter will do. Neither will anything longer; analysis in this case overruns and outrages art. Shakespeare for once has perfectly translated idea into act. Whatever the idea was, we now have only the play, and it is so clear that it becomes mysterious. For it is nothing but detail. The density of its concreteness is absolute. We do not know why Hamlet does this or that, we only know that he does it, and that we are interested in nothing else while he does it. We can no more understand him than we can doubt him. He is an enigma because he is real. We do not know why he was created or what he means. We simply and amply perceive that he exists.

Hamlet is intellectual, but we do not learn this from his thoughts, for he has none; he does not deliver himself of propositions. Of the many statements he makes there is none which is made for its own sake, and with the sense that it would be true at another time or place. In any situation only the relevant portion of the person speaks; the whole man never does, except in the play as a whole, which can be thought of as his body speaking, or rather his life. He is that unique thing in literature, a credible genius. But the reason is that Shakespeare has kept our view restricted to the surface. Here is an intellectual seen altogether from the outside. We know him as one from the way he behaves, not from the things he says he believes. We may not assume, indeed, that he believes what he says. For one thing he is a soul in agitation, his equilibrium has been lost. This glass of fashion and this mold of form, this noble mind whose harmony was once like that of sweet bells rung in tune, this courtier, soldier, scholar whose disposition has hitherto been generous and free from all contriving, this matchless gentleman who has never been known to overstep the modesty of nature, is not himself save for a few minutes at the end when his calmness comes back like magic and his apology to Laertes can almost avert the catastrophe which every event has prepared. His words elsewhere are wild and whirling; or they are cruel in their kindness; or they are simply cruel. Or they are spoken for a calculated effect—the calculation in most cases being extempore. For Hamlet is immensely sensitive to his environment, and adjusts himself with marvelous quickness to its many changes. His asides are sudden, like needles whose function is to keep both him and us awake to the farthest implications of the danger close at hand. His repartee is pistol-swift, whipped out by one forever abnormally on guard against real or imagined enemies. And his soliloquies are secret mirrors the subdued brilliance of whose shifting planes reflects the predicament that surrounds him, past and future as well as present.

Curiously then we know a man in terms of what he is not; this gentlest of all heroes is never gentle. But it is more complicated than that. Hamlet is an actor. Like any character in whom Shakespeare was greatly interested, he plays a role. He plays indeed many roles, being supreme in tragedy as Falstaff was supreme in comedy. His long interest in the theater has taught him how, but his best tutors now are the pressure of circumstance and the richness of his own nature. Like Falstaff he shows the man he is by being many men. With the exception of Horatio there is no person in the play for whose benefit he has not conceived and studied a part. He acts with the King and Queen, with Ophelia, with Polonius, with the court at large; taking on and putting off each role as occasion dictates, and at the climax of the tragedy wearing all of them simultaneously. For in the scene of the play within the play he has his audiences for the first time together. Now the fiction of Ophelia's Hamlet must harmonize with that of her father's, of the King's, of the Queen's, and with that of the general public. Only a virtuoso would succeed. But Hamlet, not to speak of Shakespeare, is a virtuoso, and he succeeds. No playwright ever attempted a subtler scene, or ever achieved it with so little show of labor. The only thing we are conscious of is the intentness with which we follow the waves of meaning across Hamlet's face. The whole meaning of the play is in vibration there, even if we cannot put it in words of our own. There is, of course, no slightest reason why we should desire to do so.

As always in Shakespeare, the style of Hamlet is the man. He is made of mercury and so has many styles, yet they are one if only because they ever are telling us of what he is made. His tongue is as flexible as his mind. It knows its way among all words, all tones, all attitudes. And it is superbly trained. The intellect of its owner is apparent in nothing so much as his literary skill. With no notice at all he can say anything, and be master of what he has said. "Well said, old mole! Canst work i' the earth so fast?" "To be honest, as this world goes, is to be one man pick'd out of ten thousand." "You cannot, sir, take from me anything that I will more willingly part withal." "Then is doomsday near." "Denmark's a prison." "O God, I could be bounded in a nutshell and count myself a king of infinite space, were it not that I have bad dreams." "To be, or not to be: that is the question." "Thus conscience does make cowards of us all." "Get thee to a nunnery, go." "I say, we will have no more marriages." "No, good mother, here's metal more attractive." "You would play upon me, you would seem to know my stops, you would pluck out the heart of my mystery." "I will speak daggers to her, but use none." "I must be cruel, only to be kind." "Not where he eats, but where he is eaten." "I see a cherub that sees them." "Where be your gibes now, your gambols, your songs, your flashes of merriment, that were wont to set the table on a roar? Not one now, to mock your own grinning? Quite chop-fallen?" "But I am very sorry, good Horatio, that to Laertes I forgot myself." "But thou wouldst not think how ill all's here about my heart." "If it be now, 't is not to come; if it be not to come, it will be now; if it be not now, yet it will come; the readiness is all." "The rest is silence." The simplicity of such utterances reveals a great man and a princely artist, an artist too much the master of his medium to be proud of what he can do with it, or even to be conscious that it is there. But Hamlet can be elaborate as well as simple, artful as well as quick. His address to the players says something which he wants them to understand, and the thing it says has been said for all time; yet the man who is speaking enjoys his speech, and may be a little proud of the nobility which knows its way so well among the short words and the long ones, the epigrams and the periods.

Speak the speech, I pray you, as I pronounc'd it to you, trippingly on the tongue; but if you mouth it, as many of your players do, I had as lief the town-crier spoke my lines. Nor do not saw the air too much with your hand, thus, but use all gently; for in the very torrent, tempest, and, as I may say, the whirlwind of passion, you must acquire and beget a temperance that may give it smoothness. O, it offends me to the soul to see a robustious periwig-pated fellow tear a passion to tatters, to very rags, to split the ears of the groundlings, who for the most part are capable of nothing but inexplicable dumb-shows and noise. I could have such a fellow whipp'd for o'erdoing Termagant. It out-herods Herod. Pray you, avoid it. . . . Be not too tame neither, but let your own discretion be your tutor. Suit the action to the word, the word to the action; with this special observance, that you o'erstep not the modesty of nature. For anything so overdone is from the purpose of playing, whose end, both at the first and now, was and is, to hold, as 't were, the mirror up to nature; to show virtue her own feature, scorn her own image, and the very age and body of the time his form and pressure. Now this overdone, or come tardy off, though it make the unskilful laugh, cannot but make the judicious grieve; the censure of the which one must, in your allowance, o'erweigh a whole theatre of others. O, there be players that I have seen play, and heard others praise, and that highly, not to speak it profanely, that, neither having the accent of Christians nor the gait of Christian, pagan, nor man, have so strutted and bellowed that I have thought some of Nature's journeymen had made men and not made them well, they imitated humanity so abominably.

(III, ii, 1-39)

"Imitated humanity so abominably," "capable of nothing but inexplicable dumb-shows and noise." Only a skilled tongue could say such phrases well, and only a proud tongue would undertake them at all. A man who can talk like that must be aware of everything in the world—except perhaps the disproportion between his discourse and its occasion. And of Shakespeare we are to remember that he never used in his play the speech which for his hero had seemed to call for so long a commentary. But then we shall be confirmed in our belief that the character of Hamlet is the character of an actor, and that the instinct of Shakespeare as a dramatic poet is to pour his fullest gifts into such persons. That Hamlet is histrionic is no less clear than that he is high-strung, cerebral, magnanimous, and sometimes obscene. Richard II had been an amateur of the boards, Jaques had been a sentimentalist spoiling to be a star, and Brutus to his own loss had been no actor at all. Hamlet is so much of a professional that the man in him is indistinguishable from the mime. His life as we have it is so naturally and completely a play that we can almost think of him as his own author, his own director, and his own protagonist. We can even think of him as his own entire cast, he is the plexus of so much humanity, the mirror in which so many other minds are registered.

We see Hamlet in other persons even more clearly than in himself. His relation to each of them is immediate and delicate; his least gesture records itself in them—in their concern, their pity, their love, their anger, or their fear. They cannot be indifferent to him, and this is one reason that we cannot. Nor is vanity in him the cause. He has not willed or desired his eminence. It is not in his nature to dominate humanity, and at last destroy it. Yet he does; this gentleman warps every other life to his own, and scatters death like a universal plague. Not quite universal, either. The world of this tragedy, like that of any other tragedy by Shakespeare, is large; Denmark is a prison and its air is close to breathe, but four times we have heard through darkness the brisk tramp of Fortinbras's feet on the bright ice beyond tragedy's frontiers. Fortinbras is Hamlet's frame. He is not completely drawn until his cannon, his drums, and his colors come on with him at the end to announce that human existence will be what it was before Hamlet lived. But then he is firmly drawn; the story of Hamlet, however morbid, has been confined. Another frame, an inner one, is Hamlet's good friend Horatio, who will live on until he has reported Hamlet and his cause aright to the unsatisfied, until he has healed a hero's wounded name. For just as Hamlet with his last breath remembers the state and thinks to give Fortinbras his dying voice for king, so he remembers that his aim had never been to strew the stage of life with corpses; to deliver Rosencrantz and Guildenstern to an English hangman, to feed Polonius to politic worms, to send Ophelia, dripping with tears and muddy death, into unsanctified ground. Within these two frames the spectacle of Hamlet is forever suspended. A merest glance from us, a chance return to any scene, and the whole movement recommences. Hamlet walks again, alone and yet surrounded: a genius of unfathomable depth who yet is in contact at every point of his clear surface with another life as sensitive to his as a still night is to sound. That honor could too much change him, that scruples too fine could distort him into a dealer of coarse death, was both his tragedy and the world's. The world could not let so destructive a man live longer, but when it sacrificed him it lost the light of its fiercest sun.

# TROILUS AND CRESSIDA

THE three comedies of Shakespeare which were written, if his chronology is rightly understood, between "Hamlet" and "Othello"—at the outset in other words of his great career in tragedy—may be said to indicate in their various ways that what he should have kept on writing at such a time was tragedy and nothing else. The comic touch of two or three years ago has been completely lost, nor will it be recovered in the last plays, though the author of them will have found an equivalent for it that will permit him another kind of success. The three comedies now at hand are in any final view unsuccessful. In "All's Well That Ends Well" the poet cannot locate his atmosphere, in "Measure for Measure" he cannot extract enough poetry from his problem, and in "Troilus and Cressida" he either lacks feeling or cannot control the feeling he has; and he cannot control the style which, however amazing in its volume and perhaps admirable in its invention, certainly runs loose.

The style of "Troilus and Cressida" is loud, brassy, and abandoned. The world which Chaucer had left so tenderly intact explodes as if a mine had been touched off beneath it, while a host of characters, conceived partly in doubt and partly in disgust, rave at the tops of their never modulated voices. All of them are angry, all of them are distrustful and mendacious; and the tone of each is hardened to rasping by some unmotivated irritation. One is tempted to suppose that the irritation was in the author before it was in them. For once he cannot write with respect either for his subject or for their styles. He composes to the limit of his energy, he laughs the loudest he has ever laughed, and still felicity is absent. He talks at the top of his lungs and still cannot say enough, or get the right thing said. Discussions are started only to end in pompous noise, as when the Greeks debate the policy of the war (I, iii), or only to fizzle out in fallacy, as when the Trojans ponder letting Helen go (II, ii). Nothing is felt enough to be finished; or something that is not expressed in the play is felt so deeply that conclusions are for the moment impossible. "Troilus and Cressida" is either Shakespeare's revenge upon mankind for losing its power to delight him or his revenge upon the theme for refusing to tell him how it should be treated. Shall it become tragedy or comedy? He does not know. So he writes the roof of his head off and at the end commits the ultimate cynicism of leaving Troilus alive, doing "mad and fantastic execution . . . with such a careless force and forceless care" as means precisely nothing (v, v, 38-40).

The writing has been admired, but for patches of roses there are acres of rank fumiter. The great speech of Ulysses on order and the specialty of rule is, merely as rant, tremendous:

> The heavens themselves, the planets, and this centre
> Observe degree, priority, and place,
> Insisture, course, proportion, season, form,
> Office, and custom, in all line of order;
> And therefore is the glorious planet Sol
> In noble eminence enthron'd and spher'd
> Amidst the other; whose medicinable eye
> Corrects the ill aspects of planets evil,
> And posts, like the commandment of a king,
> Sans check to good and bad. But when the planets
> In evil mixture to disorder wander,
> What plagues and what portents! what mutiny!
> What raging of the sea! shaking of earth!
> Commotion in the winds! Frights, changes, horrors,
> Divert and crack, rend and deracinate

The unity and married calm of states
Quite from their fixture!

(I, iii, 85-101)

His other great speech on envious and calumniating Time
breeds a dozen ideas out of one, and in any school of rhetoric
would be a model for students of the amplifying art.

Time hath, my lord, a wallet at his back,
Wherein he puts alms for oblivion,
A great-sized monster of ingratitudes.
. . . Perseverance, dear my lord,
Keeps honour bright; to have done is to hang
Quite out of fashion, like a rusty mail
In monumental mockery. . . .
For Time is like a fashionable host
That slightly shakes his parting guest by the hand,
And with his arms outstretch'd, as he would fly,
Grasps in the comer. . . .
One touch of nature makes the whole world kin,
That all, with one consent, praise new-born gawds,
Though they are made and moulded of things past,
And give to dust that is a little gilt
More laud than gilt o'er-dusted.
The present eye praises the present object.

(III, iii, 145-80)

And Troilus in at least one place is given the language to
speak wonderfully of his love:

I am giddy; expectation whirls me round.
The imaginary relish is so sweet
That it enchants my sense; what will it be,
When that the watery palates taste indeed
Love's thrice repured nectar? Death, I fear me,
Swooning destruction, or some joy too fine,
Too subtle, potent, tun'd too sharp in sweetness
For the capacity of my ruder powers.
I fear it much; and I do fear besides
That I shall lose distinction in my joys,
As doth a battle, when they charge on heaps
The enemy flying.

(III, ii, 19-30)

That Cressida is not worth all this does not damage it as
rhetoric, though it may force it as poetry; just as it does not
matter that Ulysses is a dog-fox barking platitudes, in the
one case at a ring of Grecian bullies and in the other at the
chief of all curs Achilles. Such writing has its glories, and
they must not be denied the play. But it is writing on the
loose, and when the tether is quite cut there is no glory.
"Corresponsive and fulfilling bolts" (Prologue, 18) is a great
deal too much for what needs to be let pass as merely "bolts."
Agamemnon, who divides with Nestor the honor here of
showing the most bloated tongue, can take seven lines to tell
Hector that he is welcome though an enemy.

> Understand more clear,
> What's past and what's to come is strew'd with husks
> And formless ruin of oblivion;
> But in this extant moment, faith and troth,
> Strain'd purely from all hollow bias-drawing,
> Bids thee, with most divine integrity,
> From heart of very heart, great Hector, welcome.
>
> (IV, v, 165-71)

And Hector, hearing Achilles ask the gods where he is to
give him his mortal wound, is simply preposterous in repartee:

> Think'st thou to catch my life so pleasantly
> As to prenominate in nice conjecture
> Where thou wilt hit me dead?          (IV, v, 249-51)

He is almost a match for Nestor, who tortures himself as
follows to explain that the Greeks cannot afford to send
Achilles against Hector because of what the choice of their
best warrior would symbolize:

> Our imputation shall be oddly pois'd
> In this wild action; for the success,
> Although particular, shall give a scantling
> Of good or bad unto the general;
> And in such indexes, although small pricks

> To their subsequent volumes, there is seen
> The baby figure of the giant mass
> Of things to come at large.          (I, iii, 339-46)

They all, with a fury which is regularly perverse and sometimes funny, bury themselves under mountains of hard words.
The latinism of Shakespeare's maturing style will never again
belabor the ear with so many terms like orgillous, immures
(for walls), tortive, persistive, unplausive, propugnation, re-
joindure, multipotent, impressure, and prenominate. Troilus
in one speech sounds like a neologizing schoolboy: "Why
stay we, then?" asks Ulysses when the evidence of Cressida's
perfidy has all been gathered, and her lover answers:

> To make a recordation to my soul
> Of every syllable that here was spoke.
> But if I tell how these two did co-act,
> Shall I not lie in publishing a truth?
> Sith yet there is a credence in my heart,
> An esperance so obstinately strong,
> That doth invert the attest of eyes and ears,
> As if those organs had deceptious functions,
> Created only to calumniate.          (v, ii, 116-24)

And tautology is on a rampage. The mannerism that appeared in "Henry V" has reappeared to feed upon itself.
The wind and tempest of her frown, the pride and salt scorn
of his eyes, the fan and wind of your fair sword, the unity
and married calm of states, the great swing and rudeness of
his poise, the rude brevity and discharge of one—such com-
pounds have their glory, but most of their fellows are as
coarse as handcuffs or dumbbells: vaunt and firstlings, tortive
and errant, bias and thwart, affin'd and kin, applause and ap-
probation, dialogue and sound, head and general, still and
mental, estimate and dignity, cause and question, disobedient
and refractory, passage and carriage, certain and possess'd,
tame and familiar, negligent and loose, made and molded,
still and dumb-discoursive, forfeits and subduements, dis-

solv'd and loos'd. It is of course a proper language for people who are all guile and raillery, all vanity and contempt.

Against the Trojan war as a background the love of Troilus and Cressida runs its unsmooth race. The relevant characters in each environment are brutally taken down by Shakespeare as he goes; though the level on which they begin is low enough. It is indeed so low that the two persons designed as critics of them have nothing left to do except snigger and blaspheme. Pandarus's role is to cheapen the lovers. But the quality of Cressida's coyness is so crude, each joint and motive of her body is so eloquent of the game as she passes down the row of Greeks lined up to kiss her (IV, v), and her teasing of Diomede is so gross, that to be cheaper Pandarus must be worth nothing at all. And truly enough his part has no power, it is impotent either for enlightenment or for relief.

She's making her ready, she'll come straight. You must be witty now. She does so blush, and fetches her wind so short. . . . I'll fetch her. . . . Come, come, what need you blush? Shame's a baby. . . . So, so; rub on, and kiss the mistress. . . . What, billing again? . . . How now, how now! how go maidenheads? . . . Ha, ha! Alas, poor wretch! a poor *capocchia!* hast not slept tonight? Would he not, a naughty man, let it sleep?

The role of Thersites is to cheapen the heroes. But Achilles and his brach Patroclus are such boors, Hector is so stuffed and stupid an orator, Agamemnon is such a mouther, Nestor —good old chronicle, that has so long walked hand in hand with time—is so tiresomely prolix, and Ulysses in spite of his golden tongue is so politic a rogue, that in order to sink beneath them Thersites must bubble in eternal mire. So in fact he does. And no blasphemer in Shakespeare has surpassed him in brute competence.

I would thou didst itch from head to foot and I had the scratching of thee. I would make thee the loathsom'st scab in Greece. (II, i, 29-31)

Here's Agamemnon, an honest fellow enough, and one that
loves quails; but he has not so much brain as ear-wax.

(v, i, 55-8)

How the devil Luxury, with his fat rump and potato-finger,
tickles these together! Fry, lechery, fry! (v, ii, 55-7)

But there is nothing for him to accomplish. The heroes have
accomplished their own degradation, they have shouted
themselves too hoarse and deaf to hear any wisdom out of
this filthy mouth. Nor is there any objective for Thersites
to gain in the imagination of the audience. There must be
much of him to be anything, the din about him is so loud;
the more of him the better, one might think, since he is so
far good. Yet even of good things there must be a limit, and
in his case the play has established no limit, nor did Shakespeare feel any. "Lechery, lechery; still wars and lechery;
nothing else holds fashion. A burning devil take them!" (v, ii,
195-7). Such is the conclusion of Thersites. Yet it is no conclusion for him, nor could it have been one for Shakespeare,
who nevertheless raised thus to a peak the pitch of one man's
monotonous howl in the desperate hope that it might silence
many others. It did not do so. The monotony of "Troilus
and Cressida" still has no end. The heroes and the lovers still
rave on, and the scream of no critic in the play can stop them.

# ALL'S WELL THAT ENDS WELL

"ALL'S WELL THAT ENDS WELL" is an anecdote in five acts. Its story can best be told briefly and abstractly, as a fable is told; and that is the way it had been told in most of the countries of the world before Shakespeare undertook to give it locality, detail, and atmosphere. The skeleton of the tale—and the skeleton is all—provides a man who goes away from a woman saying that she can make him recognize her as his wife only by fulfilling several impossible conditions, one of which is that she possess herself of some object he wears or otherwise owns intimately, and another of which is that she become the mother of a child by him during his absence. The man in Shakespeare's play is Bertram and the woman is Helena, and these are Bertram's conditions:

When thou canst get the ring upon my finger which never shall come off, and show me a child begotten of thy body that I am father to, then call me husband; but in such a "then" I write a "never."                                                   (III, ii, 59-63)

The tale always goes on to tell of ruses whereby the woman wins; she follows him, unseen or in disguise, and substitutes herself for another woman in his bed; and in good time he is presented with evidence which he cannot but recognize. So Helena, who by curing the King has won Bertram for her husband, pursues the unwilling youth to Florence and deceives him by seeming to be Diana. And so Bertram, confronted in the fifth act with evidence that this is true, turns to the King and says:

If she, my liege, can make me know this clearly,
I'll love her dearly, ever, ever dearly.          (v, iii, 316-7)

His jingle might be the conclusion of a clipped narrative in clever rhyme, or it might be the epilogue to an adult fairy tale. It scarcely sounds like the hero's utterance in a play by Shakespeare after he has written "Hamlet." Yet it is, and the play has been full-length and serious. "All's Well" has attempted to make drama out of anecdote, to pad a dry skeleton with living flesh, to force upon the imagination what only wit can credit. It has failed, but it is one of Shakespeare's most interesting failures.

He would appear to have known by instinct that a story whose merit depends on its brevity cannot in the nature of things be believed at length or supplied with a suitable atmosphere. It must break down somewhere, as his version does at the huddled and perfunctory finish. He made no apparent effort to forestall such a breakdown, having exhausted his interest in Bertram and Helena once the atmosphere he had conceived for them confessed its meagerness. He had conceived a meager atmosphere as the only one which his impossible problem would justify, and up to a point he had built it perfectly. But its necessary limitations were too severe, and his imagination, sensibly perhaps, stopped working.

The household in which at the opening of the play the hero and heroine are discovered, he as the young Count of Rousillon and she as his mother's penniless ward, is unique among Shakespeare's households for its poverty of spirit. It is nothing like Olivia's, Portia's, or even Rosalind's. Rosalind's uncle was cruel, but at least he held fetes and staged wrestling matches. Bertram's father is dead, and with him has died the spirit of the place. The clown with whom the elder Count had made much sport stays on by his authority, but he is a barren, unpleasant jester, "a shrewd knave and an unhappy" (IV, v, 66). Malvolio denounced Feste as barren but Malvolio was wrong, for Feste had kept his juices in the summer warmth of Olivia's world. This clown is as bleak and bitter as the air that blows through his old mistress's rooms. The Countess has been no inspiration to him, for she is old and tired. She tries once to be young with him (II, ii), but she fails. "Mine age is weak," she admits most justly of herself (III, iv, 41). She is just and kind, and Helena could not do without her; it is simply that the blood is half frozen in her veins, as it is in the veins of the play she somehow dominates. Not only has she hung her house with black in sign of her unfortunate widowhood; she oppresses it with her thin, cold way of speaking, which is like that of Lafeu, the old lord who haunts it with her, and who is as far from being a Polonius or a Menenius as a peeled stick is from being a budded stem. "Moderate lamentation is the right of the dead, excessive grief the enemy to the living," he says to Helena (I, i, 63-5), for her father has died too, though she is weeping at Bertram's departure for Paris rather than over Gerard de Narbon's death. The platitude is delivered with the least possible richness, like the platitudes which the Countess delivers to her son as he leaves her to see the world (I, i, 70-81). Polonius to this was Zeus or Apollo, and when Lafeu at court presents Helena to the King with the unlikely words,

> I am Cressid's uncle,
> That dare leave two together,          (II, i, 100-1)

he merely reminds us of the energy that had raged in "Troilus and Cressida." Here there is no surplus energy of any sort. The atmosphere at Rousillon is one of darkness, old age, disease, sadness, and death; and of superannuated people who nevertheless hold on to the chill edges of their former styles.

Bertram, an "unseason'd courtier" with arched brows, hawking eye, and youthful curls (I, i, 105), leaves this place where he has been crushed under the weight of death and generations to flourish in the freer air of the French court. But even at Paris he meets a sick king who wants to talk only

of other days and of Bertram's father. The King has no hope
that his fistula will be cured; sitting before Bertram, for he
cannot stand, he reflects that his place is soon to be filled by
younger men, and muses on the ancient manners:

> I would I had that corporal soundness now,
> As when thy father and myself in friendship
> First tried our soldiership! He did look far
> Into the service of the time, and was
> Discipled of the bravest. He lasted long;
> But on us both did haggish age steal on
> And wore us out of act. It much repairs me
> To talk of your good father. In his youth
> He had the wit which I can well observe
> Today in our young lords; but they may jest
> Till their own scorn return to them unnoted
> Ere they can hide their levity in honour
> So like a courtier. Contempt nor bitterness
> Were in his pride or sharpness; if they were,
> His equal had awak'd them, and his honour,
> Clock to itself, knew the true minute when
> Exception bid him speak, and at this time
> His tongue obey'd his hand. Who were below him
> He us'd as creatures of another place,
> And bow'd his eminent top to their low ranks,
> Making them proud of his humility,
> In their poor praise he humbled. Such a man
> Might be a copy to these younger times;
> Which, followed well, would demonstrate them now
> But goers backward. . . .
> Would I were with him! He would always say—
> Methinks I hear him now! His plausive words
> He scatter'd not in ears, but grafted them,
> To grow there and to bear,—"Let me not live,"—
> Thus his good melancholy oft began,
> On the catastrophe and heel of pastime,
> When it was out,—"Let me not live," quoth he,
> "After my flame lacks oil, to be the snuff
> Of younger spirits, whose apprehensive senses
> All but new things disdain; whose judgements are
> Mere fathers of their garments; whose constancies

Expire before their fashions." This he wish'd;
I after him do after him wish too,
Since I nor wax nor honey can bring home,
I quickly were dissolved from my hive,
To give some labourers room.            (I, ii, 24-67)

This is excellent, and bears in its grave arms the essence of
Shakespeare's ripest poetry; the play cannot be undistinguished if it contains one such passage. But Bertram has already heard too much about the past. If this is wisdom it is
not for him. He wishes at last to live like any ordinary young
fellow of France. It is his misfortune to be very ordinary—
to be "noble," as Dr. Johnson puts it, "without generosity,
and young without truth." His manners are as poor as his
imagination, and the lies he tells, once Helena has won her
wager by curing the King and getting the husband she so
strangely wants, are the work of a slim talent. He never was
cut out for the hero of a play, and had it not been for this
girl whose existence in his mother's house he had so little no-
ticed he might have pursued a decently average career in the
company of his friend Parolles—a dull braggart soldier whose
mind runs all to scarfs and bannerets, and whose contribution
to Shakespearean comedy is chiefly the contrast he offers
Falstaff, showing in himself the minimum of a comic convention and reminding us of its maximum in Prince Hal's
mighty friend. Parolles too could have had his career.

I know him a notorious liar,
Think him a great way fool, solely a coward;
Yet these fix'd evils sit so fit in him,
That they take place, when virtue's steely bones
Look bleak i' the cold wind.            (I, i, 111-5)

Thus Helena can justify him at the start. And we can respect
the line with which he departs from the scene of his unmask-
ing at Florence:
Simply the thing I am
Shall make me live.            (IV, iv, 369-70)

He was not cut out for a high comic role. He must make the best of his presence in what is after all a mirthless play.

Shakespeare could see nothing in Bertram because he could conceive no reality in a young man who would have to do the things the story calls upon him to do. He lets him have some of our sympathy at first, so that we can understand his horror of "the dark house and the detested wife" (II, iii, 309). We may even grant him a rudimentary sense of justice when he persists in defending Parolles against Lafeu and others. "It may be you have mistaken him, my lord" (II, v, 44). It may not be. Lafeu is right. But here is the decent tentativeness of an untutored boy—here, and in the quiet remark he makes when Lafeu has gone out and Parolles has denounced him as an idle lord. "I think so," says Bertram. He is not sure. But Bertram thins into a mere figure of fable as the plot wears on. He is there only because the play needs him, and because a commonplace cad will do.

If Helena thins out as well, this is not to say that she has been any sort of failure at the start. From the time she disguises herself as a pilgrim and meets Diana's mother in the streets of Florence she is no more a person than Bertram is; it is worth noting, for instance, that Shakespeare has not populated these streets as he is in the habit of doing—as he populates in his next play the streets of Vienna—and that he denies to Helena the privileges of poetry and dramatic irony which he once extended to Julia and Viola. "I know the lady," she nods and says when the widow speaks of Bertram's deserted wife; and that is about all. The play suppresses most of its possible poetry, and it is as poor in irony as it is in mirth. But up until this moment Helena has been one of Shakespeare's most interesting women. Her power is more often implied than expressed, but it is great. Her inability to speak when Bertram bids her good-by in the first scene is amply made up for by the soliloquy with which,

once she is left alone, she gives the play the only shock of
energy it is ever to have:

> I think not on my father,
> And these great tears grace his remembrance more
> Than those I shed for him. What was he like?
> I have forgot him. My imagination
> Carries no favour in 't but Bertram's.
> I am undone! There is no living, none,
> If Bertram be away. 'T were all one
> That I should love a bright particular star
> And think to wed it, he is so above me.
> In his bright radiance and collateral light
> Must I be comforted, not in his sphere.
> The ambition in my love thus plagues itself.
> The hind that would be mated by the lion
> Must die for love.                    (I, i, 90-103)

The "bright particular star" is not the only strong thing here.
Helena speaks often of stars, and the fact that she does sym-
bolizes her solitary blazing brightness in the play. But she
speaks as often in the pressing, insistent idiom of "There is
no living, none, if Bertram be away." And she is as regularly
concerned with visions of herself as an animal mating. One
of her favorite words is "nature," and there is much of it in
her. She has body as well as mind, and can jest grossly with
Parolles in the dialogue that comes next. There is nothing
frail about Helena, whose passion is secret but unmeasured.
And because her body is real her mind is gifted with a rank,
a sometimes masculine fertility. It is easy for her to achieve
the intellectual distinction of

> In his bright radiance and collateral light,

just as it is natural that she should dress her longing for Bertram in the tough language of physics and metaphysics:

> Our remedies oft in ourselves do lie,
> Which we ascribe to heaven. The fated sky
> Gives us free scope, only doth backward pull

Our slow designs when we ourselves are dull.
What power is it which mounts my love so high,
That makes me see, and cannot feed mine eye?
The mightiest space in fortune nature brings
To join like likes and kiss like native things.
Impossible be strange attempts to those
That weigh their pains in sense and do suppose
What hath been cannot be.            (i, i, 231-41)

She has in her own dark way the force of Imogen, though she inhabits an inferior play, and one whose machinery is at last too much for even her. She has done all that flesh can do to temper the chill wind her creator has set blowing through two acts. Then even that wind dies down, to the accompaniment of her self-accusing sorrow for the young man she has driven out of France:

Poor lord! is 't I
That chase thee from thy country and expose
Those tender limbs of thine to the event
Of the none-sparing war?            (iii, ii, 105-7)

Her pursuit is never softened by pity like this again. It grows mechanical like the play, for it has a tale to tell. Helena has ceased to be one of the most remarkable among those women of Shakespeare whose loves are their lives. Her life has been maneuvered into nothingness. And even while she lived it she did no more than promise to warm the steely bones that looked so bleak in Rousillon's cold wind.

# MEASURE FOR MEASURE

ONE wheel of the machinery in "All's Well" is used again in "Measure for Measure." Mariana substitutes herself for Isabella in Angelo's bed. But the resemblance ends there. Mariana is not the heroine of the new comedy; what she does is given her to be done because the playwright is interested in Isabella, not in her; there is a background of fact and event which interests him even more than Isabella does; and there is everywhere an important texture of poetry that shows in Shakespeare a relatively deep concern with his subject. If "Measure for Measure" is still unsatisfactory in some way that is difficult to define, the reason can hardly be a lack of serious attention on Shakespeare's part. He has given it thought and care, and he has written for it some of his gravest, most complex, and most effective poetry. The reason is rather that it goes against his grain to make comedy out of such matter; or perhaps that his absorption in the evil background of the tale is of such a sort as to leave his mind unfree either to judge it with detachment or to concentrate with his usual success upon the figures in the foreground, the persons of the play.

The air of Vienna is poisoned, like that of Cressida's Troy. The city stews in its vices; bawds and pimps swarm in the streets, the prisons are crowded with moral vermin, and the gentle folk have lost their goodness. Goodness exists; Isabella, if one likes, is a saint; but it is forced to be unwholesomely conscious of itself, and the universal consciousness of evil puts a certain bitter perplexity into everybody's voice. The Duke of Vienna, being perplexed in the extreme, decides to absent himself for a while and leave Angelo in authority; for

217

Angelo "scarce confesses that his blood flows"—the fantastic Lucio says this blood "is very snow-broth"—and the Duke assumes that so strict a puritan will enforce the laws against vice which he himself has "let slip" for as long as nineteen years. But the public decision of the Duke is not his private one. Shakespeare, altering his source, disguises him as a friar so that he may stand by and watch the tangle of events. His commentary will maintain the sinister tone the poet desires:

> There is so great a fever on goodness, that the dissolution of it must cure it. Novelty is only in request; and it is as dangerous to be aged in any kind of course, as it is virtuous to be constant in any undertaking. There is scarce truth enough alive to make societies secure; but security enough to make fellowships accurst. Much upon this riddle runs the wisdom of the world.
>
> (III, ii, 235-42)

And of course his presence at every crisis is our sign that all will end well. We may wonder why his omnipotence does not intervene when Angelo, who has ordered Claudio's death because he has engaged in what Lucio calls "a game of tick-tack" with Juliet, grows suddenly lecherous at the sight of Isabella and offers to pardon her brother if she will lay down the treasures of her body to him; or when, visiting Claudio in prison, his Grace lets him suffer in the thought of a death which will not come to him while the play lasts; or when Angelo, having as he supposes enjoyed the body of Isabella (but it was the body of his five-years-ago-deserted Mariana of the moated grange), breaks his promise with respect to Claudio and commands that he lose his head at once. The Duke does to be sure intervene, and no one dies. But he is torturously slow about it. His hands are sluggish in the manipulation of the dummies whose predicament he has wantonly created. Our wonderment will cease only when we realize that he is a tall dark dummy too; that it is the atmosphere of Vienna, not the hypothetical perils of Claudio and

Isabella, which interests Shakespeare. It is the somber spectacle of "a thirsty evil,"

> Like rats that ravin down their proper bane,
>
> (I, ii, 133)

rather than the motives of the Duke as spectator, or the psy-
chology of any spectator, out of which he has made the
poetry of "Measure for Measure."

That poetry is missing from the significant orations which
here and there are asked to do the work of thought and
action. Angelo's soliloquy when he finds his famous virtue
yielding ground to lust for Isabella is too conscious of itself
as document and case-history to be convincing as revelation.

> What's this, what's this? Is this her fault or mine?
> The tempter or the tempted, who sins most?
> Ha!
> Not she, nor doth she tempt; but it is I
> That, lying by the violet in the sun,
> Do as the carrion does, not as the flower,
> Corrupt with virtuous season. Can it be
> That modesty may more betray our sense
> Than woman's lightness? Having waste ground enough,
> Shall we desire to raze the sanctuary
> And pitch our evils there? O, fie, fie, fie!
> What dost thou, or what art thou, Angelo? (II, ii, 162-73)

These are the morals of melodrama, and we know them by
the questions and exclamations everywhere, the rhetorical
mold that forms on Angelo as he talks. Such talk has nothing like the force of his briefer utterances:

> We must not make a scarecrow of the law,
> Setting it up to fear the birds of prey,
> And let it keep one shape, till custom make it
> Their perch and not their terror. (II, i, 1-4)

> What's open made to justice,
> That justice seizes. What knows the laws
> That thieves do pass on thieves? (II, i, 21-3)

Nor has the celebrated cadenza by Claudio on death (III, i, 118-132) the force of a few words by the Duke on the same subject:

> Thou hast nor youth nor age,
> But, as it were, an after-dinner's sleep,
> Dreaming on both.                          (III, i, 32-4)

Nor does Isabella gain anything by being so copious, so competent, and so masculine an orator to Claudio when she realizes that his first impulse to save her from Angelo has been replaced by a nightmare of death:

> O you beast!
> O faithless coward! O dishonest wretch!
> Wilt thou be made a man out of my vice?
> Is't not a kind of incest, to take life
> From thine own sister's shame? What should I think?
> Heaven shield my mother play'd my father fair!
> For such a warped slip of wilderness
> Ne'er issu'd from his blood. Take my defiance!
> Die, perish! Might but my bending down
> Reprieve thee from thy fate, it should proceed.
> I'll pray a thousand prayers for thy death,
> No word to save thee. . . .
> O, fie, fie, fie!
> Thy sin's not accidental, but a trade.
> Mercy to thee would prove itself a bawd;
> 'T is best that thou diest quickly.        (III, i, 136-51)

Her tirade against Angelo for his misuse of authority had been in an absolute sense much better:

> Could great men thunder
> As Jove himself does, Jove would ne'er be quiet;
> For every pelting, petty officer
> Would use his heaven for thunder,
> Nothing but thunder! Merciful Heaven,
> Thou rather with thy sharp and sulphurous bolt
> Splits the unwedgeable and gnarled oak
> Than the soft myrtle; but man, proud man,
> Dress'd in a little brief authority,

Most ignorant of what he's most assur'd,
His glassy essence, like an angry ape,
Plays such fantastic tricks before high heaven
As makes the angels weep; who, with our spleens,
Would all themselves laugh mortal.          (II, ii, 110-23)

Yet even there her strength had somehow not been personal; and here, railing at her brother, she outdoes Angelo in fie, fies and fierce questions. The trouble with Isabella is partly of course the trouble with all women in story who have to debate whether they will "give themselves" for a consideration. The situation in itself makes virtue theoretical—and makes their own goodness problematical, a thing to be discussed, a commodity to be weighed and measured. The paradox of goodness is that when it is most real it weighs the least, and thinks least of itself. Isabella, for all she is "enskied and sainted" (I, iv, 34), and the words are Lucio's, is the most ponderous of Shakespeare's good women and therefore the most negligible. We do not see her in her goodness; we only hear her talking like a termagant against those who doubt it. This is because Shakespeare is not primarily in love with it in his capacity as poet, any more than he is in love with the subject of Mariana's sorrows. He gives Mariana a pretty moat to live by, a pretty garden-house to meet Angelo in, and a more than pretty song to hear sung:

Take, O, take those lips away,
    That so sweetly were forsworn;
And those eyes, the break of day,
    Lights that do mislead the morn.          (IV, i)

But he does not fill out the figure of a girl who exists only to knit his plot, much in the same way that Isabella exists to reinforce it with declamation.

The atmosphere of Vienna is the thing. It curls like acrid smoke through all the crannies of the plot, and in more secret ways than we know presents itself to our senses. The odor of it is in the Duke's words,

> And quite athwart
> Goes all decorum.                          (i, iii, 30-1)

It is strong in Angelo's words sometimes:

> Blood, thou art blood.
> Let's write good angel on the devil's horn;
> 'T is not the devil's crest.               (ii, iv, 15-7)

And it hangs like a bitter scent above the humor of the play, which is as rank and real as anything in Shakespeare. "Measure for Measure" has for its clown a pimp, a parcel-bawd, whose twirling tongue is practiced in the art of delaying justice—come now in the form of Elbow, who deposes that his wife has stumbled upon evidence of Mistress Overdone's iniquity. Pompey explains, or has the air of explaining, just how it was:

> Sir, she came in great with child, and longing, saving your honour's reverence, for stew'd prunes. Sir, we had but two in the house, which at that very distant time stood, as it were, in a fruit-dish, a dish of some threepence. Your honours have seen such dishes; they are not china dishes, but very good dishes. . . .
> (ii, i, 91-7)

But there is a clown beyond Pompey, for there is the cynic fop Lucio, who does not guess the trouble he is making for himself when he abuses the Duke as one who would "eat mutton on Fridays" and "mouth with a beggar though she smelt brown bread and garlic" (iii, ii, 191-5). The friar he confides this to is none other than the Duke, to whom he sticks like a burr, scratching poison, until in the last scene the Duke pulls off his hood and resumes his terror. The exposure of Lucio is finally more interesting than that of Angelo, for of the two men Lucio has the greater dramatic integrity and is the better acclimated to the play. And the Duke's harshness to him, sentencing him to be whipped and hanged, or at any rate to marry a punk he has got with child, has no parallel in Hal's settlement with Falstaff for slander,

Henry V's paying off of Michael Williams, or even Bertram's dismissal of Parolles from his service. It is harshness unrelieved, as befits the quality of the evil in which "Measure for Measure" has chosen to steep itself.

Above all there is the prison where Abhorson the executioner instructs Pompey in the new "mystery" of hanging, and where one Ragozine, a most notorious pirate, dies of a cruel fever in time to supply his head in place of Claudio's; and where Barnardine is too drunk to be present at his own execution:

> *Abhorson.* Sirrah, bring Barnardine hither.
> *Pompey.* Master Barnardine! You must rise and be hang'd, Master Barnardine!
> *Abhorson.* What, ho, Barnardine!
> *Barnardine.* (*Within.*) A pox o' your throats! Who makes that noise there? What are you?
> *Pompey.* Your friends, sir; the hangman. You must be so good, sir, to rise and be put to death.
> *Barnardine.* (*Within.*) Away, you rogue, away! I am sleepy.
> *Abhorson.* Tell him he must awake, and that quickly too.
> *Pompey.* Pray, Master Barnardine, awake till you are executed, and sleep afterwards.
> *Abhorson.* Go in to him, and fetch him out.
> *Pompey.* He is coming, sir, he is coming. I hear his straw rustle.                                              (IV, iii, 22-38)

The rustling of that straw will be louder in our memory of "Measure for Measure" than Claudio's outcry in the face of death, or Angelo's perverse mutterings, or Isabella's panegyrics to her chastity. It is the permanent symbol for a city, itself all earth and rotting straw, with which Shakespeare at the moment can do no more than he had been able to do with the diseased bones of Pandarus's Troy. All he can do is stir it until its strench fills every street and creeps even into the black holes of prisons. In a tragedy he might have done more, for tragedy is a cleansing stroke, like lightning. Perhaps in this year he was not up to tragedy, however soon he was to write "Othello." But comedy has its lightnings too, and none of them strikes Vienna. The bank of dark cloud above her forehead is never burned away.

# OTHELLO

THE evil in "Othello" is more than an atmosphere. It is a force, and its origin, like the origin of everything else in the tragedy, is the character of the hero. Othello is both the best and the worst of men, he is both superior to passion and its slave. That is why his career can develop into tragedy; and why, since Shakespeare has now recovered his formula, it truly does. To speak only of Othello's deception by Iago, and of the accidents, the misunderstandings, the coincidences which make this deception work smoothly, is to overemphasize the mechanics of the catastrophe; or it is not to see them all. The superb machinery of "Othello" shows us more than a man whom various tricks of external fate combine in an awful moment to render pitiful. There is the pity of it, but there is also the terror. Othello is a great and fearful man; one who generates his own tragic atmosphere as he goes; and one therefore to whom nothing that happens is utterly accidental. The precarious balance in his nature between the monstrous and the tender, the giant and the lover, the soldier and the man, is a balance of powers no one of which can be denied its reality. Add the conflict in him between the past and the present, the remote and the local, the free and the confined; add once again his genius for extending and expressing himself in the whole atmosphere of the world at whose center he moves; and it will be seen that he deserves his tragedy. It is both his punishment and his privilege: his punishment, because in the permanent order of things dimensions like his must be reduced; his privilege, because they are his dimensions and his alone.

His love for Desdemona is first presented to us in a shrill and hideous light: at night, in a street of Venice, and to the accompaniment of obscene and blasphemous cries. Roderigo beats on Brabantio's windows and bawls until the old gentleman is awake so that he may tell him his daughter is transported

> To the gross clasps of a lascivious Moor. (1, i, 127)

But such language is gentleness itself compared with Iago's

> Even now, now, very now, an old black ram
> Is tupping your white ewe. (1, i, 88-9)

And neither announcement contains the whole of the hardness, the loudness, which characterizes the outrage of this opening scene. The love of Romeo and Juliet had to struggle for its existence, but not against a hostility so heartless, a cynicism so noisily and blackly brutal. The only match for such blasphemy is that which Othello is to achieve himself. His howls are to be even louder, his obscenity is to surpass Iago's as a hero's always may surpass a villain's. There is much noble stillness in "Othello," and there is harmonious music of a sort. But the clatter of its opening balances only too well the clamor which waits in Othello's soul to make itself hideously heard, just as the cynicism of Iago is a malign promise of that which is to work such havoc in his master's mind.

Iago is nothing if not cynical. Othello in his idiom is not merely an old black ram, he is a Barbary horse; and love is a thing for goats and monkeys, or for the beast with two backs. Money and love are married in his mind for convenience, not as in "The Merchant of Venice" for the generation of further love and a fairer beauty.

> Faith, he tonight hath boarded a land carack.
> If it prove lawful prize, he's made for ever. (1, ii, 50-1)

That is the way he announces Othello's good fortune to Cassio, whose generous eloquence he in turn despises as the

volubility of a knave (II, i, 241-5), whose innocent disposition he doubts, and the "daily beauty" of whose life (v, i,
19) makes his own life ugly in some way which even his remarkable intelligence never fathoms. Courtesy to him is but
a coating over lechery (II, i, 260-1), reputation has only fictitious value, and love is but the absurd antics of men who
do not own themselves. Roderigo is a sick fool

> Whom love hath turn'd almost the wrong side out;
> (II, iii, 54)

though Iago does not put it that way in conversation with
his gull. For Roderigo's benefit he frames it flatteringly.
"They say, base men being in love have then a nobility in
their natures more than is native to them" (II, i, 217-9).
"They say"—the sentiment is contemptuously referred to
those who cherish it. And the sentiment, if Roderigo only
knew Iago, is in itself contemptible because it concerns itself
with nobility. Roderigo has merely thought himself flattered.
Nothing in fact is more nauseous to Iago than nobility. "The
Moor," he admits, "is of a constant, loving, noble nature"
(II, i, 298), but the admission is tantamount to a slur, for
Iago is least at home where love and nobility walk together—
with, in the bargain, constancy to something other than self-
interest. His jealousy of the Moor may have one far root in
Emilia, but the near root and the deep one is in himself: in
the fury he feels before one who is guileless.

> The Moor is of a free and open nature,
> That thinks men honest that but seem to be so.
> (I, iii, 405-6)

If everybody's epithet for Iago is "honest," Othello uses it
most often; it is Othello whom he can most easily deceive,
and whom therefore he most unmitigably hates. Hamlet's
best friend Horatio had not been passion's slave, and so
Hamlet had worn him comfortably in his heart's core.
Othello's worst friend seems also to have a heart "that pas-

sion cannot rule" (III, iii, 124), and "certain," says Othello, "men should be what they seem." But the maxim, repeated though it is from Iago's lips (III, iii, 126), is the hero's, not the fiend's. Iago is not what he seems, and if he has any morality it tells him not to be what he seems—"full of love and honesty," says Othello. Honesty is as absurd as love, and both are but strings whereon a clever man plays wry music. Iago's cynicism consists finally of his believing that he knows the strings, and knows the utmost of their melody. The passions of men are toys for him to play with, tools to use; they are means to his end, not to their own end, which is more and better feeling. They have their limits and their certainties, which he knows almost as well as if he had contrived them himself. He did not do that, but his life is spent in watching them work. He likes nothing better than to make plans which other men's emotions will execute: Montano's, Roderigo's, Cassio's, and of course Othello's.

> As he shall smile, Othello shall go mad.   (IV, i, 101)

Cassio's manipulated merriment will produce a certain result in Desdemona's husband. Iago knows what it is, and itches to weigh it on the scales of his expectation. He is wickeder than Aaron and cleverer than Richard III because his cleverness *is* his wickedness. It rests upon an absolute cynicism with respect to good men, a cynicism which consists not of denying that good men exist but of saying that better men do also—men who like himself can take the measure of nobility and thereby be above it. Of saying, in other words, that goodness is small enough to see around. There is no such cynicism in Emilia his wife, who wears her virtue loosely, says Dr. Johnson, but does not cast it off. There is none whatever in Cassio, none even in Roderigo. Only in Othello is there anything to answer it. "Goats and monkeys!" cries the Moor, remembering his ancient's lecture on salt lust. Nothing that is in Iago is absent from Othello, though there is much in Othello of which Iago never dreamed. It would be misleading to say that Iago is an extension of Othello, for Iago is complete in himself. But it may be illuminating to point out that the response of one to the other is immediate, or if not immediate, sure; and that Othello in the end is huge enough to produce the impression of Iago's disappearance somewhere between his evil and his good, or perhaps in some recess of his infinite, impossible, unextenuated error.

"Fie, there is no such man; it is impossible," says Iago with secret irony to Emilia and Desdemona (IV, ii, 134), who do not know they have been describing him. And to his master's cry,

> Farewell! Othello's occupation's gone! (III, iii, 357)

his response is simply: "Is't possible, my lord?" It is a phrase that he has picked up from the play, but neither Desdemona nor Othello ever uses it with irony, or at any rate with the calculated irony of liars. To both of them things hitherto held impossible are happening; and in Othello's case an element of mystery and magic, native to his original environment and in the meantime only half-forgotten, would seem to have become operative again. His voice and his very clothes have brought the scent of it along. Brabantio had perhaps been right in the main when he accused the Moor of winning his daughter with charms, drugs, minerals, spells, and medicines. Othello's denial that he had resorted to mixtures, poisons, and drams, to conjuration and mighty magic, is not a denial that Desdemona had caught the scent of wonder from one who could sweep strange distances with his travel's history:

> Wherein of antres vast and deserts idle,
> Rough quarries, rocks, and hills whose heads touch heaven,
> It was my hint to speak,—such was my process,—
> And of the Cannibals that each other eat,
> The Anthropophagi, and men whose heads
> Do grow beneath their shoulders. (I, iii, 140-5)

"This only is the witchcraft I have us'd," he insists to the senators. But an infusion of magic does tincture the play—even Iago can call his jealousy of the Moor "a poisonous mineral" that gnaws his inwards (II, iii, 306)—and its source is somehow in Othello. Without his presence it would not be here: his presence, and his extraordinary susceptibility to any suggestion of it. When he speaks of Desdemona's eyes as "charms" (v, i, 35) he means everything that convention has forgotten in the term. And there is the handkerchief, the antique token which his mother had given him and which, in ways he cannot yet realize, is his own fatal gift to Desdemona.

> She, dying, gave it me;
> And bid me, when my fate would have me wiv'd,
> To give it her. I did so; and take heed on't;
> Make it a darling like your precious eye.
> To lose 't or give 't away were such perdition
> As nothing else could match.            (III, iv, 63-8)

"Is 't possible?" gasps Desdemona, in terror because she has already lost the handkerchief, and because she only now grasps its significance both to him and to her. His reply clouds all the play with that scent of strangeness, now grown sinister:

> 'T is true; there's magic in the web of it.
> A sybil, that had numb'red in the world
> The sun to course two hundred compasses,
> In her prophetic fury sew'd the work;
> The worms were hallowed that did breed the silk;
> And it was dy'd in mummy which the skilful
> Conserv'd of maidens' hearts.

"Sure, there's some wonder in this handkerchief," broods Desdemona when he is gone; and she is thinking not so much of the sybil and the maidens' hearts—symbols which he has employed with deliberate, angry exaggeration—as of the truly devilish jest that chance has played. It is such a jest as

Othello's atmosphere might generate. For irony in his world is more than something to be simply and passively noted; it is animated, it has will behind it, it expresses malice and the motives of devils. "Devil" is what Othello instinctively calls Desdemona when madness returns him to his old mind; and it is what in the end he almost literally believes Iago to be— looking at the captured villain's feet to see if they are cloven. "But that's a fable" (v, ii, 286), he mutters, poising himself on the threshold of sanity; then resuming his oldest self with the desperate line:

> If that thou be'st a devil, I cannot kill thee.

"Devil" is more than something that Othello says; it is something that he means, just as he means, when he tells Iago his heart has turned to stone, that it is a piece of rock. "I strike it, and it hurts my hand" (iv, i, 193). So the word "bitter," spoken so frequently in this play, has literal force, as if each occurrence of it were a drop of poison glittering in its line. And so the mind of the hero lives everywhere close to the ominous, the miraculous.

> O, it comes o'er my memory,
> As doth the raven o'er the infected house,
> Boding to all.                    (iv, i, 20-2)

> It is the very error of the moon;
> She comes more nearer earth than she was wont,
> And makes men mad.                    (v, ii, 109-11)

It is entirely natural for Othello to speak thus. In the first place he is the hero of a tragedy as intense as it is mature; Richard III had had a heart of stone, but it was rhetoric rather than poetry that told us so. And in the second place he is the kind of man whose imagination has lived with green-eyed monsters; whose career has been among disastrous chances; and whose multitude of memories might have left him inarticulate had not a sudden and subtle love converted him by awful magic into one of the greatest of poets.

When Iago dismisses Othello as an "erring barbarian" (i, iii, 362) he does not guess the confusion of riches in a man as much greater than he as lions are greater than adders. The potencies of Othello are vast and seldom expressed; and when they are expressed it is as if words had been given their way unwillingly. Wonderfully as Othello talks, he would rather not talk at all. His voice is deep, his throat dusky, and strangely for one whose eloquence is so overpowering his tone is difficult, reluctant, forced. His eloquence overpowers and engulfs him. One whose life has been all silent act poisons his own peace now with bursts of speech, with the clangor of huge sounds. "To hear music," says the clown at Cyprus, "the general does not greatly care" (iii, i, 17-8). He prefers stillness, for his ears are sensitive to noise. "Silence that dreadful bell," he cries when the island rings with alarms of Cassio's misdeeds (ii, iii, 175). Yet he is to lose himself in the dark music of his own voice; he is to say things he should not say; he is to be swept away on a current of uncontrolled vocables. Or if they are controlled, it is from a source as unfamiliar to him as the refinements of super-subtle love; his greatest poetry is unpremeditated. His tongue is not the practiced tongue of Hamlet, at home along the entire scale of sound. His vowels and consonants are the heavy ones; the weight they swing is enormous. "O monstrous! monstrous!" "O, blood, blood, blood!" "Damn her, lewd minx! O, damn her! damn her!" "O Desdemon! dead, Desdemon! dead! Oh! Oh!" "O fool! fool! fool!" Despair drives him thus to repeat himself in words that take on the quality of brute moans; and the style of the play supports him in this, for there are frequent passages in which a significant term echoes fatefully from mouth to mouth in desperate dialogue:

*Othello.* Is he not honest?
*Iago.* 　　　　　　　　Honest, my lord?
*Othello.* 　　　　　　　　Honest! ay, honest.
*Iago.* 　　My lord, for aught I know.

*Othello.* What dost thou think?
*Iago.*              Think, my lord?
*Othello.*                Think, my lord!
      By heaven, he echoes me,
      As if there were some monster in his thought
      Too hideous to be shown.        (III, iii, 103-8)

*Othello.* Thy husband knew it all.
*Emilia.* My husband!
*Othello.* Thy husband.
*Emilia.* That she was false to wedlock?
*Othello.* Ay, with Cassio. . . .
*Emilia.* My husband!
*Othello.* Ay, 't was he that told me on her first. . . .
*Emilia.* My husband!
*Othello.* What needs this iterance, woman? I say thy husband.
*Emilia.* O mistress, villainy hath made mocks with love!
      My husband say that she was false!
*Othello.*                              He, woman;
      I say thy husband; dost understand the word?
      My friend, thy husband, honest, honest Iago.
                        (v, ii, 139-54)

But the style of the play at its grandest is the style of his
longer speeches, his full outpourings. And these are either
clogged with latinisms:

      And all indign and base adversities
      Make head against my estimation!      (I, iii, 274-5)

                Exchange me for a goat,
      When I shall turn the business of my soul
      To such exsufflicate and blown surmises,
      Matching thy inference;      (III, iii, 180-83)

or sonorous with full-throated o's and r's, and bodied with
the most substantial consonants the language knows:

      Farewell the plumed troop, and the big wars,
      That makes ambition virtue! O, farewell!
      Farewell the neighing steed, and the shrill trump,
      The spirit-stirring drum, the ear-piercing fife,

The royal banner, and all quality,
Pride, pomp, and circumstance of glorious war!
And, O you mortal engines, whose rude throats
The immortal Jove's dread clamours counterfeit,
Farewell! (III, iii, 349-57)

If thou dost slander her and torture me,
Never pray more; abandon all remorse;
On horror's head horrors accumulate. (III, iii, 368-70)

Never, Iago. Like to the Pontic Sea,
Whose icy current and compulsive course
Ne'er feels retiring ebb, but keeps due on
To the Propontic and the Hellespont,
Even so my bloody thoughts, with violent pace,
Shall ne'er look back, ne'er ebb to humble love,
Till that a capable and wide revenge
Swallow them up. (III, iii, 453-60)

Cold, cold, my girl!
Even like thy chastity. O cursed, cursed slave!
Whip me, ye devils,
From the possession of this heavenly sight!
Blow me about in winds! roast me in sulphur!
Wash me in steep-down gulfs of liquid fire!
(v, ii, 274-80)

O, insupportable! O heavy hour!
Methinks it should be now a huge eclipse
Of sun and moon, and that the affrighted globe
Did yawn at alteration. (v, ii, 98-101)

In many such lines the voice of Othello sounds, and it is a
hoarse voice, unused to hearing its own rages. He has another one at the beginning.

Keep up your bright swords, for the dew will rust them.
(I, ii, 59)

Most potent, grave, and reverend signiors,
My very noble and approv'd good masters. . . .
She lov'd me for the dangers I had pass'd,
And I lov'd her that she did pity them. (I, iii, 76-168)

And still a third one, reminiscent of this but richer, ushers in his dying speech:

> Soft you; a word or two before you go. . . .
> Speak of me as I am; nothing extenuate,
> Nor set down aught in malice. Then must you speak
> Of one that lov'd not wisely but too well;
> Of one not easily jealous, but being wrought
> Perplex'd in the extreme. (v, ii, 338-46)

Othello's rages, in other words, are enclosed like Hamlet's madness within a frame of courtesy and noble quietness, of gentle reason and ruled sound.

> If after every tempest come such calms,
> May the winds blow till they have waken'd death!
> (ii, i, 187-8)

There is but one tempest in Othello's soul, and that is what the play is about. But there are two calms, before and after, and they tell us as much about him as the tempest tells us.

The jungle in Othello is ever enemy to his garden. The ordered rows of his princely manner are in constant danger of being overwhelmed by a wild-beast growth, savage in its strength and monstrous in its form. Twice in Iago's presence he speaks of this hinterland.

> For know, Iago,
> But that I love the gentle Desdemona,
> I would not my unhoused free condition
> Put into circumscription and confine
> For the sea's worth. (i, ii, 24-8)

> Excellent wretch! Perdition catch my soul,
> But I do love thee! and when I love thee not,
> Chaos is come again. (iii, iii, 9c-2)

In both cases he opposes it to his love for Desdemona, which it would appear he imperfectly understands and will never absorb. She is his world, his one entire and perfect chryso-

lite (v, ii, 145), and when he rejoins her at Cyprus it seems
to him that his life is at last complete.

> If it were now to die,
> 'T were now to be most happy; for, I fear,
> My soul hath her content so absolute
> That not another comfort like to this
> Succeeds in unknown fate.              (II, i, 191-5)

Yet it is not complete, and she is not his world. Even apart
from the thing that Iago will do to destroy him, first with
doubt and then with certainty, there is a wildness in him that
will not be organized. In one breath he calls his old life free
and in another he calls it chaos. Which was it? He does not
know, for he is not intelligent. There is a great gentleman
in him:

> Keep up your bright swords, for the dew will rust them;

but there is also the barbarian who will chop Desdemona
"into messes" (IV, i, 211). This barbarian is very close to the
surface; he is most of the mixture which is the Moor, and one
drop of Desdemona, however clear and serene, will not pre-
cipitate it. Othello is all of the past trying to forget itself in
a moment, he is Africa trying to breathe in Venice. That is
his struggle, that is what threatens his peace; and that, over
and above the wiles of Iago, is the source of our feeling that
explosion will follow calm. He is articulate about particulars:

> Haply, for I am black
> And have not those soft parts of conversation
> That chamberers have, or for I am declin'd
> Into the vale of years,—yet that's not much;
>                                     (III, iii, 263-6)

and Iago hints still another particular when he sets the appetite of Desdemona against Othello's "weak function" (II, iii,
354). But Othello has no words for the general danger he is
in, for the animal whose cage is so inadequately barred. He
has no words because there are none. There is only the play

"Othello," suggesting as it proceeds that success is quite unthinkable; that the great Moor will die upon his kiss. And it
proceeds, as he himself does, with an appalling rapidity.
Othello's farewell to his occupation (III, iii) is scarcely mo-
tivated by anything Iago has so far said; he blows all his fond
love to heaven (III, iii, 444-6) before an ordinary man would
have taken breath; he falls into a trance, barking incompre-
hensible prose (IV, i, 34-44), sooner than reason and psychol-
ogy can explain; and in a single scene (IV, i) he destroys the
reputation which years of careful, proud soldiership have
kept intact. "Is this the nature," exclaims Lodovico after
Othello has struck Desdemona and run out,

> Whom passion could not shake? whose solid virtue
> The shot of accident nor dart of chance
> Could neither graze nor pierce?          (IV, i, 276-9)

It is. But Lodovico has known only the nature that could
bow to senators and call them

> Most potent, grave, and reverend signiors,
> My very noble and approv'd good masters.

He has not known the giant whom the shot of Iago's accident and the dart of Desdemona's chance could bring down
all at once. Othello was no better armed against the perfection of Desdemona than against the cunning of Iago. It was
a new perfection, too fine and small for one large Moor to
master. He failed pitifully, but there was grandeur in the fall
of one who at his death took pains to make it clear that he
had been a man

> whose hand,
> Like the base Indian, threw a pearl away
> Richer than all his tribe.

"For he was great of heart," said Cassio. And had Desdemona
been alive she would have said the same thing.

# KING LEAR

"TO judge of Shakespeare by Aristotle's rules," said Pope, "is like trying a man by the laws of one country who acted under those of another." But if the truth about poetry is everywhere the same, and if Aristotle's analysis of the art was sound, he will tell us as much about Shakespeare as he told us about Sophocles. He tells us a great deal about "King Lear" when he remarks that tragedies have a beginning, a middle, and an end. The first scene of "King Lear" is a beginning, but all the rest is end. The initial act of the hero is his only act; the remainder is passion. An old and weary king, hungry for rest, banishes the one daughter who would give it him and plunges at once into the long, loud night of his catastrophe. An early recognition of his error does not save him. The poet does not wish to save him, for his instinct is to develop a catastrophe as none has been developed before or since. Henceforth King Lear is a man more acted against than active; the deeds of the tragedy are suffered rather than done; the relation of events is lyrical instead of logical, musical instead of moral. Such a play, if it is destined like this one to become the most tremendous of poems, must enrich itself with magnificent and immediate effects, with sensational tempests and intolerable tortures. It must incur the risk of seeming monstrous rather than terrible; it must have villains of enormous size—Edmund, Regan, Goneril—and it must give them the hearts of wolves. Edmund is Iago with a club and stilts, and Lear's dog-hearted daughters, scowling with their thunder-brows, are like no other women in Shakespeare or the world. Such a play must also, since it cannot order its events by intellect or law, deal heav-

ily in sound. It must suggest, as "King Lear" does, an analogy
with the complexest imaginable music. "King Lear" had to
be a symphony to be anything at all; though only a giant's
genius could have built it into the symphony it is. Its movement is not spearlike as "Hamlet's" is, a single curve of speed;
it is glacial, inexorable, awful, and slow, pushing everything
before it as its double front advances over Britain from west
to east, from Lear's inland palace to the cliffs of Dover.

For its front is double; its theme, vast as it is, is worked out
on two levels. Again it can be said that if "King Lear" was
to be as great as it is it needed the addition of the Gloucester
story—woe piled on woe, music answering to music. But to
meet the need required all of Shakespeare's daring, and all of
his capacity. Nothing in his plays is more skillful than this
parallel of Lear and Gloucester, and nothing is more mean-
ingful. The careers of the two old men lie parallel, but one
runs well below the other; they never cross, for if they did
they would lose their mutual power, they would cease to
reflect each other. The difference between them is no less
audible than the resemblance is visible. The two catastrophes
look alike; Gloucester banishes his one good son Edgar as
Lear banishes his one good daughter Cordelia, and both of
them suffer and die through a mistaken trust in their remaining offspring, who show themselves to be kites of the same
detested feather by mingling in adulterous flight across rain-
beaten England. And there are many identities of detail, as
well as many points of contact: both sufferers grope their
way stubbornly towards Dover, Edgar encounters Lear and
becomes his "philosopher," each father meets and fails to
know his banished child, and the thoughts of one are echoed
in the other—both make the same discoveries and arrive at
the same conclusions. But it is here that the resemblance
ceases. Lear and Gloucester do not sound alike. The first is
a great poet, articulate to the limit of speech; the second is a
plain man whose tongue's prose cannot save him from de-

scent into dumb-animal agony when his eyes are gouged out by Cornwall and he stumbles on in full knowledge of his injustice to Edgar. As Lear rises on the wings of metaphor Gloucester lowers his voice to a mumble. The keen violins and the trombone blasts of the King's self-pity are balanced and tempered by the simple bass of the earl, who if he thinks of himself does not know how to say so. Each music serves the other—Gloucester's to measure the height of Lear's, and Lear's to pour meaning into the lowly goodness and modesty of Gloucester's. Gloucester may be the better man, but Lear is the better artist. And only to him is given the inestimable privilege of madness. The earl envies him this.

> The King is mad; how stiff is my vile sense
> That I stand up and have ingenious feeling
> Of my huge sorrows! Better I were distract;
> So should my thoughts be sever'd from my griefs,
> And woes by wrong imaginations lose
> The knowledge of themselves.            (IV, vi, 286-91)

For he cannot go mad any more than he can make great music with his mind and tongue. Nothing is more characteristic of him than the muttered brevity of his response to Edgar at one of the immortal moments in the play:

> *Edgar.* What, in ill thoughts again? Men must endure
> Their going hence, even as their coming hither;
> Ripeness is all. Come on.
> *Gloucester.*                   And that's true too.
>                                         (V, ii, 9-11)

And when he and the King are concerned with a cognate theme it is the King who does the talking:

> *Lear.*      Thou must be patient; we came crying hither.
> Thou know'st, the first time that we smell the air,
> We wawl and cry. I will preach to thee; mark.
> *Gloucester.* Alack, alack the day!
> *Lear.*      When we are born, we cry that we are come
> To this great stage of fools.       (IV, vi, 182-7)

"Alack, alack the day!" The words say nothing, though the man has suffered everything. Gloucester's epithets are conventional—"base," "brutish," "abhorrent," "abominable," "common"—and the key of his poetry, such as it is, is correspondingly low. "Here, take this purse," he says to the miserable Edgar,

> thou whom the heavens' plagues
> Have humbled to all strokes. That I am wretched
> Makes thee the happier; heavens, deal so still!
> Let the superfluous and lust-dieted man,
> That slaves your ordinance, that will not see
> Because he does not feel, feel your power quickly;
> So distribution should undo excess,
> And each man have enough.             (IV, i, 67-74)

This is in his best style, but how much better Lear can talk may be seen at a glance in the passage which parallels it:

> Poor naked wretches, wheresoe'er you are,
> That bide the pelting of this pitiless storm,
> How shall your houseless heads and unfed sides,
> Your loop'd and window'd raggedness, defend you
> From seasons such as these? O, I have ta'en
> Too little care of this! Take physic, pomp;
> Expose thyself to feel what wretches feel,
> That thou mayst shake the superflux to them,
> And show the heavens more just.        (III, iv, 28-36)

Gloucester's lines are never brilliant like that, nor is his spirit in consequence ever freed by the satisfactions which the articulation of grief can give. Our feelings are spared after his eyes are out by hearing one servant say to another:

> I'll fetch some flax and whites of eggs
> To apply to his bleeding face.         (III, vii, 106-7)

Lear does not need such help, nor is he given it; his own poetry is his medicine, his ability to reach the extremes of statement has somehow made all even. A wounded animal may be pitied in a sick silence, but an eloquent man can soar beyond sympathy. The luxuries of rhetoric are denied the Earl of Gloucester, who to be sure can say that he loves Edgar "tenderly and entirely," and can announce, after another "Alack," that

> the night comes on, and the high winds
> Do sorely ruffle,                                    (II, iv, 303-4)

and can mount to at least one potent generality:

> As flies to wanton boys, are we to the gods,
> They kill us for their sport,                        (IV, i, 38-9)

but who for the most part must carry wounds that language cannot lick. His longest speech, beginning "These late eclipses in the sun and moon portend no good to us" (I, ii, 112-27), and going on to connect mutinies, disorders, divisions, and treasons with the irregularities of the stars, is immediately derided by Edmund, who dismisses any interest in "planetary influence" as "an admirable evasion of whoremaster man." Edmund is as evil as Iago, but his annihilation of Gloucester's fallacy is complete, and we shall remember the cynic son longer than the inspired father: a sort of thing that could never conceivably happen to Lear, who cries down all competitors, animate or inanimate, in lines we cannot choose but remember. Finally too it is significant that Gloucester crawls out of the play to die. We learn simply from Edgar that the old man's heart,

> 'Twixt two extremes of passion, joy and grief,
> Burst smilingly.                                     (v, iii, 198-9)

We neither hear nor see his end, for it happens inside him where he has always lived. He has not lived in language, like King Lear.

The reach of Lear's rhetoric reveals itself as early as the first scene, which is better suited to the remainder of the play than many admit.

> The barbarous Scythian,
> Or he that makes his generation messes
> To gorge his appetite                    (I, i, 118-20)

—that looks forward to

> Blow, winds, and crack your cheeks! Rage! Blow!
> You cataracts and hurricanoes, spout
> Till you have drench'd our steeples, drown'd the cocks!
>                                          (III, ii, 1-3)

and to

> Down from the waist they are Centaurs,
> Though women all above;
> But to the girdle do the gods inherit,
> Beneath is all the fiends';               (IV, vi, 126-9)

and in its different way to

>                       No, you unnatural hags,
> I will have such revenges on you both
> That all the world shall—I will do such things,—
> What they are, yet I know not; but they shall be
> The terrors of the earth.                 (II, iv, 281-5)

In its different way; for Lear commands both trumpets and strings, he can be as limpid in some lines as he is loud in others. This old man whose first announcement to us is that he wishes to rid himself of all his cares so that he may "unburden'd crawl toward death" (I, i, 42), whose thoughts of rest have been set on the kind nursery of Cordelia (I, i, 125-6), and whose broken sinews, once he has banished her, are never to be bound up by "our foster-nurse of nature" (IV, iv, 12), can be as plaintive as a child. Macbeth in his prime is dissolved to desperation by insomnia; Lear, unable to sleep or rest, is reduced sometimes to the merest petulance. The reason may be that he has reached his second childhood, yet Regan remembers no other father: " 'T is the infirmity of his age; yet he hath ever but slenderly known himself" (I, i, 296-7). "We came crying hither," he reminds Gloucester;

and he will go crying hence. Meanwhile he has been a proud, spoiled man, a play-king who fancied that his gestures really ruled the world. He still makes enough of them in Goneril's house for her to have some show of right when she rebukes him. He still expects mankind to come running when he claps his hands. "Where's my Fool, ho? I think the world's asleep" (I, iv, 51-2). When the Fool comes he is not altogether fool, observes Kent (I, iv, 165). His bitter tongue tells truths that a king only half knows. The great scene he dominates with his comedy (I, iv) bears no resemblance to the great comic scene of "Hamlet" (v, i) where the Prince jested with grave-diggers; that scene enhanced its hero by showing that he had recovered his sense of humor and his philosophy, whereas this one throws the weakness of Lear into full tragic relief. "Thou shouldst not have been old till thou hadst been wise," concludes the bitter Fool (I, v, 48). Now he will never be wise. He will rend the air with his self-pity:

> You see me here, you gods, a poor old man;    (II, iv, 275)

> The little dogs and all,
>   Tray, Blanch, and Sweetheart, see, they bark at me;
>                                         (III, vi, 65-6)

but he will never understand as Gloucester does that another's misery can be deeper than his own (IV, vi, 221-3). He will make the heavens shrill with prayers for the patience he is deluded into thinking he once had, but he will never be a king over his passion as Cordelia, pattern of grief, is a queen over hers:

>                       You have seen
>   Sunshine and rain at once: her smiles and tears
>   Were like a better way. . . . In brief,
>   Sorrow would be a rarity most beloved,
>   If all could so become it.          (IV, iii, 19-26)

He will implore: "O, let me not be mad, not mad, sweet heaven!" Yet it will be madness of which he becomes the pattern in all poetry, not patience as he supposes.

Matter and impertinency are mixed in his madness, which is never insanity of the sort that obliterates the connection between cause and effect. Persons who are demented beyond the memory of their woes cannot be used in poetry; irrelevance has no value in any art. Lear's farthest range of wildness keeps within dramatic meaning. His progress is through irony, which in the beginning is so natural an expression of his self-absorption that he does not suspect the direction in which it is taking him. "Are you our daughter?" "Your name, fair gentlewoman?" This is mere sarcasm, and Goneril can dismiss it as a "prank" (i, iv, 259). But it opens the way to wider ironies when it dawns on Lear that the answers to his rhetorical questions are after all not obvious in a household whose indifference to him is draining his very identity away. And when he is convinced of his homelessness in either daughter's castle he is ready for the final irony of his desire to go homeless among the elements. The ruined king will become a ruined piece of nature too. Hamlet had been isolated in the society of Elsinore, but the King of Britain must be as naked in the universe as he is destitute of human love. The great wheel of Fortune which comes full circle for Edmund, and which grinds remorselessly for Edgar until his only comfort is to say:

> The lamentable change is from the best;
> The worst returns to laughter,                    (iv, i, 5-6)

must grow for Lear into a wheel of fire that turns with him down into a hell of his own making. The theme of exposure announces itself early in the play, and thenceforward is never out of mind. Kent's wish to Cordelia in the first scene is that the gods take her "to their dear shelter" (185), as if the world were suddenly without roofs. And Edgar as poor Turlygod, poor Tom, presents himself naked to the winds and persecutions of the sky before Lear does. Lear has had a hint from the Fool of the vision which will underlie his desire.

*Lear.* Dost thou call me fool, boy?

*Fool.* All thy other titles thou hast given away; that thou
wast born with. (I, iv, 162-4)

The vision is of himself as naked as nature had made him—
naked not only of clothes but of titles, ties, possessions, duties,
rights, and even memories. It grows upon him with bewilder-
ing rapidity, and controls all his thought throughout the
heart of the play.

> Return to her, and fifty men dismiss'd!
> No, rather I abjure all roofs, and choose
> To wage against the enmity o' the air;
> To be a comrade with the wolf and owl,—
> Necessity's sharp pinch. (II, iv, 210-4)

> O, reason not the need! Our basest beggars
> Are in the poorest thing superfluous.
> Allow not nature more than nature needs,
> Man's life is cheap as beast's. (II, iv, 267-70)

As the third act opens we listen to a gentleman telling Kent
that Lear has made the plunge: he has disappeared into a
world which is all foul weather and inhuman storm, he tears
his white hair in the blast and

> Strives in his little world of man to out-scorn
> The to-and-fro-conflicting wind and rain. (III, i, 10-11)

Then we see the thing itself, and hear it:

> Rumble thy bellyful! Spit, fire! Spout, rain!
> Nor rain, wind, thunder, fire, are my daughters.
> I tax not you, you elements, with unkindness.
> (III, ii, 14-6)

But we have yet to learn that Lear does not feel thunder and
rain as other men feel them; that they have become symbols
under which he can find a sort of shelter. He explains to
Kent at the hovel:

> Thou think'st 't is much that this contentious storm
> Invades us to the skin; so 't is to thee;

But where the greater malady is fix'd,
The lesser is scarce felt. . . . When the mind's free,
The body's delicate; the tempest in my mind
Doth from my senses take all feeling else
Save what beats there.                        (III, iv, 6-14)

And we have yet to listen as he tears off both his actual and his mental clothes, pressing fiercely against the nude secret of nature in the mad hope of entering it at last.

Thou wert better in a grave than to answer with thy uncover'd body this extremity of the skies. Is man no more than this? Consider him well. Thou ow'st the worm no silk, the beast no hide, the sheep no wool, the cat no perfume. Ha! here's three on's are sophisticated! Thou art the thing itself; unaccommodated man is no more but such a poor, bare, forked animal as thou art. Off, off, you lendings! come, unbutton here.

(III, iv, 105-14)

Man delighted not Hamlet, but he was still accommodated, if only with suits of woe upon his body and with a pestilent congregation of vapors over his head. Lear has stripped himself to the thing itself, and it is poor and bare. Not that he is satisfied, for his thirst is absolute and cannot be quenched.

They flatter'd me like a dog, and told me I had the white hairs in my beard ere the black ones were there. To say "ay" and "no" to everything that I said! . . . Go to, they are not men o' their words: they told me I was everything; 't is a lie, I am not ague-proof.                                    (IV, vi, 98-107)

They told him he was everything, and now he must be nothing. So must the world with its mockery virtues; he will tear the fine clothes off of every simpering lecher this side of hell. Like Hamlet and Othello, and like Timon later, he grows suddenly and cynically gross, laying the whip of obscenity on:

I pardon that man's life. What was thy cause?
Adultery?

Thou shalt not die. Die for adultery! No:
The wren goes to 't, and the small gilded fly
Does lecher in my sight.
Let copulation thrive; for Gloucester's bastard son
Was kinder to his father than my daughters
Got 'tween the lawful sheets.
To 't, luxury, pell-mell! for I lack soldiers.
Behold yon simp'ring dame,
Whose face between her forks presages snow,
That minces virtue, and does shake the head
To hear of pleasure's name,—
The fitchew, nor the soiled horse, goes to 't
With a more riotous appetite.
Down from the waist they are Centaurs,
Though women all above;
But to the girdle do the gods inherit,
Beneath is all the fiends';
There's hell, there's darkness, there's the sulphurous pit,
burning, scalding, stench, consumption; fie, fie, fie! pah, pah!
Give me an ounce of civet; good apothecary, sweeten my
imagination.                                    (IV, vi, 111-33)

Such is the terrible progress of Lear to the point where at last
he has no longer the strength to rage and is found by the sen-
tries of Cordelia, whose giving him into the hands of a doctor
does not save him any more than Edmund's repentance saves
her. No happy ending was thinkable for a hero who had
learned so much so late. There is a lull before the end, a hesi-
tation on the brink of serenity that reminds us of Hamlet
when he returns from England and talks with Horatio in the
churchyard, or even of Othello when Emilia says "he looks
gentler than he did" (IV, iii, 11). "The great rage, you see,"
says the doctor to Cordelia, "is kill'd in him" (IV, vii, 78-9).
But the ominous tide has set too firmly in to be withstood.
The catastrophe has been too long preparing not to shatter
the final rock.

The world of the play has been too sinister and comfort-
less for any warmth to come at sunset. The ceiling of Lear's

world is low, the atmosphere is murky. The wet earth creeps with treacherous, slimy-weather beasts; rats, toads, wild dogs and wolves, eels, pole-cats, snakes, and vultures. The wild flowers in Lear's hair are not flowers at all; he is crowned, says Cordelia,

> with rank fumiter and furrow-weeds,
> With hardocks, hemlock, nettles, cuckoo-flowers,
> Darnel, and all the idle weeds that grow
> In our sustaining corn. (IV, iv, 3-6)

The dark sky is oppressive, and clouds of enormous weight hang low in it to torture human beings with their bulk. The play is rich in recognition scenes which increase rather than relieve the prevailing gloom. The function of recognition scenes in tragedy is to light pain and death with understanding; and their effect upon the audience is normally, by compressing two or more past lives into the excitement of a single moment, by bringing all the forces of the play to bear upon one glance, one gesture, one exclamation, to discharge a load of emotion which has become intolerable. The discharge in "King Lear" is instantaneous, but it is incomplete. For few of the recognitions are mutual. Gloucester never knows Edgar, or Lear his faithful Kent. Lear takes Gloucester's blindness for a squint, and calls him Cupid (IV, vi, 140-1). And not until we are past the expectation of relief does Lear plainly recognize his daughter. "We two alone will sing like birds i' the cage," he says (V, iii, 9). But the power of that line is nothing like the power of

> Do not laugh at me;
> For, as I am a man, I think this lady
> To be my child Cordelia. (IV, vii, 68-70)

The genius of the play is working there—in the interest, perhaps, of that part of tragedy which is pity rather than towards that whole for which there can be no common name. Such recognition scenes enlarge our misery without enlight-

ening it. Edgar has to make sure that Edmund knows him at
the end:

> My name is Edgar, and thy father's son.
>
> (v, iii, 169)

And the line is as welcome as lightning over a lost road, or
as a trumpet when the suspense of stillness has lasted too long.
But Edgar has existed in the play for his father's sake rather
than for his own, and Edmund ceases at once to be the man
he was. The tragedy has not been chiefly theirs:

> The oldest hath borne most; we that are young
> Shall never see so much, nor live so long.  (v, iii, 325-6)

The tragedy has been that of two old men who learned too
much too late.

Shakespeare, who spares us nothing in this play, knows also
how to let us have it all at once from time to time in little
speeches, in single pregnant lines that pierce us literally to the
heart. If the whole is as vast and shaggy as the cosmos is to
fearful man, the parts are fitted in with wonderful refinement. Nothing in all his work is more impressive than these
two extremes of skill. Line after line carries in its apparently
frail body the immense burden of the whole. Such lines—or
they may be less than lines—come everywhere, but naturally
they thicken towards the close. Then they imply so much
that their context cannot be suggested short of a reference
to all that has happened. In themselves they are of the utmost
simplicity, and seem to mean nothing:

> I stumbled when I saw.                    (iv, i, 21)
>
> Too well, too well.                       (iv, vi, 66)
>
> You do me wrong to take me out o' the grave.
>
> (iv, vii, 45)
>
> I fear I am not in my perfect mind.       (iv, vii, 63)
>
> No cause, no cause.                       (iv, vii, 75)

Ripeness is all. Come on.
                    And that's true too.          (v, ii, 11)

Is this the promis'd end?                        (v, iii, 263)

            Her voice was ever soft,
Gentle, and low; an excellent thing in woman.
                                (v, iii, 272-3)
Why should a dog, a horse, a rat, have life,
And thou no breath at all? Thou 'lt come no more,
Never, never, never, never, never!          (v, iii, 306-8)

In "King Lear," however, they mean everything. What the play means it means all of the time; which must be the last way now of saying that it is not only wide but deep, not only pitiful but huge.

# MACBETH

THE brevity of "Macbeth" is so much a function of its brilliance that we might lose rather than gain by turning up the lost scenes of legend. This brilliance gives us in the end somewhat less than the utmost that tragedy can give. The hero, for instance, is less valuable as a person than Hamlet, Othello, or Lear; or Antony, or Coriolanus, or Timon. We may not rejoice in his fall as Dr. Johnson says we must, yet we have known too little about him and have found too little virtue in him to experience at his death the sense of an unutterable and tragic loss made necessary by ironies beyond our understanding. He commits murder in violation of a nature which we can assume to have been noble, but we can only assume this. Macbeth has surrendered his soul before the play begins. When we first see him he is already invaded by those fears which are to render him vicious and which are finally to make him abominable. They will also reveal him as a great poet. But his poetry, like the poetry of the play, is to be concerned wholly with sensation and catastrophe. "Macbeth" like "Lear" is all end; the difference appearing in the speed with which doom rushes down, so that this rapidest of tragedies suggests whirlwinds rather than glaciers, and in the fact that terror rather than pity is the mode of the accompanying music. "Macbeth," then, is not in the fullest known sense a tragedy. But we do not need to suppose that this is because important parts of it have been lost. More of it would have had to be more of the same. And the truth is that no significant scene seems to be missing. "Macbeth" is incomparably brilliant as it stands, and within its limits perfect. What it does it does with flawless force. It hurls a universe against a

man, and if the universe that strikes is more impressive than
the man who is stricken, great as his size and gaunt as his soul
may be, there is no good reason for doubting that this is what
Shakespeare intended. The triumph of "Macbeth" is the con-
struction of a world, and nothing like it has ever been constructed in twenty-one hundred lines.

This world, which is at once without and within Macbeth,
can be most easily described as "strange." The word, like the
witches, is always somewhere doing its work. Even in the
battle which precedes the play the thane of Glamis has made
"strange images of death" (I, iii, 97), and when he comes
home to his lady his face is "as a book where men may read
strange matters" (I, v, 63-4). Duncan's horses after his murder turn wild in nature and devour each other—"a thing most
strange and certain" (II, iv, 14). Nothing is as it should be
in such a world. "Who would have thought the old man to
have had so much blood in him?" There is a drift of disorder
in all events, and the air is murky with unwelcome miracles.

It is a dark world too, inhabited from the beginning by
witches who meet on a blasted heath in thunder and lightning, and who hover through fog and filthy air as they leave
on unspeakable errands. It is a world wherein "men must not
walk too late" (III, vi, 7), for the night that was so pretty in
"Romeo and Juliet," "A Midsummer Night's Dream," and
"The Merchant of Venice" has grown terrible with ill-smell-
ing mists and the stench of blood. The time that was once a
playground for free and loving spirits has closed like a trap,
or yawned like a bottomless pit. The "dark hour" that Banquo
borrows from the night is his last hour on an earth which
has lost the distinction between sun and gloom.

> Darkness does the face of earth entomb,
> When living light should kiss it.          (II, iv, 9-10)

The second of these lines makes a sound that is notable in
the play for its rarity: the sound of life in its normal ease and

lightness. Darkness prevails because the witches, whom Banquo calls its instruments, have willed to produce it. But Macbeth is its instrument too, as well as its victim. And the weird sisters no less than he are expressions of an evil that employs them both and has roots running farther into darkness than the mind can guess.

It is furthermore a world in which nothing is certain to keep its shape. Forms shift and consistencies alter, so that what was solid may flow and what was fluid may congeal to stone.

> The earth hath bubbles, as the water has,
> And these are of them,                    (I, iii, 79-80)

says Banquo of the vanished witches. Macbeth addresses the "sure and firm set earth" (II, i, 56), but nothing could be less firm than the whole marble and the founded rock he has fancied his life to be. At the very moment he speaks he has seen a dagger which is not there, and the "strange infirmity" he confesses at the banquet will consist of seeing things that cannot be. His first apostrophe to the witches had been to creatures

> That look not like the inhabitants o' the earth,
> And yet are on 't.                         (I, iii, 41-2)

So now a dead man lives; Banquo's brains are out but he rises again, and "this is more strange than such a murder is."

> Take any shape but that, and my firm nerves
> Shall never tremble.                       (III, iv, 102-3)

But the shape of everything is wrong, and the nerves of Macbeth are never proof against trembling. The cardinal instance of transformation is himself. Bellona's bridegroom has been turned to jelly.

The current of change pouring forever through this universe has, as a last effect, dissolved it. And the dissolution of so much that was solid has liberated deadly fumes, has thick-

ened the air until it suffocates all breathers. If the footing
under men is less substantial than it was, the atmosphere they
must push through is almost too heavy for life. It is confin-
ing, swarming, swelling; it is viscous, it is sticky; and it
threatens strangulation. All of the speakers in the play conspire to create the impression that this is so. Not only do the
witches in their opening scene wail "Fair is foul, and foul is
fair," but the military men who enter after them anticipate
in their talk of recent battle the imagery of entanglement to
come.

> Doubtful it stood,
> As two spent swimmers that do cling together
> And choke their art. . . .
> The multiplying villainies of nature
> Do swarm upon him. . . .
> So from that spring whence comfort seem'd to come
> Discomfort swells.                     (i, ii, 7-28)

Macbeth's sword is reported to have "smok'd with bloody
execution," and he and Banquo were "as cannons over-
charg'd with double cracks;" they

> Doubly redoubled strokes upon the foe.

The hyperbole is ominous, the excess is sinister. In the third
scene, after what seemed corporal in the witches has melted
into the wind, Ross and Angus join Banquo and Macbeth to
report the praises of Macbeth that had poured in on Duncan
"as thick as hail," and to salute the new thane of Cawdor.
The witches then have been right in two respects, and Macbeth says in an aside:

> Two truths are told,
> As happy prologues to the swelling act
> Of the imperial theme.                (i, iii, 127-9)

But the imagined act of murder swells in his mind until it is
too big for its place, and his heart beats as if it were choking
in its chamber.

Why do I yield to that suggestion
Whose horrid image doth unfix my hair
And make my seated heart knock at my ribs,
Against the use of nature? Present fears
Are less than horrible imaginings.
My thought, whose murder yet is but fantastical,
Shakes so my single state of man that function
Is smother'd in surmise, and nothing is
But what is not.                              (I, iii, 134-42)

Meanwhile Lady Macbeth at home is visited by no such fears.
When the crisis comes she will break sooner than her husband does, but her brittleness then will mean the same thing
that her melodrama means now: she is a slighter person than
Macbeth, has a poorer imagination, and holds in her mind
less of that power which enables it to stand up under torture.
The news that Duncan is coming to her house inspires her to
pray that her blood be made thick; for the theme of thickness is so far not terrible in her thought.

Come, thick night,
And pall thee in the dunnest smoke of hell,
That my keen knife see not the wound it makes,
Nor heaven peep through the blanket of the dark
To cry, "Hold, hold!"                              (I, v, 51-5)

The blanket of the dark—it seems to her an agreeable image,
and by no means suggests an element that can enwrap or
smother. With Macbeth it is different; his soliloquy in the
seventh scene shows him occupied with images of nets and
tangles: the consequences of Duncan's death may coil about
him like an endless rope.

If it were done when 't is done, then 't were well
It were done quickly. If the assassination
Could trammel up the consequence, and catch
With his surcease success; that but this blow
Might be the be-all and the end-all here,
But here, upon this bank and shoal of time,
We'd jump the life to come. But in these cases

We still have judgement here, that we but teach
Bloody instructions, which, being taught, return
To plague the inventor.                    (I, vii, 1-10)

And his voice rises to shrillness as he broods in terror upon
the endless echo which such a death may make in the world.

                              His virtues
Will plead like angels, trumpet-tongu'd, against
The deep damnation of his taking-off;
And pity, like a naked new-born babe
Striding the blast, or heaven's cherubin hors'd
Upon the sightless couriers of the air,
Shall blow the horrid deed in every eye,
That tears shall drown the wind.           (I, vii, 18-25)

It is terror such as this that Lady Macbeth must endeavor to
allay in what is after all a great mind. Her scolding cannot
do so. She has commanded him to screw his courage to the
sticking-point, but what is the question that haunts him when
he comes from Duncan's bloody bed, with hands that can
never be washed white again?

        Wherefore could not I pronounce "Amen"?
I had most need of blessing, and "Amen"
Stuck in my throat.                        (II, ii, 31-3)

He must not consider such things so deeply, his lady warns
him. But he does, and in good time she will follow suit. That
same night the Scottish earth, shaking in a convincing sympathy as the Roman earth in "Julius Caesar" never shook,
considers the grievous state of a universe that suffocates in
the breath of its own history. Lamentings are heard in the
air, strange screams of death, and prophecies of dire combus-
tion and confused events (II, iii, 61-3). And the next morning, says Ross to an old man he meets,

              By the clock 't is day,
And yet dark night strangles the travelling lamp.
                                          (II, iv, 6-7)

Macbeth is now king, but his fears "stick deep" in Banquo (III, i, 50). The thought of one more murder that will give him perhaps the "clearness" he requires (III, i, 133) seems for a moment to free his mind from its old obsessive horror of dusk and thickness, and he can actually invoke these conditions—in the only verse he ever uses with conscious literary intention.

> Come, seeling night,
> Scarf up the tender eye of pitiful day,
> And with thy bloody and invisible hand
> Cancel and tear to pieces that great bond
> Which keeps me pale! Light thickens, and the crow
> Makes wing to the rooky wood;
> Good things of day begin to droop and drowse,
> While night's black agents to their preys do rouse.
>
> (III, ii, 46-53)

The melodrama of this, and its inferiority of effect, may warn us that Macbeth is only pretending to hope. The news of Fleance's escape brings him at any rate his fit again, and he never more ceases to be "cabin'd, cribb'd, confin'd" (III, iv, 24). He is caught in the net for good, his feet have sunk into quicksands from which they cannot be freed, his bosom like Lady Macbeth's is "stuff'd" with "perilous stuff which weighs upon the heart" (V, iii, 44-5)—the figure varies, but the theme does not. A strange world not wholly of his own making has closed around him and rendered him motionless. His gestures are spasmodic at the end, like those of one who knows he is hopelessly engulfed. And every metaphor he uses betrays his belief that the universal congestion is past cure:

> What rhubarb, senna, or what purgative drug,
> Would scour these English hence?        (V, iii, 55-6)

The answer is none.

The theme never varies, however rich the range of symbols employed to suggest it. One of these symbols is of course the fear that shakes Macbeth as if he were an object not human; that makes him start when the witches call him "King here-after," that sets his heart knocking at his ribs, that wrings from him unsafe extremities of rhetoric, that reduces him to a maniac when Banquo walks again, that spreads from him to all of Scotland until its inhabitants "float upon a wild and violent sea" of terror (iv, ii, 21), and that in the end, when he has lost the capacity to feel anything any longer, drains from him so that he almost forgets its taste (v, v, 9). Another symbol, and one that presents itself to several of our senses at once, is blood. Never in a play has there been so much of this substance, and never has it been so sickening. "What bloody man is that?" The second scene opens with a mes-senger running in to Duncan red with wounds. And blood darkens every scene thereafter. It is not bright red, nor does it run freely and wash away. Nor is it a metaphor as it was in "Julius Caesar." It is so real that we see, feel, and smell it on everything. And it sticks. "This is a sorry sight," says Macbeth as he comes from Duncan's murder, staring at his hands. He had not thought there would be so much blood on them, or that it would stay there like that. Lady Macbeth is for washing the "filthy witness" off, but Macbeth knows that all great Neptune's ocean will not make him clean; rather his hand, plunged into the green, will make it all one red. The blood of the play is everywhere physical in its looks and gross in its quantity. Lady Macbeth "smears" the grooms with it, so that when they are found they seem "badg'd" and "unmannerly breech'd" with gore, and "steep'd" in the colors of their trade. The murderer who comes to report Banquo's death has blood on his face, and the "blood-bolter'd Banquo" when he appears shakes "gory locks" at Macbeth, who in deciding upon the assassination has reflected that

> I am in blood
> Stepp'd in so far that, should I wade no more,
> Returning were as tedious as go o'er.      (iii, iv, 136-8)

Richard III had said a similar thing, but he suggested no veritable pool or swamp of blood as this man does; and his victims, wailing over their calamities, did not mean the concrete thing Macduff means when he cries, "Bleed, bleed, poor country!" (IV, iii, 31). The world of the play quite literally bleeds. And Lady Macbeth, walking in her sleep, has definite stains upon the palms she rubs and rubs. "Yet here's a spot. . . . What, will these hands ne'er be clean? . . . Here's the smell of the blood still; all the perfumes of Arabia will not sweeten this little hand."

A third symbol, of greater potency than either fear or blood, is sleeplessness. Just as there are more terrors in the night than day has ever taught us, and more blood in a man than there should be, so there is less sleep in this disordered world than the minimum which once had been required for health and life. One of the final signs of that disorder is indeed the death of sleep.

> Methought I heard a voice cry, "Sleep no more!
> Macbeth does murder sleep. . . .
> Glamis hath murder'd sleep, and therefore Cawdor
> Shall sleep no more; Macbeth shall sleep no more."
>
> (II, ii, 35-43)

Nothing that Macbeth says is more terrible than this, and no dissolution suffered by his world is more ominous. For sleep in Shakespeare is ever the privilege of the good and the reward of the innocent. If it has been put to death there is no goodness left. One of the witches knows how to torture sailors by keeping sleep from their pent-house lids (I, iii, 19-20), but only Macbeth can murder sleep itself. The result in the play is an ultimate weariness. The "restless ecstasy" with which Macbeth's bed is made miserable, and

> the affliction of these terrible dreams
> That shake us nightly                    (III, ii, 18-9)

—such things are dreadful, but his final fatigue is more dreadful still, for it is the fatigue of a soul that has worn itself out

with watching fears, wading in blood, and waking to the
necessity of new murders for which the hand has no relish.
Macbeth's hope that when Macduff is dead he can "sleep in
spite of thunder" (iv, i, 86) is after all no hope. For there is
no sleep in Scotland (iii, vi, 34), and least of all in a man
whose lids have lost the art of closing. And whose heart has
lost the power of trembling like a guilty thing.

> The time has been, my senses would have cool'd
> To hear a night-shriek, and my fell of hair
> Would at a dismal treatise rouse and stir
> As life were in 't. I have supp'd full with horrors;
> Direness, familiar to my slaughterous thoughts,
> Cannot once start me.
>
> (v, v, 10-15)

Terror has degenerated into tedium, and only death can follow, either for Macbeth who lacks the season of all natures
or for his lady who not only walks but talks when she should
sleep, and who will not die holily in her bed.

Meanwhile, however, another element has gone awry, and
it is one so fundamental to man's experience that Shakespeare has given it a central position among those symbols
which express the disintegration of the hero's world. Time is
out of joint, inoperative, dissolved. "The time has been," says
Macbeth, when he could fear; and "the time has been" that
when the brains were out a man would die, and there an
end (iii, iv, 78-80). The repetition reveals that Macbeth is
haunted by a sense that time has slipped its grooves; it
flows wild and formless through his world, and is the deep
cause of all the anomalies that terrify him. Certain of these
anomalies are local or specific: the bell that rings on the night
of the murder, the knocking at the gate, the flight of Macduff into England at the very moment Macbeth plans his
death, and the disclosure that Macduff was from his mother's
womb untimely ripp'd. Many things happen too soon, so that
tidings are like serpents that strike without warning. "The
King comes here tonight," says a messenger, and Lady Macbeth is startled out of all composure: "Thou 'rt mad to say

it!" (I, v, 32). But other anomalies are general, and these are the worst. The words of Banquo to the witches:

> If you can look into the seeds of time,
> And say which grain will grow and which will not,
>
> (I, iii, 58-9)

plant early in the play a conception of time as something which fulfills itself by growing—and which, the season being wrong, can swell to monstrous shape. Or it can find crannies in the mold and extend secret, sinister roots into dark soil that never has known them. Or it can have no growth at all; it can rot and fester in its place, and die. The conception wavers, like the courage of Macbeth, but it will not away. Duncan welcomes Macbeth to Forres with the words:

> I have begun to plant thee, and will labour
> To make thee full of growing.        (I, iv, 28-9)

But Macbeth, like time itself, will burgeon beyond bounds. "Nature's germens" will

>                               tumble all together,
> Even till destruction sicken.        (IV, i, 59-60)

When Lady Macbeth, greeting her husband, says with excited assurance:

> Thy letters have transported me beyond
> This ignorant present, and I feel now
> The future in the instant,        (I, v, 57-9)

she cannot suspect, nor can he, how sadly the relation between present and future will maintain itself. If the present is the womb or seed-bed of the future, if time is a succession of growths each one of which lives cleanly and freely after the death of the one before it, then what is to prevail will scarcely be recognizable as time. The seed will not grow; the future will not be born out of the present; the plant will not disentangle itself from its bed, but will stick there in still birth.

> Thou sure and firm set earth,
> Hear not my steps, which way they walk, for fear
> Thy very stones prate of my whereabout,
> And take the present horror from the time,
> Which now suits with it,                    (II, i, 56-60)

prays Macbeth on the eve of Duncan's death. But time and horror will not suit so neatly through the nights to come; the present moment will look like all eternity, and horror will be smeared on every hour. Macbeth's speech when he comes back from viewing Duncan's body may have been rehearsed and is certainly delivered for effect; yet he best knows what the terms signify:

> Had I but died an hour before this chance,
> I had liv'd a blessed time; for, from this instant,
> There's nothing serious in mortality.     (II, iii, 96-8)

He has a premonition even now of time's disorders; of his own premature descent into the sear, the yellow leaf (V, iii, 23); of his failure like any other man to

> pay his breath
> To time and mortal custom.               (IV, i, 99-100)

"What, will the line stretch out to the crack of doom?" he cries when Banquo's eight sons appear to him in the witches' cavern (IV, i, 117). Time makes sense no longer; its proportions are strange, its content meaningless. For Lady Macbeth in her mind's disease the minutes have ceased to march in their true file and order; her sleep-walking soliloquy (V, i) recapitulates the play, but there is no temporal design among the fragments of the past—the blood, the body of Duncan, the fears of her husband, the ghost of Banquo, the slaughter of Lady Macduff, the ringing of the bell, and again the blood —which float detached from one another in her memory. And for Macbeth time has become

> a tale
> Told by an idiot, full of sound and fury,
> Signifying nothing.                      (V, v, 26-8)

Death is dusty, and the future is a limitless desert of tomor-
rows. His reception of the news that Lady Macbeth has died
is like nothing else of a similar sort in Shakespeare. When
Northumberland was told of Hotspur's death he asked his
grief to wait upon his revenge:

> For this I shall have time enough to mourn.
>
> ("Henry IV," 2-1, i, 136)

And when Brutus was told of Portia's death he knew how to
play the stoic:

> With meditating that she must die once,
> I have the patience to endure it now.
>
> ("Julius Caesar," iv, iii, 191-2)

But Macbeth, drugged beyond feeling, supped full with
horrors, and tired of nothing so much as of coincidence in
calamity, can only say in a voice devoid of tone:

> She should have died hereafter;
> There would have been a time for such a word.
>
> (v, v, 17-8)

There would, that is, if there were such a thing as time. Then
such words as "died" and "hereafter" would have their meaning. Not now, however, for time itself has died.

Duncan was everything that Macbeth is not. We saw him
briefly, but the brilliance of his contrast with the thane he
trusted has kept his memory beautiful throughout a play
whose every other feature has been hideous. He was "meek"
and "clear" (i, vii, 17-8), and his mind was incapable of sus-
picion. The treachery of Cawdor bewildered him:

> There's no art
> To find the mind's construction in the face.
> He was a gentleman on whom I built
> An absolute trust                    (i, iv, 11-14)

—this at the very moment when Macbeth was being brought
in for showers of praise and tears of plenteous joy! For Dun-

can was a free spirit and could weep, a thing impossible to
his murderer's stopped heart. The word "love" was native to
his tongue; he used it four times within the twenty lines of
his conversation with Lady Macbeth, and its clear beauty as
he spoke it was reflected that night in the diamond he sent
her by Banquo (II, i, 15). As he approached Macbeth's castle
in the late afternoon the building had known its only moment of serenity and fairness. It was because Duncan could
look at it and say:

> This castle hath a pleasant seat; the air
> Nimbly and sweetly recommends itself
> Unto our gentle senses.                    (I, vi, 1-3)

The speech itself was nimble, sweet, and gentle; and Banquo's
explanation was in tone:

> This guest of summer,
> The temple-haunting martlet, does approve,
> By his loved masonry, that the heaven's breath
> Smells wooingly here; no jutty, frieze,
> Buttress, nor coign of vantage, but this bird
> Hath made his pendent bed and procreant cradle.
> Where they most breed and haunt, I have observ'd
> The air is delicate.

Summer, heaven, wooing, and procreation in the delicate air
—such words suited the presence of a king who when later on
he was found stabbed in his bed would actually offer a fair
sight to guilty eyes. His blood was not like the other blood
in the play, thick and fearfully discolored. It was bright and
beautiful, as no one better than Macbeth could appreciate:

> Here lay Duncan,
> His silver skin lac'd with his golden blood
>                                     (II, iii, 117-8)

—the silver and the gold went with the diamond, and with
Duncan's gentle senses that could smell no treachery though
a whole house reeked with it. And Duncan of course could

sleep. After life's fitful fever he had been laid where nothing could touch him further (III, ii, 22-6). No terrible dreams to shake him nightly, and no fears of things lest they come stalking through the world before their time in borrowed shapes.

Our memory of this contrast, much as the doings of the middle play work to muffle it, is what gives power to Malcolm and Macduff at the end.

> Angels are bright still, though the brightest fell.
>
> (IV, iii, 22)

Scotland may seem to have become the grave of men and not their mother (IV, iii, 166); death and danger may claim the whole of that bleeding country; but there is another country to the south where a good king works miracles with his touch. The rest of the world is what it always was; time goes on; events stretch out through space in their proper forms. Shakespeare again has enclosed his evil within a universe of good, his storm center within wide areas of peace. And from this outer world Malcolm and Macduff will return to heal Scotland of its ills. Their conversation in London before the pious Edward's palace (IV, iii) is not an interruption of the play; it is one of its essential parts, glancing forward as it does to a conclusion wherein Macduff can say, "The time is free" (V, viii, 55), and wherein Malcolm can promise that deeds of justice, "planted newly with the time," will be performed "in measure, time, and place" (V, viii, 64-73). Malcolm speaks the language of the play, but he has recovered its lost idiom. Blood will cease to flow, movement will recommence, fear will be forgotten, sleep will season every life, and the seeds of time will blossom in due order. The circle of safety which Shakespeare has drawn around his central horror is thinly drawn, but it is finely drawn and it holds.

# ANTONY AND CLEOPATRA

I F "Antony and Cleopatra" was written first among the three tragedies in which Shakespeare returned to Plutarch for his source, the writing of it involved the removal of his imagination to a distance that almost staggers measurement. The poet of "King Lear" and "Macbeth" now works freely under a great dome of lighted sky which knows no clouds except an occasional illusory and indistinct one, and which feels no wind beyond the soft one of its own effortless breathing. The world of "Antony and Cleopatra" is so immense that time yawns in it; and this is not because time is going to die as it did in "Macbeth" but because it luxuriates in a sense of perfect and endless health. The mandragora that Cleopatra wants to drink so that she may "sleep out this great gap of time" (I, v, 5) while Antony is away needs scarcely to be drunk in a universe already drugged with a knowledge of its own size. It is all the world that Plutarch knew or that Shakespeare knows as he writes: the Mediterranean world where opulent Africa lies across a gleaming sea from Spain, Italy, and Greece, and where innumerable kingdoms stretch eastward to the horizon. Nor is there terror in such distances. Men are at home in "the wide arch of the rang'd empire," and call each other naturally the most glorious names: "triple pillar of the world," "demi-Atlas of this earth," "senators alone of this great world," "world-sharers," "universal landlord," "sole sir o' the world." There is no terror because there is so much light. When Iras says

> the bright day is done,
> And we are for the dark,                    (v, ii, 193-4)

she is bidding good-by to an afternoon which has been long
with life; and the dark for which she is destined seems somehow to have no blackness in it, for the same reason that when
Cleopatra utters her command:

> Darkling stand
> The varying shore o' the world     (IV, xv, 10-11)

we cannot imagine that any cliff or headland has ceased to be
luminous even though the sun has burned the great sphere
it moves in. Light plays on everything with undiscouraged
luxury: on land, on rivers, on islands, and on the sea. We
are never far away from the limpid and life-giving element
of water, which, rather than forming like dew as it did in "A
Midsummer Night's Dream," now spreads a rich iridescent
film over the whole of a vast daylight existence. There is of
course the sea, and Antony is one who with his sword

> Quarter'd the world, and o'er green Neptune's back     3
> With ships made cities.                    (IV, xiv, 58-9)

But there is also the Nile, whose "slime and ooze," creative
of "flies and gnats" as well as crocodiles, we are kept no less
conscious of than we are kept conscious of flowing streams
wherein "tawny-finn'd fishes" play, where swan's down-
feathers float at full of tide, and from which rise swifts and
mallards. It is a world of languid and abundant life which
cannot surprise us with news that swallows have built their
nests in Cleopatra's sails (IV, xii, 3-4), or that the river of
Cydnus fell in love with her barge as it burned on its water.

> The oars were silver,
> Which to the tune of flutes kept stroke, and made
> The water which they beat to follow faster,
> As amorous of their strokes.          (II, ii, 199-202)

At night, since night must be, there is nevertheless the moon,
whose fleeting terrene visits keep Italy and Egypt flooded
with yellow light. And by day again there is certain to be
music—"moody food," says Cleopatra (II, v. 1-2), "of us that

trade in love." But it is not music played in a chamber, like the music of "Twelfth Night," or on the lawn of a great lady's estate as in "The Merchant of Venice." It has the dome of the world to fill, so that it plays "far off" while Cleopatra fishes (ii, v, 11), and runs both through the air and underground when

> the god Hercules, whom Antony loved,
> Now leaves him.                                    (iv, iii, 16-7)

Such a world needs a special style, and the play triumphantly provides it. The units of this style, curiously enough, are very brief. Nothing is drawn out as with too little thought we might have expected it to be. The action is broken into as many as forty-two scenes; our attention is constantly shifted from one to another portion of the single scene which is the earth. And so with the speech, the characteristic unit of which is almost breathlessly short. There are no rolls of rhetoric, no attempts to loop the universe with language. This universe is too large to be rendered in anything but fragments, too much alive in its own right to care for extended compliment and discourse. It can be handled only by a process of constantly reassembling its many small parts—moving them about in an always flexible mosaic. For the world of "Antony and Cleopatra" shows its strength in nothing so much as its flexibility. Any part, examined closely, yields the whole, just as any speech, once it is made, escapes into some far altitude of the air without exactly losing itself; in the long run it will count. The action expresses itself in many ripples, like a resting sea. The climate in which Antony and Cleopatra so completely love each other permits them the luxury of little phrases, as if with their breath it panted the tale of its own endless well-being. Accommodating itself to its heroine, it utters itself with a refined sensuousness, opening its lips and pronouncing delicious words in which the light sounds of i, short a, s, st, l, and ing predominate.

                    By the fire
That quickens Nilus' slime, I go from hence
Thy soldier, servant.                    (I, iii, 68-70)

                    This common body,
Like to a vagabond flag upon the stream,
Goes to and back, lackeying the varying tide,
To rot itself with motion.                    (I, iv, 44-7)

                    Think on me,
That am with Phoebus' amorous pinches black,
And wrinkled deep in time?                    (I, v, 27-9)

How much unlike art thou Mark Antony!
Yet, coming from him, that great medicine hath
With his tinct gilded thee.                    (I, v, 35-7)

By Isis, I will give thee bloody teeth.                    (I, v, 70)

                              She
In the habiliments of the goddess Isis
That day appear'd.                    (III, vi, 16-8)

That which is now a horse, even with a thought
The rack dislimns, and makes it indistinct,
As water is in water.                    (IV, xiv, 9-11)

With thy sharp teeth this knot intrinsicate
Of life at once untie.                    (v, ii, 307-8)

This is an aspic's trail; and these fig-leaves
Have slime upon them, such as the aspic leaves
Upon the caves of Nile.                    (v, ii, 354-6)

The speech of any person in the play is likely to spill itself
in agreeable gasps, as if it came through gills; and the blank-
verse line of the earlier dramas has almost lost its form in the
fluid element that surrounds it.

     Let Rome in Tiber melt, and the wide arch
     Of the rang'd empire fall! Here is my space.
     Kingdoms are clay; our dungy earth alike
     Feeds beast as man; the nobleness of life
     Is to do thus, when such a mutual pair
     And such a twain can do 't.                    (I, i, 33-8)

Nay, pray you, seek no colour for your going,
But bid farewell, and go. When you sued staying,
Then was the time for words; no going then;
Eternity was in our lips and eyes,
Bliss in our brows' bent; none our parts so poor,
But was a race of heaven. They are so still,
Or thou, the greatest soldier of the world,
Art turn'd the greatest liar.              (I, iii, 32-9)

My salad days,
When I was green in judgement; cold in blood,
To say as I said then! But, come, away;
Get me ink and paper.
He shall have every day a several greeting,
Or I'll unpeople Egypt.                     (I, v, 73-8)

I will o'ertake thee, Cleopatra, and
Weep for my pardon. So it must be, for now
All length is torture; since the torch is out,
Lie down, and stray no farther. Now all labour
Mars what it does; yea, very force entangles
Itself with strength.                      (IV, xiv, 44-9)

Such a style suits lovers who make up as quickly as they have
quarreled; the anger of Antony and Cleopatra has a short
memory, and pardons succeed curses with little shift of accent.
                    Courteous lord, one word.
    Sir, you and I must part, but that's not it;
    Sir, you and I have lov'd, but there's not it;
    That you know well. Something it is I would,—
    O, my oblivion is a very Antony,
    And I am all forgotten.                (I, iii, 86-91)

That will do for Cleopatra's text after any altercation; and
Antony, who played with half the bulk of the world as he
pleased and had superfluous kings for messengers, can humble himself as briefly:

        Fall not a tear, I say; one of them rates
        All that is won and lost. Give me a kiss.
        Even this repays me.               (III, xi, 69-71)

Their misunderstandings are waves which there are other waves to check, just as the bits of acting they practice on each other are chopped short because they know that neither can be deceived.

> Cleopatra.              Good now, play one scene
> Of excellent dissembling; and let it look
> Like perfect honour.
> Antony.              You'll heat my blood. No more.
> Cleopatra. You can do better yet; but this is meetly.
> Antony.    Now, by my sword,—
> Cleopatra.              And target.—Still he mends;
> But this is not the best.              (I, iii, 78-83)

This banter is from a queen who is herself a consummate actress, and she knows Antony knows it. Once she fails to see through him, but that is when he is acting for men only and she does not catch the style. As he opens an old vein of oratory and contrives tremulos for the benefit of certain servitors on the eve of battle (IV, ii) she appeals to Enobarbus who is standing by: "What means this?" Enobarbus puts her off by saying that it is an odd trick of sorrow; Antony is affected by thoughts of the next day. But as the instrument plays on she asks again: "What does he mean?" And Enobarbus, who knows his master even better than she knows her lover, has to confess: "To make his followers weep." It is mere wanton art, an expert's oratory. There is of course a final quarrel and a final attempt at deception, for the play is a tragedy and Cleopatra will not be able to undo her subterfuge of the monument (IV, xiii-xv). Yet even there the established style will prevail, and modify the tragedy. And long before that it will have subdued every item of the action to the tone of its own unique refinement. The drunkenness of the generals on board Pompey's galley (II, vii) is as little gross as the love of Antony and Cleopatra is voluptuous. As wine makes the world-sharers witty, and steeps their senses at last in "soft and delicate Lethe," so love turns the lead of

Antony and Cleopatra into gold. Pompey credits the Queen
with sultry powers that keep the brain of her lover fuming,
but the love we see is light with jest and mellow with amuse-
ment. This is because Cleopatra is really queen of her world.
When Enobarbus pays her his famous tribute:

> Age cannot wither her, nor custom stale
> Her infinite variety. . . . She makes hungry
> Where most she satisfies, for vilest things
> Become themselves in her,                (II, ii, 240-44)

he is placing her in that world which the style of the play is
forever creating: a world which is ancient yet not stale, com-
placent yet still hungry, and as becoming in its vileness as it
is cultivated in its virtues. Its infinite variety is a quality of its
air, its land, its water, its animals, its clouds, its language, and
its people. All are the creation of a style whose imponderable
atoms are ever in graceful dance, no sooner combining to
produce forms than separating to dissolve them. The next
question is whether action is possible in such an atmosphere,
and if so, what kind of action.

In one sense "Antony and Cleopatra" is actionless. A world
is lost, but it is so well lost that it seems not to have been lost
at all; its immensity was not disturbed. The peculiar greatness of this poetry defeats any conceivable dramatic end.
Line for line it is perhaps the richest poetry Shakespeare
wrote, but the reward it reaps is paradoxical: it builds a universe in which nothing can happen, or at any rate one in
which the conflicts and crises of persons cannot be of the
first importance. This explains, if it is granted that the gods
ordained some sort of greatness for the play, the nakedness
of its verbal intensity. The writing has to be wonderful because it is not supported by anything that Aristotle would
have called a plot. And it is wonderful. Merely as expression
it has that final force which permits many of its passages to
stand alone, without the need of a context to recommend

them. If they gain from being read in place, the place is an atmosphere rather than an action. The intensity of Hamlet, Othello, Lear, and Macbeth was derived from their respective predicaments; the intensity of Antony and Cleopatra seems to be generated in themselves, and in the poet who is writing their speeches. This will tend to be true of all the plays to come. Shakespeare's last plays contain his richest writing but they are not his best plays. Though Timon, Pericles, Imogen, and Leontes are not surpassed by any of Shakespeare's poets, their stories leave them at a disadvantage. If the disadvantage is less conspicuous in the case of "Antony and Cleopatra," the reason may be that its poetry has come as near as poetry can come to the performing of miracles: the play has lifted itself by its language. This appears most regularly in the passages of praise which glisten everywhere as others like them will glisten through the later dramas. The final poet in Shakespeare is content to be lyrical. Praise becomes with him an occupation in itself. The explanation may be that he now has things to say about humanity which must be said directly; or that he cannot find, in the stories available to him, persons to match his thought; or that his dramatic energies have declined. Whatever the explanation, his lyre labors continually at the task of praise, and labors with regal result. Consider Lepidus on Antony:

> I must not think there are
> Evils enow to darken all his goodness.
> His faults in him seem as the spots of heaven,
> More fiery by night's blackness; hereditary,
> Rather than purchas'd; what he cannot change,
> Than what he chooses.          (I, iv, 10-15)

Or Euphronius on Antony:

> Such as I am, I come from Antony.
> I was of late as petty to his ends
> As is the morn-dew on the myrtle-leaf
> To his grand sea.          (III, xii, 7-10)

Or Caesar on Antony:

> The breaking of so great a thing should make
> A greater crack. The round world
> Should have shook lions into civil streets,
> And citizens to their dens. The death of Antony
> Is not a single doom; in the name lay
> A moiety of the world. (v, i, 14-9)

Or Cleopatra on Antony:

> O, see, my women,
> The crown o' the earth doth melt. My lord!
> O, wither'd is the garland of the war,
> The soldier's pole is fall'n! Young boys and girls
> Are level now with men; the odds is gone,
> And there is nothing left remarkable
> Beneath the visiting moon. (IV, xv, 62-8)

Or Cleopatra on Antony again—and this would seem to be the goal in the play toward which both panegyric and poetry had been striving, for there is no better speech in Shakespeare:

> His legs bestrid the ocean; his rear'd arm
> Crested the world; his voice was propertied
> As all the tuned spheres, and that to friends;
> But when he meant to quail and shake the orb,
> He was as rattling thunder. For his bounty,
> There was no winter in 't; an autumn 't was
> That grew the more by reaping. His delights
> Were dolphin-like, they show'd his back above
> The element they liv'd in. In his livery
> Walk'd crowns and crownets; realms and islands were
> As plates dropp'd from his pocket. (v, ii, 83-92)

In another sense "Antony and Cleopatra" has all the action it desires and deserves. There is as much drama in the deaths of its hero and heroine as there can be in the deaths of two persons who lived, at least while we knew them, without illusion; or lived, it may be more accurate to say, in the full light of accepted illusion. Change is a fairy toy for Theseus in

"A Midsummer Night's Dream," and for Macbeth it is a growing terror. For Antony and Cleopatra it is what must be expected, and they have seen so much of it that more cannot surprise them. The changeableness of life is the only thing that does not change; they know this, and to that extent cannot be touched. Their love has been too thoroughly tested to be shaken now. It is founded on its own fact, and on the humorous knowledge they have of each other. Shakespeare put their case perfectly in his 138th sonnet:

> When my love swears that she is made of truth,
> I do believe her, though I know she lies. . . .
> O, love's best habit is in seeming trust,
> And age in love loves not to have years told.

Yet not quite perfectly, either. Each knows the other to be a liar, and ultimately does not care if this is so; but one of their pastimes is telling their years. Their days are past the best, and they know this as well as Enobarbus knows that Antony is an old lion (III, xiii, 95), or as well as Caesar knows, or thinks he knows, that his rival is an old ruffian (IV, i, 4). Antony's remark that gray in both of them has something mingled with their younger brown (IV, viii, 19-20) is only a courteous reference to the white hairs he elsewhere takes to himself (III, xi, 13). And Cleopatra is content with the boast:

> Though age from folly could not give me freedom,
> It does from childishness.                    (I, iii, 57-8)

As lovers go, then, they are old. That is why they can do without illusion—or, better still, why they know what to do with it. They prefer each other's untruth to any truth that has yet to be tried. This does not make them easy material for tragedy. It makes them indeed the most intractable material of all; for tragedy works with delusions, and they have none. They would seem to have been cut out for comedy, and indeed there is much comedy here. Only a supreme effort at writing keeps the play on its tragic keel. And even

then it must do without the sense in any line that death is terrible. Tragedy counts, both in its hero and in us, upon the
fear of death for its great effects. But these lovers, far from
fearing death, embrace it as a third lover. Enobarbus says of
Cleopatra: "I do think there is mettle in Death, which commits some loving act upon her, she hath such a celerity in
dying" (I, ii, 147-9). He is satirical, and refers to the actress
who puts on shows of death in order to hold her lord. But his
intelligence has penetrated to the symbol which Antony no
less than she will employ to express an ultimate passion. "I'll
make Death love me," swears Antony as he prepares for battle (III, xiii, 193), and as he falls on his sword he elaborates
the image:

>                    I will be
>      A bridegroom in my death, and run into 't
>      As to a lover's bed.                    (IV, xiv, 99-101)

Cleopatra, however, gives it its most sophisticated form:

>      The stroke of death is as a lover's pinch,
>      Which hurts, and is desir'd.             (V, ii, 298-9)

Antony is a great man, but his dimensions do not express
themselves in drama. The play, such as it is, pauses while his
praise is sung by Lepidus, by Euphronius, by Caesar, and
again and again by Cleopatra. He deserves that such things
should be said of him, but we must not expect to see them
exemplified in act. They are often negative things: there are
not enough evils to darken his goodness, his death is not a
single doom, nothing is left remarkable since he is gone, his
bounty had no winter in it. And there is a further negative:

>      Who tells me true, though in his tale lie death,
>      I hear him as he flatter'd. . . .
>      Speak to me home, mince not the general tongue.
>                                              (I, ii, 102-9)

He does not trade in untruths. We learn much from such
negatives, but we learn it directly, through lyric statement

while the action rests. His delights were dolphin-like, they show'd his back above the element they liv'd in—the movement there goes on outside our practical vision, in a remote kingdom by the sea of metaphor. Nothing more interesting was ever said about any man, but it has to be said, it cannot be shown. Antony is finally ineffable, and Shakespeare has the tact to let him tower alone. Bounty, as the first half of "Timon of Athens" proves, is not a dramatic virtue; nor is there any attempt in this play to make it seem one, though the suicide of Enobarbus (IV, vi) states it powerfully, and Cleopatra's encomium is majestic in its range. The virtues of Antony cannot be dramatized because they are one virtue and its name is magnanimity. Actor though he is and orator though he has been, at his best he shows his back above the element he lives in. He can be moved to anger, jealousy, and pride, he can laugh within a minute after he has raged, he can be a man of forty moods; yet our last vision is of one whose spirit has grown stationary. For all his shrewdness Enobarbus does not see what has happened. He speaks of "a diminution in our captain's brain" (III, xiii, 198), but he is wholly wrong. There has been an expansion, not a contraction. Great as is the world of Roman thoughts, and Caesar reveals the limit of that greatness, Antony has found a greater world—one whose soft sky is of infinite size, and one where thoughts melt into one another as water does in water. A soothsayer warns Antony to keep space between himself and Caesar (II, iii, 23), but the space is already there. The discomfort Antony feels in Caesar's presence is based on more than political rivalry between an old lion and a young fox; it is based on an inability to tell Caesar or any other man why Egypt is so attractive. The reason is Egypt's air, which cannot be felt until it is withdrawn; when it must be found and breathed again, for a full breath cannot be taken in any other. Antony grows until he occupies the whole of Egypt's and Cleopatra's air. And his final act of occupation is his death—which, if it withdraws him from us, leaves us an exact equivalent in the greatness of that air.

Cleopatra's dimensions express themselves on the other hand with an excess of drama—in many little plays rather than in one that is round and single. She comes at us in waves, each of which breaks before it reaches us, but the total number of which is great and beautiful. She is fickle, she is spoiled—

> Pity me, Charmian,
> But do not speak to me—                    (ii, v, 118-9)

she is vain, she is cowardly, she is incorrigibly unserious; yet she is a queen "whom everything becomes" (i, i, 49). Antony says that, and he means it even of one who is "cunning past man's thought"; her cunning becomes her too, and the holy priests bless her when she is riggish (ii, ii, 244-5). For her variety is infinite; she perfectly expresses the elasticity of Egypt's air. Antony's immobility measures its amount, but its quality can be fingered only in her. She is mercury, she is changeable silk, she is a serpent of old Nile whose movements are too many to count. The messenger's description of Octavia is nicely calculated for the woman to whom it is delivered:

> She creeps;
> Her motion and her station are as one;
> She shows a body rather than a life,
> A statue than a breather.                    (iii, iii, 21-4)

Cleopatra is not like that; she is a breather, and her life is still more fascinating than her body. It is her life that makes her love so interesting. "There's beggary in the love that can be reckon'd" (i, i, 15)—Antony has learned this from her, and from the boundless air of Egypt. She teaches him even while she tortures him; that is why he can forgive her the long, ghastly effort to die which her lie about the monument imposes upon him (iv, xiv). His pleasure in her alternates with pain, and in fact the play deals more with the pain than it does with the pleasure. But between the lines we read that he could have endured as much again from one whose behavior has never been what Octavia's is, "holy, cold, and still" (II, vi, 131). Cleopatra is too seldom at rest to be easily understood; we shall never be sure, any more than Antony would have been sure, what her intentions were with respect to the treasure she withheld from Caesar (v, ii, 138-92), and whether her decision to die was inspired by loathing for Roman triumphs or by love for the "husband" to whom death would bring her. When the basket of asps arrives she announces to her people:

> My resolution's plac'd, and I have nothing
> Of woman in me; now from head to foot
> I am marble-constant; now the fleeting moon
> No planet is of mine.          (v, ii, 238-41)

Yet her demeanor in dying has no marble in it. She is still all mercury and lightness, all silk and down. "I have immortal longings in me" is said with a smile at the expense of the rural fellow who has just gone out wishing her joy of the worm and insisting that its bite is "immortal"; she must have on her robe and crown before she feels the loving pinch of death; when Iras precedes her in death she pretends to worry lest Antony's first kiss in heaven be wasted on another woman; she saves enough breath to call Caesar "ass unpolicied," and spends the last of it in likening the immortal worm to a baby at her breast. Charmian, surviving her a moment, echoes "ass unpolicied" with "lass unparallel'd," and bothers to straighten her mistress's crown before she dies. The scene is great and final, yet nothing in it seems to be serious; and the conversation between Caesar and his train when they come in concerns a spectacle that is pretty rather than painful.          She looks like sleep,

> As she would catch another Antony
> In her strong toil of grace.          (v, ii, 349-51)

The strength of Cleopatra has never appeared more clearly than in the charm with which she yields herself to death. Her greatness cannot be distinguished from her littleness, as water may not be defined in water.

# CORIOLANUS

THE movement of "Coriolanus" is rhetorical. As in "Julius Caesar," but more bleakly than there, the streets of Rome are conceived as rostrums where men meet for the sole purpose of discussing something —the character of the hero and its effect upon a certain political situation. Shakespeare is interested in the character and the situation, but he is conscious of being interested; he is addressing himself with all the sobriety of his intelligence to a subject which has not been created by the play itself or even by its respected godfather Plutarch. It is a subject whose existence does not depend upon dramatic art, nor is the artist in this case wholly absorbed in it as he was in the subject of "Hamlet," whatever that is. We do not know what the subject of "Hamlet" is; we only know that the play is of inexhaustible interest. The interest of "Coriolanus" is not easily exhausted; many things in it are meritorious, and the writing has a steady, dogged strength which the judicial critic may admire; but it has its limits, and these are clearly defined by a list of the things Shakespeare has taken out in talk.

Coriolanus is a tragic hero whom we listen to and learn about entirely in his public aspect. His heroic fault, which is pride, is announced in the first scene as a theme for discussion; and the play is that discussion. He is almost never alone with himself, and when he is, in the soliloquy at Antium (IV, IV, 12-26), he has nothing to say to himself that we do not already know. Passionate as he is, and eccentric too, he is somehow not personal. His character is of that clear kind which calls for statement; but in poetry and drama statement is one of the obscurer mediums. Groups of people—tribunes,

citizens, servants, officers laying cushions in the Capitol, trav-
elers on the highway, the ladies of his household—are forever
exchanging opinions on the subject of Coriolanus. And the
individuals who share with him the bulk of our attention are
here for no other purpose than to make leading remarks
about him. Competent as the scene is (i, iii) which introduces
the ladies to us, and adroitly as they are distinguished from
one another throughout the play, the "faint puling and lament" of the wife Virgilia always contrasting with the antique Roman rage of the mother Volumnia, the lady who
emerges farthest from the group, Volumnia herself, exists
first and last as a setting for her son. The pleasure she would
have taken in sacrificing a dozen such sons for Rome (i, iii,
23-7), the fact that she can exclaim:

> Now the red pestilence strike all trades in Rome,
> And occupations perish,                         (iv, i, 13-4)

and the very brevity with which she can sum herself up in
"Anger's my meat" (iv, ii, 50)—these things show where
Coriolanus came from, just as her strictures upon his extreme
behavior show that he has come too far. And his old friend
Menenius, who speaks exceedingly well in garrulous prose,
speaks nevertheless to the end that we shall understand Coriolanus as well as speeches from any external source could
persuade us to. "What I think, I utter" (ii, i, 58), says
Menenius, who is willing to be known as "a humourous pa-
trician," one that "converses more with the buttock of the
night than with the forehead of the morning," so long as he
can have his say. He is accused by the tribune Brutus of
being "a perfecter giber for the table than a necessary
bencher in the Capitol" (ii, i, 90-2), and his old man's mind
does run by preference on food. This bestows upon him a
particularity which is welcome in so generalized a play, and
his tongue has oftentimes clean skill, as when he says of
Coriolanus: "There is no more mercy in him than there is

milk in a male tiger" (v, iv, 30-1). Yet we have only to perceive the parallel between him and Polonius to know how
far he comes from existing in his own right as Ophelia's father did. He as much as anyone in "Coriolanus" keeps it
wordy—witness the way he rubs irony in with six repetitions
of "You have made good work" (iv, vi)—though it would
be wordy enough without him. Blood in the play is once
again what it was in "Julius Caesar," verbal. We hear that
Coriolanus has lost more blood than he had in him by many
an ounce, that he is "smear'd" with it as if it were paint,
that he looks like one flayed, that at Corioli he was "a thing
of blood" from face to foot. But this is political blood laid on
in metaphor, just as the death of the hero is a catastrophe cut
into the fable from a point without. The death of Coriolanus
is inevitable not because of his character or because of his
career as we have followed it, but because Aufidius hates him.
This hatred, engraved on the surface of the tragedy as many
as seven times, is a sign that cannot be missed, but it has
nothing to do with the essential theme. Its origin is earlier
than the play and has to do with a rivalry between two leaders. The central conflict is between the leader and the led.

The political "meaning" of the play is considerably less
simple than it may seem. If it has to do with the difference
between the many and the one, that difference is viewed
from both directions. The many, the Roman mob, are criticized without mercy, but so is Coriolanus as the one. The
tribunes of the people are convicted of his pride (ii, i, 41),
and there is something in Volumnia's charge that it is they
rather than he by whom the rabble becomes incensed (iv, ii,
33). Certainly they are represented as dishonest demagogues
(ii, iii), and their complete wrongness with respect to the
possibility of an attack from Aufidius (iv, vi) renders them
as statesmen contemptible. The mob, as usual in Shakespeare,
behaves badly, and even permits one of its members to casti-
gate its many-headedness (ii, iii, 19-26). But Coriolanus in

turn is as relentlessly dissected. His impossible pride is the subject of the play, which makes no attempt to ennoble this pride as a tendentious toryism might like to do—merely, that is, by elevating it above the animal authority of the mob.

His pride is animal too. The vigor of speech which scalds citizens with epithets—"rogues," "scabs," "slaves," "minnows," "measles," "mutable rank-scented many"—is the vigor of a man whose voice can sound exactly like Caliban's:

> All the contagion of the south light on you,
> You shames of Rome! you herd of—Boils and plagues
> Plaster you o'er, that you may be abhorr'd
> Further than seen, and one infect another
> Against the wind a mile!                    (I, iv, 30-34)

And the pride with which he "pays himself" (I, i, 33-4) is sometimes of that subhuman sort which consists of insulting those who would offer praise. Menenius urges Coriolanus to take his honor with his form, but Coriolanus is deficient in form. It is not merely that he cannot take compliments and gifts with grace; he cannot take them at all, and this is true whether they come from his inferiors or from his equals. The fastidiousness of the duke in "Measure for Measure" which robbed him of any relish in the "aves vehement" of his people is reproduced in Coriolanus's scorn of all "acclamations hyperbolical" (I, ix, 51), but he goes much farther than that. "Sir, praise me not," he cuts in curtly when Titus Lartius, a fellow-general, has noted his worthy wounds (I, v, 17); and when the entire Roman camp shouts his new name he mutters: "I will go wash" (I, ix, 68). He cannot prevent his mother's praises, for she is a better orator than he, but he can and does insist upon silence from Rome, by whose dignitaries he will not have his "nothings monster'd" (II, ii, 81). This is not the modesty of nature or the magnanimity of a man who knows himself. It is bad manners, and it is disruptive of that very social order which Coriolanus claims to consider more important than himself. Modesty in a great man permits him to accept the praise that is due him. Coriolanus's rejection of praise leaves him still great but leaves him less a man—leaves him, in fact, the "lonely dragon" he says he is (IV, i, 30). Honor and responsibility must pay for themselves by being seen. Coriolanus would like to do famous deeds and remain unknown. It is a contradiction in terms, but so is his pride a monster that confounds itself with many contradictions.

"His nature," says Menenius, "is too noble for the world" (III, i, 255), but the fault is his as well as the world's. He can be the world's servant in only one way, his own (II, i, 219), for he is utterly rigid. "You are too absolute," Volumnia tells him,

> Though therein you can never be too noble,
> But when extremities speak.                    (III, ii, 40-1)

The extremity she has in mind is none other than the fate of Rome, and still Coriolanus cannot bring himself to "trouble the poor with begging" (II, iii, 76) or to behave as though he were "common in my love" (II, iii, 101). He goes to the Forum a second time promising to answer the people mildly; but he mumbles the word "mildly" like a mastiff (III, ii, 142-5), and once he is among the "common cry of curs" he bares his teeth and invites the exile which will conduct him to his death. The art of calling names finds him too easily its master; he cannot hold his tongue any more than he can keep his mind from working, and his intelligence tells him many true things.

> What custom wills, in all things should we do 't,
> The dust on antique time would lie unswept,
> And mountainous error be too highly heapt
> For truth to o'er-peer.                    (II, iii, 125-8)

His intellect, indeed, almost makes him magnificent in his pride. The reasons that it cannot do so finally are left for bystanders to state. A shrewd citizen makes one point:

Now, to seem to affect the malice and displeasure of the people
is as bad as that which he dislikes, to flatter them for their love.
                                                    (II, ii, 23-6)

Volumnia makes another:

> You might have been enough the man you are,
> With striving less to be so.        (III, ii, 19-20)

And Aufidius presents the summary:

> Whether 't was pride,
> Which out of daily fortune ever taints
> The happy man; whether defect of judgement,
> To fail in the disposing of those chances
> Which he was lord of; or whether nature,
> Not to be other than one thing, not moving
> From the casque to the cushion, but commanding peace
> Even with the same austerity and garb
> As he controll'd the war; but one of these,—
> As he hath spices of them all—not all,—
> For I dare so far free him,—made him fear'd;
> So, hated; and so, banish'd: but he has a merit
> To choke it in the utterance.          (IV, vii, 37-49)

This is noble analysis, but the fact that it is not especially
characteristic of the speaker reminds us that Shakespeare has
been writing the kind of play which needs such anomalies.
The kind of play which calls on its characters to say what it
means—to do in other words the author's work—may be admirable, as "Coriolanus" is, but it cannot be attractive. "Coriolanus" remains—a strange thing for Shakespeare—cold, and
its hero continues until his death to be a public man whom
we are not permitted to know closely enough either for understanding or for love.

# TIMON OF ATHENS

IF Aristotle was right when he called plot the soul of tragedy, "Timon of Athens" has no soul. There are those who claim to know that Shakespeare's soul is in it, exposed at a crisis which experts on the inner lives of authors can read at a glance; but that is an additional way of saying that the play does without complications. Its action is the simplest that can be imagined. Upon the refusal of four friends to lend him money when he needs it Timon passes from the extreme of prodigality to the extreme of misanthropy. "The middle of humanity," whence tragedy no less than comedy derives its strength, he never knows; he knows "but the extremity of both ends." The words are those of Apemantus, who as the churl of the piece is privileged also to say that Timon's transformation is from a madman to a fool, from a flashing phoenix to a naked gull. Apemantus is a harsh critic, but he is a critic. The author's interest is entirely confined to the absolutes of Timon's illusion and disillusion. Not only has he taken no pains to motivate his hero's change of mind, for the episode of the friends' ingratitude is perfunctory; he has taken no pains whatever to put more than lyric force into Timon's utterances before and after. The play is two plays, casually joined at the middle; or rather two poems, two pictures, in swan white and raven black. The contrast is all. This is where the spiritual biographers of Shakespeare come in. The poetry of either half being radical in its intensity and impossible to ignore, they argue that the feeling behind it must be Shakespeare's instead of Timon's, and that the play was never anything but an excuse to rid the poet's bosom of its perilous stuff—granted, to be sure, that he is responsible for all of it as it stands. Assuming that he is, we can agree that the play as written leaves him open to the charge of having expressed himself rather than his theme. But the field of conjecture is so wide that any step taken across it may be in the right direction, and we may wish to escape into an alternative theory which starts from the supposition that "Timon of Athens" is Shakespeare's last tragedy and that it was never finished. If this was the case, then he may have been tired of tragedy—through with it as an artist and exhausted by its tensions. This alone could account for his relapse into the lyric mode, for the concentration of his interest upon the things his hero says rather than upon the meaning of the fact that he says them. It may not matter to criticism what theory we hold, so long as we recognize the limits of the play before us.

No play of Shakespeare's confesses its limits more frankly. It is content to be abstract, to leave unclothed the symbols of which its poetry is made. The hall in Timon's house where he dispenses bounty is allegorical in its splendor, a chamber prepared for the performance of generous miracles, not an inhabitable portion of one man's dwelling. Timon as its host, moving gracefully to music while servants bear in urns of fruit and caskets of jewels, bowing to friends as though they were gods and receiving gifts from them—two brace of greyhounds, four milk-white horses trapped in silver—as blissfully as he bestows his own gifts in return, clapping his hands to summon a masque of ladies dressed as Amazons so that the lords his guests may dance with them to the strains of lutes and hautboys, and now and then giving golden voice to his inexpressible love:

> I could deal kingdoms to my friends,
> And ne'er be weary                    (i, ii, 226-7)

—this Timon is not so much a man as a figure representing Munificence, an abstraction in whom madness may not matter. For we see some meaning in Apemantus's epithet when we overhear the steward's attempts to convince Timon that he is bankrupt, and when we realize that he is giving away borrowed wealth. But he is already fantastic, and our fears for him are not real. Neither is our pity for him real when later on we listen to his rages as he stands in the middle of an empty plain outside of Athens and digs in the bare ground for symbols barer still—"one poor root" and "yellow, glittering, precious gold."

> This yellow slave
> Will knit and break religions, bless the accurs'd,
> Make the hoar leprosy ador'd, place thieves
> And give them title, knee, and approbation
> With senators on the bench. This is it
> That makes the wappen'd widow wed again;
> She, whom the spital-house and ulcerous sores
> Would cast the gorge at, this embalms and spices
> To the April day again. Come, damn'd earth,
> Thou common whore of mankind, that puts odds
> Among the rout of nations, I will make thee
> Do thy right nature.                    (IV, iii, 33-44)

Such a speech has its terrors, and with many another speech in the play it belongs somewhere near the top of Shakespeare's poetry. But it is not terrible that Timon should be saying such things as it was terrible that Lear should say the things he said. Gold has been a symbol wherewith Timon could express his love. Now it is a symbol wherewith he can express his hate. That is all. It is as naked a piece of poetic property as the hole he stands in, as the root he throws up, as the cave he enters and leaves, and as the sea by which he is to die. Nakedness itself becomes a symbol in this play— nakedness as something which Timon's extremity desires and as something which he has in death, for he makes his everlasting mansion where the light foam of the sea may beat his grave-stone daily (IV, iii, 379-80), and where the only tears will be those of vast Neptune (V, iv, 78). The scene is not populated as Lear's Britain was, nor does what happens to its hero concern us so much. The parallel is suggested not only by the action as a whole but by a particular speech of Apemantus:

> Call the creatures
> Whose naked natures live in all the spite
> Of wreakful heaven, whose bare unhoused trunks,
> To the conflicting elements expos'd,
> Answer mere nature; bid them flatter thee.
>
> (IV, iii, 227-31)

Here might be the king who in his own extremity discovered the existence of poor naked wretches with houseless heads and unfed sides. But Timon, though he goes farther in speech than Lear ever went, moves us not half so deeply, and in fact does not move us at all. Lear's obscenity was innocence to this:

> Hold up, you sluts,
> Your aprons mountant. . . . Be whores still;
> And he whose pious breath seeks to convert you,
> Be strong in whore, allure him, burn him up;
> Let your close fire predominate his smoke,
> And be no turncoats. . . . Whore still;
> Paint till a horse may mire upon your face;
> A pox of wrinkles! (IV, iii, 134-48)

But it was heart-breaking to hear, as this is not because there is no heart in Timon to break, or any other organ. He is pure mouth-piece, even when his poetry is best:

> Go, live rich and happy;
> But thus condition'd: thou shalt build from men;
> Hate all, curse all, show charity to none,
> But let the famish'd flesh slide from the bone,
> Ere thou relieve the beggar. (IV, iii, 532-6)

He himself is pure symbol, a misanthrope and not a man.

The play confesses as much in the conduct of such action as it has. Schematism is everywhere apparent. There are three malcontents: Timon, Apemantus, and Alcibiades. Three servants enter Timon's hall bearing gifts (I, ii). Three friends refuse money to Timon in three consecutive scenes (III, i, ii, iii), and three strangers comment upon the triple outrage (III, ii). In his solitude Timon is visited by three significant individuals: Alcibiades, Apemantus, Flavius. And the banditti who come are three in number. This is obviously the work of a playwright who does not care how much his machinery shows, just as the poetry is the work of a man who does not mind announcing his themes—in the first half they are friendship, music, love, praise, and summer tears, in the second half they are hate, rage, roots, gold, bleak earth and sky, unvesseled sea, and winters too hard for weeping.

If the spiritual experts are right and "Timon of Athens" is a personal play, its interest, over and above the intrinsic interest of its poetry, is in the limit of pessimism it reaches. There could scarcely be more railing and cursing in five acts than we have here, and indeed there is to be no more of these commodities in Shakespeare. One is free to conjecture that in Timon's tomb Shakespeare buried his own bitterness —in a bleak, open, timeless place where the only tears are Neptune's, and where a "sea of air" broods in its vast empty arc above another sea whose waves are without memory. It is not necessary to conjecture thus, and if one wishes to do so it is well to remember that on the subject of Shakespeare's inner life there can be no authority. The great dead deserve whatever peace is possible. The temptation, however, is real in view of the mood which dominates four comedies still to come. Whatever the truth about Shakespeare was, "Timon of Athens" is some kind of transition between his last tragedies and his last comedies—or, as the term goes, his romances. It looks both ways: backward through "Lear" to the pestilent congregation of vapors in which Hamlet was befouled, and forward with "Antony and Cleopatra" to thick amber air and the rich difficult sunset of reconciliation.

# PERICLES

ANY one of the four "last" plays of Shakespeare—
"Pericles," "Cymbeline," "The Winter's Tale,"
and "The Tempest"—gains by being known in
company with the other three. The interest of each is singular and great, but the interest of the group is greater still.
The group has so much the air of being last—the final seg-
ment of a long curve—that criticism will always be torn between the theory that Shakespeare was writing "finis" to his
thought and the theory that he had merely shifted, following
perhaps the fashion of his craft, to a new form, the form of
the dramatic romance. Both theories are good, and neither
would explain success in the case of a lesser playwright. In
the case of a playwright like Shakespeare the professional
motive must always have been important without the personal motive needing to be less so. Whatever his reason for
writing these four plays, he felt them deeply; and if their
form had first been fashioned by other hands he may have
been grateful to it because it offered him a license which
neither tragedy nor comedy had so far wholly permitted.
This would be the license to ignore plausibility, to range the
wide world of imaginable event in search of nothing but
scenes that might give his speculations scope and be a medium for his memories. It would be an invitation to escape
from the necessary into the possible, and to create such a
universe as men might like to end their days believing in.
The form of the romance, shuttling as it did between the
ups and downs of fortune, and encouraging the invention of
fantastic evil to match fantastic good, directed him to go on
painting the dark sky he was all too familiar with; yet an-

other of its laws was that from time to time the clouds should part, permitting sunshine—even artificial sunshine—to burst through. His subject, in other words, must still be man's affliction, but its taste could be "as sweet as any cordial comfort" ("The Winter's Tale," v, iii, 76-7).

The mischance most common in the four romances is family separation—husband from wife, brother from brother, parent from child. There may seem to be nothing new in this, since Shakespeare has handled such business before and since it is business which always has been fundamental to story. But it is precisely the fundamental nature of family ties, and in consequence their symbolic value, that interests Shakespeare now. He has, for instance, been interested in fathers and daughters before: in Capulet and Juliet, in Polonius and Ophelia, in Lear and Cordelia. But never has he used them to say more than in themselves they mean. The relation tends now to become abstract, and, because it is abstract, to be realized with a special intensity in the persons who embody it. It is as if their destiny were to express it through misfortunes in their lives which fixed it as something sacred, even magic, in their minds. And they are sorely beset—they, together with other members here of separated families—by misfortunes not of their own making. Misunderstanding, jealousy, cruelty, and fraud are calamities out of the sky; they come whole and naked, without motivation or excuse, as lightning or pestilence might come, or storms at sea that wreck the best-intentioned ships. Literal shipwrecks are frequent in the four plays; so frequent, in fact, as to seem at last not literal at all. The shipwreck is Shakespeare's final symbol. There is "a wild dedication" of his people "to unpath'd waters, undream'd shores" ("The Winter's Tale," iv, iv, 576-7); there is separation by sea; and then there is recovery home. "Though the seas threaten, they are merciful" ("The Tempest," v, i, 178). It is of course Shakespeare who makes the seas merciful, just as it is he who has

decided that "Fortune brings in some boats that are not
steer'd" ("Cymbeline," IV, iii, 46). Hence the importance in
these plays of recognition scenes, which often fill the fifth
act and have unspeakable power. For they are also scenes of
reconciliation. A husband is being reconciled with a wife, a
father with a daughter; and it may be that Shakespeare is
being reconciled with the world.

Meanwhile there has been much episode, and most of it has
been sensational; the plots are hard to remember, as melo-
dramas are. We have visited the extremes of character, and
been shocked by sudden juxtapositions of innocence and vice
—Marina in the brothel, Miranda in danger of rape by Caliban. We have seen problems solved by supernatural means;
gods have been invoked, oracles have intervened, and magic
has been worked. But what is more important for poetry, we
have heard Shakespeare playing his ripest music on a few repeated themes. These themes come in pairs, for contrast. Age
in its selfish gruffness and its unthinking or thinking cruelty
is set against youth in its soft purity. The heroines have not
the wit and realism of Beatrice and Rosalind, nor do they
have such names. They are named for their qualities—Marina,
Perdita, Miranda—and although their innocence is high-
willed it is tender-hearted; they are angels, or fairy ladies,
bearing flowers. Fathers need to be careful lest their justice
"prove violence" and be piteously wild ("The Winter's
Tale," II, i, 127-8; 181-2), but justice in daughters is no less
natural than song. They are to their elders as summer is to
winter, as love is to hate, as loyalty is to treachery, as peace
is to discord, as trust is to distrust. For not only do the themes
appear in pairs; the pairs are finally one pair. Music conquers
misery, harmony puts the wild sea to sleep.

> Mark how one string, sweet husband to another,
> Strikes each in each by mutual ordering,
> Resembling sire and child and happy mother,
> Who all in one, one pleasing note do sing.

Those four lines of the eighth sonnet were curiously prophetic of what their author would be thinking and writing years later. Music sounds everywhere through his last plays: as song, as instrument, as metaphor, as idea. It may accompany a dance, or it may be merely a power to which reference is made. It is the solver of mysteries, the smoother of waves. And it is the maker of Shakespeare's last great poetry. For his final writing, congested as it sometimes is, gleams with lines whose effortlessness is not inconsistent with the richest and mellowest of ambiguities. Their meaning is like music's meaning, clear yet full five fathom deep.

It is generally agreed that Shakespeare did not write the first two acts of "Pericles"; they are different from the last three acts, and inferior to them. But there is a resemblance as well as a difference, and inferiority, which is always a matter of opinion, in this case is also a matter of degree. It is not impossible to believe that Shakespeare, new to the looseness inherent in the romantic form, abused his license in the beginning and hurried on to the only portion of the story that interested him: the separation of Pericles from his wife Thaisa and his infant daughter Marina, their sufferings apart from one another, and their mutual recognition at the end. If this cannot be believed, at least it can be seen that the first two acts, whoever wrote them, are necessary as temporal background to the rest; the early wanderings of Pericles, before he meets Thaisa, help to explain the special value he places upon a wife and daughter once he has them, and add their weight to the recognition scenes which are the glory of the play. If this is seen, and if furthermore it is noted that the second act is an improvement over the first, and supplies a perfect approach to the third, then it must be admitted that Shakespeare found a fragment miraculously suited to his purpose. Whatever the truth, and doubtless the truth will never be known, "Pericles" has more unity than it is the convention to acknowledge, and is of greater interest throughout.

The narrative technique with which it begins is abandoned
as soon as its function has been performed—as soon, that is,
as it has established the hero as homeless—and gives way to
the various techniques of concentration in which Shakespeare
is master. It is convenient to consider the play as one, however many its authors.

So considered, "Pericles" completely typifies the group of
plays it introduces. The emphasis here is upon father and
daughter, not husband and wife, though Thaisa's plight has
power to move us too. The story of Pericles and Marina is
the essential one—as, knowing Shakespeare's tendency to
counterpoint his main effects, we might guess from the presence in the first act of a contrasted story. The episode of
Antiochus and his daughter would be irrelevant except that
the incestuous relations between the two will be remembered
against the purity of Pericles's paternal love and Marina's
filial passion, and will give a depth to that purity such as
only the hidden sympathy beneath such contrasts can ever
give. And the later threat to Marina's chastity in the brothel
at Mytilene will balance this. As for the shipwrecks of which
"the sea-tost Pericles" is perpetually the victim, they cost
him Thaisa rather than Marina, and Thaisa is perhaps in the
foreground there. For a shipwreck landed him on her father's
shores in the first place; and the poet of the play lavishes
some of his finest lines upon her loss:

> A terrible childbed hast thou had, my dear;
> No light, no fire;                                    (III, i, 57-8)

as later upon the miracle of her awakening in Cerimon's
house:

> Gentlemen,
> This queen will live. . . . See how she gins to blow
> Into life's flower again! . . .
>                          She is alive; behold,
> Her eyelids, cases to those heavenly jewels

Which Pericles hath lost,
Begin to part their fringes of bright gold.

(III, ii, 92-101)

Yet it is Marina, born in this very tempest, to whom we are indebted for its details:

*Marina.*    When I was born, the wind was north.
*Leonine.*                                   Was 't so?
*Marina.*    My father, as nurse says, did never fear,
           But cried "Good seamen!" to the sailors, galling
           His kingly hands, haling ropes;
           And, clasping to the mast, endured a sea
           That almost burst the deck,—
*Leonine.*   When was this?
*Marina.*    When I was born;
           Never was waves nor wind more violent;—
           And from the ladder-tackle washes off
           A canvas-climber. "Ha!" says one, "wilt out?"
           And with a dropping industry they skip
           From stem to stern. The boatswain whistles, and
           The master calls, and trebles their confusion.

(IV, i, 52-65)

And between her recognition scene (v, i) and Thaisa's (v, iii) there can be no choice: the first one is the masterpiece.

Meanwhile the themes of the romances all find places in the play. Extremes of character appear not only in Antiochus and Pericles but in the bad queen Dionyza and the good queen Thaisa, not to speak of the bawds and pandars who infest Mitylene—"the poor Transylvanian is dead that lay with the little baggage" (IV, ii, 23-4). Queens are as important here as they are in fairy-tales, and there must be both kinds. The very word would seem to have taken on a special value, judging by its repetition throughout the central shipwreck scene (III, i):

How does my queen?

           Take in your arms this piece
Of your dead queen.

> Here's all that is left living of your queen.

> Sir, your queen must overboard.

Cerimon will echo it two scenes later:

> Gentlemen,
> This queen will live;

and Florizel will take it to its limit two plays later in an ultimate compliment to Perdita:

> All your acts are queens.

The pagan gods are continually referred to and invoked;
Cerimon seems to Pericles as much a god as any man can be
(v, iii, 62-3); when the hero hears of his father's death he
asks the heavens to make a star of him (v, iii, 79); and of
course Thaisa in retirement is Diana's priestess. Cerimon is
not so much a god as a magician; like Prospero he has studied
the "secret art" of physic and therefore knows

> the blest infusions
> That dwells in vegetives, in metals, stones.
>
>                                   (III, ii, 35-6)

A third father in the play, Simonides, puts on a harshness
which is not his when he pretends to think Pericles a villain
and traitor who has bewitched Thaisa; it is like the feigned
harshness of Prospero with Ferdinand, and it is prophetic of
Polixenes's actual cruelty to Florizel. On the other hand his
daughter Thaisa, like her daughter Marina, attracts the epithet "absolute" (II, v, 19; IV, Chorus, 31); for daughters here
are perfect in virtue, and Marina in the brothel is indeed "a
piece" of it (IV, vi, 118). Marina brings flowers to deck the
grave of her nurse Lychorida, and scatters their names in the
very teeth of threatened death, for Dionyza has decided that
Leonine shall kill her:

> No, I will rob Tellus of her weed,
> To strew thy green with flowers. The yellows, blues,

> The purple violets and marigolds
> Shall as a carpet hang upon thy grave
> While summer-days doth last. Ay me! poor maid,
> Born in a tempest, when my mother died,
> This world to me is like a lasting storm,
> Whirring me from my friends.          (IV, i, 14-21)

And when the identity of this untouchable maid who

> never spake bad word, nor did ill turn
> To any living creature          (IV, i, 76-7)

first dawns upon her father he has to be assured of her reality:

> But are you flesh and blood?
> Have you a working pulse, and are no fairy?
> Motion?          (V, i, 154-6)

The terms "fear" and "grief" weave a web throughout the play with "peace" and "pity." Grief flows freely from the good people—Pericles, Cerimon, Marina—and is rebuked only by the bad, as when Dionyza scolds Marina for her "unprofitable woe" (IV, i, 26). So Claudius had rebuked Hamlet; and so by this time Shakespeare has made up his mind, in spite of Richard II and Constance, to prefer those who can weep to those who cannot. Perhaps it was Leonato in "Much Ado" who settled it for him:

> But there is no such man; for, brother, men
> Can counsel and speak comfort to that grief
> Which they themselves not feel; but, tasting it,
> Their counsel turns to passion, which before
> Would give preceptial medicine to rage,
> Fetter strong madness in a silken thread,
> Charm ache with air and agony with words. . . .
> For there was never yet philosopher
> That could endure the toothache patiently.
>
>           (V, i, 20-36)

At any rate it is settled, and the marriage between tears and integrity is permanent. Unjust men cannot weep, though their victims can:

The blind mole casts
Copp'd hills towards heaven, to tell the earth is throng'd
By man's oppression; and the poor worm doth die for 't.
                                              (i, i, 100-2)

And neither can they sleep, or lie in peace, or hear sweet
music.

Pericles, says Simonides, is "Music's master" (ii, v, 30);
and though the younger man is in his own opinion "the worst
of all her scholars," in Shakespeare's mind he is worthy of
the most musical end yet given to any play. The "rough and
woeful music" which sounds while Cerimon opens Thaisa's
coffin, and the pretty strains of Marina's lute, as later of her
voice—these are of marked importance, but they are nothing
to what the father hears when he knows his daughter. First
there is the cry of his own voice—"Ho, Helicanus!"—breaking into her narrative like a trumpet. Then come the syllables, always potent in the later plays, of "sea" and "shore."
When Pericles had first suspected his daughter in the girl
before him he had said:

                Pray you, turn your eyes upon me.
        You are like something that—What country-woman?
        Here of these shores?                  (v, i, 102-4)

And she had answered:

        No, nor of any shores.

Now he entreats:

        O Helicanus, strike me, honoured sir;
        Give me a gash, put me to present pain;
        Lest this great sea of joys rushing upon me
        O'erbear the shores of my mortality,
        And drown me with their sweetness.     (v, i, 192-6)

After which there comes the climax:

Pericles.    Give me my robes. I am wild in my beholding.
             O heavens bless my girl! But, hark, what music?
             Tell Helicanus, my Marina, tell him

O'er, point by point, for yet he seems to doubt,
How sure you are my daughter. But, what music?

*Helicanus.* My lord, I hear none.

*Pericles.* None!
The music of the spheres! List, my Marina.

*Lysimachus.* It is not good to cross him; give him way.

*Pericles.* Rarest sounds! Do ye not hear?

*Lysimachus.* Music, my lord? I hear.

*Pericles.* Most heavenly music!
It nips me unto listening, and thick slumber
Hangs upon mine eyes. Let me rest.

*Lysimachus.* A pillow for his head.
So, leave him all.

(v, i, 224-38)

# CYMBELINE

THE separated persons in "Cymbeline" are husband and wife; or, since Posthumus is banished so soon after his marriage to Imogen, lover and lover. And no separation in Shakespeare is attended by so many ills. Slander and poison infect every portion of the air which these pre-Christian Britons breathe; the husband plots the wife's death and believes it has been accomplished; there is a vast deal of dangerous coming and going; and it takes a bloody war with Rome to bring the sufferers close enough together for reconcilation. The action is so complicated that only an expert can remember it. It is too complicated of course for tragedy, where the Folio classified it; and Dr. Johnson, who still considered "Cymbeline" a tragedy, had in so far some reason for writing: "To remark the folly of the fiction, the absurdity of the conduct, the confusion of the names and manners of different times, and the impossibility of the events in any system of life, were to waste criticism upon unresisting imbecility, upon faults too evident for detection, and too gross for exaggeration." The problem is to explain a certain fascination which the play nevertheless exerts, and to justify the weakness which one may well have for imbecility, if that is the word, so unresisting as to suggest that there was method in it after all. The first thing to do is to remember that "Cymbeline" is not a tragedy. And the second is to see how Shakespeare, coasting the farthest limits of romantic form, turned sensation and coincidence into gold which he could carry home.

Even among the romances "Cymbeline" is extreme. Its king is meaninglessly stern, banishing the hero with extravagant words:

> Away!
> Thou 'rt poison to my blood,        (i, i, 127-8)

and dismissing the grief of the heroine, his own daughter,
with this harsh command:

> Nay, let her languish
> A drop of blood a day; and, being aged,
> Die of this folly!        (i, i, 156-8)

Its queen is sinister in her craft; she brews poison out of innocent violets, cowslips, and primroses (i, v, 83), she knows
how to make sleep look like death, and she lectures the heroine coldly against grief, ignorant that it can be a medicine
too, as Imogen once says (iii, ii, 33). And her son Cloten,
whom Imogen had been ordered to marry instead of Posthumus, is, as the villain of the piece, so utterly out of bounds
that he becomes a clown; "this ass," as the lords at court call
him, swears horrendously that he will ravish Imogen in her
husband's clothes, but he swears with "snatches in his voice,
and burst of speaking" (iv, ii, 105-6), and is but a whining
parody of Aaron the Moor. The fairy element loses some of
its force through being associated with the rigmarole of two
princes, sons of Cymbeline, who since their abduction as
babes have been brought up in a Welsh cave and yet are
princes still; for, as Belarius their abductor says, it is hard "to
hide the sparks of nature" (iii, iii, 79). And the divine element, pursued to a point where Jupiter descends in thunder
and lightning, sitting on an eagle, to say that the sleeping
Posthumus will be all the happier for his affliction, and to
leave on his chest a riddling tablet which once interpreted
will make all clear, is perhaps grotesque.

Furthermore, the structure of romance is here fantastically
ornate. Imogen, seeking her husband in Wales, passes the
very cave where her kidnaped brothers dwell, and of course
enters it for food and rest; and this leads on to a scene such
as only a virtuoso would attempt—the funeral of a living girl,

thought to be dead by two boys who have mistaken her for
a boy and called her "brother" when in fact, and unknown
to them or her, they are her brothers, and princes at that.
Nor is this all; for when she wakes from her sleep that
looked like death she finds herself lying by one truly dead—
the headless Cloten, whom, since he is dressed in her husband's clothes, she passionately mourns. That the scene is
very affecting, and by some miracle of poetry natural, does
not for the moment matter. It is certainly fantastic, as the
"curious mantle" and the "sanguine star" by which the boys
are proved to be princes must be set down as the baggage
of romance, and as the multiple recognition scene which requires almost five hundred lines merely to suggest its possibilities—"this fierce abridgement," says Cymbeline,

> Hath to it circumstantial branches, which
> Distinction should be rich in. . . .
>                          but nor the time nor place
> Will serve our long inter'gatories—          (v, v, 382-92)

might seem to have been designed as a recognition scene to
end all recognition scenes, since it has everything in it and
more. That the scene is by some double miracle of poetry
and humanity moving, and in certain places immensely so,
does not altogether answer the epithet extreme.

Where, then, does "Cymbeline" gets its power, for it has
power? The answer is the uses to which Shakespeare has put
his extremes. In plausibility he was perhaps not interested at
all, absorbed as he must have been in the opportunities his
plot gave him for saying absolute things absolutely, and for
following to its end in Imogen the vision of an absolutely
faithful woman—absolutely faithful because absolutely in
love. But the heroine of the play cannot be understood before its style, which is the richest and most elaborate of
Shakespeare's styles thus far. The opening speech, by a
nameless gentleman of Cymbeline's court, accustoms us at
once to involution:

> You do not meet a man but frowns. Our bloods
> No more obey the heavens than our courtiers
> Still seem as does the King.

The proportion in the second sentence is less obvious than we expected, and leaves us with a sense that we should have listened more closely. The sense will be with us always, whether it is prose we hear:

He was then of a crescent note, expected to prove so worthy as since he hath been allowed the name of;          (I, iv, 2-4)

You speak of him when he was less furnish'd than now he is with that which makes him both without and within;

(I, iv, 8-10)

or whether it is verse, tangling us in excesses of syntax:

> I have given him that
> Which, if he take, shall quite unpeople her
> Of liegers for her sweet, and which she after,
> Except she bend her humour, shall be assur'd
> To taste of too.          (I, v, 78-82)

Syntax would seem with this poet to have become an occupation in itself; complex sentences, not to be parsed by thoughtless ears, are his special pleasure. And he takes a further pleasure in making familiar words do unfamiliar work: "rather than story him in his own hearing," "to the madding of her lord," "when we shall hear the rain and wind beat dark December," "in simple and low things to prince it much beyond the trick of others," "thy memory will then be pang'd by me," "to winter-ground thy corse," "the holy eagle stoop'd, as to foot us." This is always the privilege of poets, and Shakespeare has made full use of the privilege before; but he has never been so ingenious at coining verbs. His style is on the stretch. To the brevity of phrase that distinguished "Antony and Cleopatra" are added further brevities, sometimes perverse, and still more nervous tensions. It is the style of a man whose determination is to reach extremes

of statement with as few preliminaries as possible. His people
are deadly earnest in their exaggeration:

> I'll drink the words you send,
> Though ink be made of gall.                    (I, i, 100-1)

> Should we be taking leave
> As long a term as yet we have to live,
> The loathness to depart would grow.            (I, i, 106-8)

> I am senseless of your wrath; a touch more rare
> Subdues all pangs, all fears.                   (I, i, 135-6)

> Such boil'd stuff
> As well might poison poison!                    (I, vi, 125-6)

> Why should I write this down, that's riveted,
> Screw'd to my memory?                           (II, ii, 43-4)

> What shall I need to draw my sword? The paper
> Hath cut her throat already.                    (III, iv, 34-5)

> I had rather
> Have skipp'd from sixteen years of age to sixty,
> To have turn'd my leaping-time into a crutch,
> Than have seen this.                            (IV, ii, 198-201)

> So I'll die
> For thee, O Imogen, even for whom my life
> Is every breath a death.                        (V, i, 25-7)

This is the speech of persons for whom there are but two
alternatives, all and none; as when Posthumus puts an end to
Iachimo's slander of Imogen with the desperate words:

> Spare your arithmetic; never count the turns;
> Once, and a million!                            (II, iv, 142-3)

The music of praise has never in Shakespeare been so elaborate. The gentleman of the opening scene says of Posthumus
that he
> is a creature such
> As, to seek through the regions of the earth
> For one his like, there would be something failing

In him that should compare. I do not think
So fair an outward and such stuff within
Endows a man but he.

And when the second gentleman remarks that this is far
praise indeed, the first insists:

I do extend him, sir, within himself,
Crush him together rather than unfold
His measure duly.

Posthumus is not only a sample to the youngest, he is a guide
for dotards—he is all that man can be, and the final proof of
this is that such a woman as Imogen has elected him husband.
Not that the praise of Imogen will always be indirect.
Iachimo, setting eyes on her, exclaims to himself:

All of her that is out of door most rich!
If she be furnish'd with a mind so rare,
She is alone, the Arabian bird.              (I, vi, 15-7)

And if he is disingenuous when he tells her that Posthumus
sits among men like a descended god (I, vi, 169), he will be
sincere when in his confession at the end he calls his injured
friend "the best of all amongst the rar'st of good ones" (v, v,
159-60). Nor will good old Belarius fail of conviction as he
deifies Fidele:

By Jupiter, an angel! or, if not,
An earthly paragon! Behold divineness
No elder than a boy;                         (III, vi, 43-5)

or as he anoints the princes whose natural father he can no
longer seem to be:

I must lose
Two of the sweet'st companions in the world.
The benediction of these covering heavens
Fall on their heads like dew! for they are worthy
To inlay heaven with stars.              (v, v, 348-52)

The language of praise in this play has found its absolute
grammar—as, when Imogen hears Cloten call Posthumus a

base slave, the reverse language of denunciation comes correspondingly into its own:

> Wert thou the son of Jupiter and no more
> But what thou art besides, thou wert too base
> To be his groom. Thou wert dignified enough,
> Even to the point of envy, if 't were made
> Comparative for your virtues, to be styl'd
> The under-hangman of his kingdom, and hated
> For being preferr'd so well . . .
> He never can meet more mischance than come
> To be but nam'd of thee. His meanest garment
> That ever hath but clipp'd his body, is dearer
> In my respect than all the hairs above thee,
> Were they all made such men.     (II, iii, 130-41)

Imogen is one of the great women of Shakespeare or the world. The absoluteness of her fidelity comes from the absoluteness of her love, the intensity of which has more than saved the play—has endowed it with a unique fascination. Her virtue is not a named thing like Isabella's, nor is she conscious of it as virtue. And her devotion is to Viola's as avalanches are to aromas—swift, full-bodied, not to be withstood. Neither has it any of the rankness which reduced Helena's at times to the level of barbarism. Being complete, it has its pressing tendernesses, its urgent delicacies, its passionate reserves. Its influence spreads through all of the play that can contain it; makes Iachimo by contact a great poet, and fills the figure of Posthumus with seriousness which otherwise it would have lacked. Posthumus exists through Imogen, as Iachimo through both. Her speech has everywhere a force beyond which poetry can scarcely go, and this is true whether she is expressing herself in short, sharp, compendious queries and interjections: "Will my lord say so?", "Not he, I hope," "Am I one, sir?", "Let me hear no more," "You make amends," "To pieces with me!", "Soft, soft, we'll no defence," "Do 't, and to bed then," "Talk thy tongue weary; speak," "What, good fellow, what shall I do the while? Where bide? How live?", "Nay, be brief"; or whether she is delivering her mind of sudden metaphors: "In a great pool a swan's nest" (III, iv, 142), "but if there be yet left in heaven as small a drop of pity as a wren's eye" (IV, ii, 303-5); or whether she is pursuing to its limit in long discourse the theme of her incomparable attachment. The dialogue which opens the third scene would alone distinguish the play, and certainly it lets us feel, before we have gone any farther, the fierceness along with the beauty of our heroine's temper.

*Imogen.* I would thou grew'st unto the shores o' the haven,
And question'dst every sail. If he should write
And I not have it, 't were a paper lost,
As offer'd mercy is. What was the last
That he spake to thee?
*Pisanio.* It was his queen, his queen!
*Imogen.* Than wav'd his handkerchief?
*Pisanio.* And kiss'd it, madam.
*Imogen.* Senseless linen! happier therein than I!
And that was all?
*Pisanio.* No, madam; for so long
As he could make me with this eye or ear
Distinguish him from others, he did keep
The deck, with glove, or hat, or handkerchief,
Still waving, as the fits and stirs of 's mind
Could best express how slow his soul sail'd on,
How swift his ship.
*Imogen.* Thou shouldst have made him
As little as a crow, or less, ere left
To after-eye him.
*Pisanio.* Madam, so I did.
*Imogen.* I would have broke mine eye-strings; crack'd them, but
To look upon him, till the diminution
Of space had pointed him sharp as my needle;
Nay, follow'd him, till he had melted from
The smallness of a gnat to air, and then
Have turn'd mine eye and wept.

Imogen in her urgency, her insistence which is never quite
hysteria, creates Posthumus through her love, and even
brings his servant to the point of being a fine poet. For Pisanio shares with her the moments when she speaks best—
the moment, for another instance, when she reads the letter
from Posthumus which he has given her:

> O, for a horse with wings! Hear'st thou, Pisanio?
> He is at Milford-Haven. Read, and tell me
> How far 't is thither. If one of mean affairs
> May plod it in a week, why may not I
> Glide thither in a day? Then, true Pisanio,—
> Who long'st, like me, to see thy lord; who long'st,—
> O, let me bate,—but not like me—yet long'st,
> But in a fainter kind;—O, not like me,
> For mine's beyond beyond—say, and speak thick,—
> Love's counsellor should fill the bores of hearing,
> To the smothering of the sense—how far it is
> To this same blessed Milford; and by the way
> Tell me how Wales was made so happy as
> To inherit such a haven.            (III, ii, 50-63)

This is not hysteria, it is rapture. The woman who bears
down upon Pisanio and us with such a rush of eagerness,
such tornadoes of joy, is herself whole and strong.

The authenticity of her passion is what converts the make-
believe of her "funeral" into one of Shakespeare's most successful scenes. The "death" of Juliet in her father's house had
been affecting, but the ritual of this burial is profound in its
sweetness.

> With female fairies will his tomb be haunted,
> And worms will not come to thee.      (IV, ii, 217-8)

The fairy theme is restored to its dignity there, as the flower
theme is rescued from the degradation to which the Queen
has condemned it.

> With fairest flowers
> Whilst summer lasts and I live here, Fidele,
> I'll sweeten thy sad grave. Thou shalt not lack

The flower that's like thy face, pale primrose, nor
The azur'd harebell, like thy veins, no, nor
The leaf of eglantine, whom not to slander,
Out-sweet'ned not thy breath. The ruddock would,
With charitable bill . . . bring thee all this;
Yea, and furr'd moss besides, when flowers are none,
To winter-ground thy corse. . . .
Here's a few flowers; but 'bout midnight, more.
The herbs that have on them cold dew o' the night
Are strewings fitt'st for graves.      (IV, ii, 218-29; 283-5)

And the chanting of her funeral song by boys whose voices
are changing so that they cannot sing "Fear no more the heat
o' the sun" is in itself a symbol of her clear, pure seriousness.
But there is another scene which she saves for greatness. The
recognition scene (v, v) draws all of its power from her;
first when she fixes her eyes on Iachimo across the room,
saying                                I see a thing
          Bitter to me as death,                        (103-4)

and later when, having been struck to the floor by Posthumus in the rage which precedes recognition, and having
had at last a few moments of silence with him while Cymbeline and Cornelius speak, she teases him with the question:

          Why did you throw your wedded lady from you?
          Think that you are upon a rock, and now
          Throw me again.                                (261-3)

To which, whether "rock" (precipice) or "lock" (as in
wrestling) is the word Shakespeare wrote, and either would
fit the speaker, Posthumus's response is adequate at last:

                    Hang there like fruit, my soul,
          Till the tree die!

# THE WINTER'S TALE

"THE WINTER'S TALE" tells of grievous divisions between friend and friend (Leontes and Polixenes), king and queen (Leontes and Hermione), father and daughter (Leontes and Perdita); and, after sixteen years, between father and son (Polixenes and Florizel). The "wide gap of time" which goes unchronicled between the third and fourth acts might seem to give us two plays instead of one, but there is only one. It is conceived in contrast, and it is dedicated to the task of stating with all the force of which poetry is capable the opposition between age and youth, cruelty and goodness, jealousy and faith. The abstract symbols it employs are winter and spring: winter with its blasts of January and storm perpetual, spring with its virgin branches and its daffodils that come before the swallow dares. But its concrete symbols are of course human beings; Leontes and Perdita divide this great poem between them—the one an obsessed husband and ruthless father, the other a faultless daughter, ignorant of her parentage, who grows up in a cottage, not a court, and who restores to the final plays that maiden image which Imogen had for the moment obscured. "A sad tale's best for winter," Mamillius tells Hermione, and a series of happy endings does not make this poem gay. Leontes's half is never lost in Perdita's, however much its memory is softened. The play is one but its halves are two, and each of them underlines the other.

Leontes infects the whole of the first three acts with the angry sore of his obsession. There is no more jealous man in literature. Once being jealous Othello could go mad, but the jealousy of Leontes is madness from the start, and it has a curious way of feeding on itself, so that the delusion which inspires it is worse than irresistible; it is nothing less than the condition of its victim's life, and the expression of it gives him in some perverse way a horrible pleasure. The intensity of his speech is out of all proportion to its cause; there is no cause, nor has Shakespeare bothered to prove that this is so, his interest being confined to the deep, straight line he wants to draw, the instance of evil he needs to begin with. We are not shown that Hermione is innocent of adultery with Leontes's boyhood friend Polixenes, the King of Bohemia who has been visiting him so many months. We assume that she is, even though the Sicilian court is a brilliantly and frankly sensual place, the heavy richness of whose life and the animal leisureliness of whose pleasures we gather at once from the courtesy of the first scene and from the luxury of the second. Both are baroque, and it cannot be said of the two kings that they who once were "pretty lordings" and "twinn'd lambs" have grown into ascetics, or that Hermione, queen to Leontes, longs delicately for compliment.

> I prithee tell me; cram 's with praise, and make 's
> As fat as tame things. One good deed dying tongueless
> Slaughters a thousand waiting upon that.
> Our praises are our wages; you may ride 's
> With one soft kiss a thousand furlongs ere
> With spur we heat an acre.                      (I, ii, 91-6)

We assume that Hermione is innocent; and go on to understand why the delusion of Leontes should be so luxuriant, why the poetry in which he embalms it should seem to be that of a man whose appetite for expressing himself is fierce and unnatural, as if it fed riotously on words and heated itself to a fever with wild phrases. His speech is not the clear, cool, perfect speech of Perdita sixteen years later. It is mad with its own riches, and fiery-red with a rash of exaggeration. His first aside, after he has commanded Hermione to urge upon their guest a still longer stay and she has done so

by placing her hand in that of Polixenes, opens his whole
mind to us:

>                    Too hot, too hot!
> To mingle friendship far is mingling bloods.
> I have *tremor cordis* on me; my heart dances,
> But not for joy; not joy. This entertainment
> May a free face put on, derive a liberty
> From heartiness, from bounty, fertile bosom,
> And well become the agent; 't may, I grant;
> But to be paddling palms and pinching fingers,
> As now they are, and making practis'd smiles,
> As in a looking-glass; and then to sigh, as 't were
> The mort o' the deer;—O, that is entertainment
> My bosom likes not, nor my brows!        (I, ii, 108-19)

It is a mind in which images of his betrayal work like mag-
gots, swarming and increasing with every moment of his
thought. The good Camillo's denial that Hermione can be
false brings on a fury of evidence, all of it perversely imagined; and there is more of it now than there was a few minutes past:

>                    Is whispering nothing?
> Is leaning cheek to cheek? Is meeting noses?
> Kissing with inside lip? stopping the career
> Of laughter with a sigh?—a note infallible
> Of breaking honesty;—horsing foot on foot?
> Skulking in corners? wishing clocks more swift?
> Hours, minutes? noon, midnight? and all eyes
> Blind with the pin-and-web but theirs, theirs only,
> That would unseen be wicked? Is this nothing?
> Why, then the world and all that's in 't is nothing;
> The covering sky is nothing; Bohemia nothing;
> My wife is nothing; nor nothing have these nothings,
> If this be nothing.                      (I, ii, 284-96)

The mind of Leontes always rushes. A single epithet or conceit is rarely sufficient to express his nerve-racked bitter madness; he must find others at once and pile them on, or he
must extend the one he has by repetition and hyperbole:

Inch-thick, knee-deep, o'er head and ears a fork'd one!

(I, ii, 186)

                    Was this taken
By any understanding pate but thine?
For thy conceit is soaking,—will draw in
More than the common blocks. Not noted, is 't,
But of the finer natures? By some severals
Of head-piece extraordinary? Lower messes
Perchance are to this business purblind?          (I, ii, 222-8)

He must develop every idea until it is grotesque, and his brain exhausts itself in a search for terms and analogies; though it soon is itself again, and rages on. He is sometimes so difficult that we cannot follow the twists of his thinking:

Affection! thy intention stabs the centre.
Thou dost make possible things not so held,
Communicat'st with dreams;—how can this be?—
With what's unreal thou coactive art,
And fellow'st nothing. Then 't is very credent
Thou mayst co-join with something; and thou dost,
And that beyond commission.          (I, ii, 138-44)

This is the obscurest passage in Shakespeare, and it is no wonder that Polixenes puts in: "What means Sicilia?" Leontes means in general that the impossible has become all too possible, but the particulars of his meaning are his own. His utterances are half to himself, fitting the creases of his thought rather than the form of any truth; and they exactly, insanely, fit:

                    There have been,
Or I am much deceiv'd, cuckolds ere now;
And many a man there is, even at this present,
Now while I speak this, holds his wife by the arm,
That little thinks she has been sluic'd in 's absence
And his pond fish'd by his next neighbour, by
Sir Smile, his neighbour.          (I, ii, 190-6)

                    How blest am I
In my just censure, in my true opinion!
Alack, for lesser knowledge! How accurs'd

In being so blest! There may be in the cup
A spider steep'd, and one may drink, depart,
And yet partake no venom, for his knowledge
Is not infected; but if one present
The abhorr'd ingredient to his eye, make known
How he hath drunk, he cracks his gorge, his sides,
With violent hefts. I have drunk, and seen the spider.

(II, i, 36-45)

Nor night nor day no rest. It is but weakness
To bear the matter thus; mere weakness. If
The cause were not in being,—part of the cause,
She the adulteress; for the harlot king
Is quite beyond mine arm, out of the blank
And level of my brain, plot-proof; but she
I can hook to me: say that she were gone,
Given to the fire, a moiety of my rest
Might come to me again.                (II, iii, 1-9)

He is never at a loss for something to say; ideas or pieces of
ideas pour into his brain pell-mell, so that he cannot find
enough room there to make all of them comfortable. The
epithets he lays upon the good Paulina—"gross hag," "a callat
of boundless tongue," "a mankind witch," "a most intelli-
gencing bawd"—seem to torture him as well as slander her;
and the fallacies his mind commits are such as only frenzy
can account for, as when he answers Hermione's appeal to
his memory of her honorable behavior with this outrageous
logic:                        I ne'er heard yet
          That any of these bolder vices wanted
          Less impudence to gainsay what they did
          Than to perform it first.        (III, ii, 55-8)

Leontes is an artist of jealousy, an expert in self-hurt, and
he so utterly dominates the first half of the play as to keep
other speakers, brilliant though they may also be, secondary
to himself. Polixenes, for instance, who shares with his old
friend the fashion of intricate speech, is buried under that
same friend's abuse. Paulina, whose tirades are no more won-

derful than the eight words she addresses to Leontes when
Hermione swoons:

> Look down
> And see what Death is doing,        (III, ii, 149-50)

shines only in her antagonism to a king's injustice. Even
Hermione, who can say

> I love thee not a jar o' the clock behind
> What lady she her lord,               (I, ii, 43-4)

who remembers her father and wishes he were alive to behold his daughter's trial, and who knows how to make up
with tenderness and story-telling for the irritation her preg-
nancy has made her feel in the presence of the boy Mamillius
(II, i), is lost in the less admirable figure of Leontes. Leontes
is less admirable than anybody, but the disease of his suspi-
cion is one whose progress we watch spellbound. And from
the first it declares itself as a disturbance from which the play
cannot be expected wholly or at any rate blithely to recover.
It is an absolute crime, and he will never be able to expiate it
without the help of grace; sixteen years of "saint-like sorrow" will not teach him how to forget a fit of jealousy so
extreme, so baseless, as to have needed the oracle of Delphi
for its correction. He has done damage that cannot ade-
quately be undone; first of course to Hermione, and through
her to Mamillius, but after that to the infant daughter he has
refused to recognize as his and sent with the good Antigonus
—for the play has its trio of ineffectual saints—to death on the
seacoast of Bohemia. That the exposed infant does not die,
but is found in a transition scene by two ineffable shepherds
along with the fairy gold Antigonus has left for the finder,
gives us Perdita, and Perdita will grow up in a shepherd's
cottage to be Leontes's grace. From now on it is Perdita's
play, and her delicious presence in it will restore "spring to
the earth" (V, i, 152). Yet even in her presence the past of
Leontes will not be forgotten, nor will the world of the play

be wholly what it was before he drank the spider. The formula of reconciliation is honored, but the second half of "The Winter's Tale" still has its gravity, its veins of dark iron across an otherwise untroubled pattern.

The famous scene of the sheep-shearing (IV, iv) balances all that Leontes has been, and Florizel, son of Polixenes, begins it with a pretty compliment to the maiden across whose "father's" ground his falcon has flown: Perdita, he says, seems in her unusual weeds to be

> no shepherdess, but Flora,
> Peering in April's front.

Yet it is not April, nor is it any other month of spring. When Polixenes comes in disguise, hoping to catch his heir in the act of wooing a poor nobody, the flowers she offers him are "flowers of winter."

> Sir, the year growing ancient,
> Not yet on summer's death, nor on the birth
> Of trembling winter, the fairest flowers o' the season
> Are our carnations and streak'd gillyflowers,
> Which some call Nature's bastards. Of that kind
> Our rustic garden's barren; and I care not
> To get slips of them.                    (IV, iv, 79-85)

Perdita, whose preference for nature over art is so simple and stubborn that the King's quibble about art as the offspring of nature has no effect upon her whatever, lives here in the light of the last sun, not the first. She has "flowers of middle summer" to bestow upon her guests of middle age, but there are no "flowers o' the spring" to deck the youth of Florizel.

> O Proserpina,
> For the flowers now, that frighted thou let'st fall
> From Dis's wagon! daffodils,
> That come before the swallow dares, and take
> The winds of March with beauty; violets dim,
> But sweeter than the lids of Juno's eyes
> Or Cytherea's breath; pale primroses,

> That die unmarried, ere they can behold
> Bright Phoebus in his strength—a malady
> Most incident to maids; bold oxlips and
> The crown imperial; lilies of all kinds,
> The flower-de-luce being one! O, these I lack.
>
> (IV, iv, 116-27)

This is a sad speech, not a merry one; it is homesick for blossoms which an older generation will never see again in their original innocence. Perdita does not know this, nor does Florizel, for both of them will laugh in many springs; but their special charm resides for us in the fact that they stand adoring each other in the sunset of the year, in a glow whose depth they are too young to measure. Such a compliment as Florizel pays Perdita when she recovers from her eloquence and asks his pardon for her Whitsun-pastoral pose is not to be found anywhere else in Shakespeare, late or early:

> What you do
> Still betters what is done. When you speak, sweet,
> I'd have you do it ever; when you sing,
> I'd have you buy and sell so, so give alms,
> Pray so; and for the ord'ring your affairs,
> To sing them too. When you do dance, I wish you
> A wave o' the sea, that you might ever do
> Nothing but that; move still, still so,
> And own no other function. Each your doing,
> So singular in each particular,
> Crowns what you are doing in the present deeds,
> That all your acts are queens.       (IV, iv, 135-46)

Shakespeare only now has the art—and the feeling—to write so profoundly well. But that is because he sees a shadow falling across his perfect pair even while they feed on each other's smiles. All the merriment of this long scene, with its masques and dances and the surpassing roguery of Autolycus:

Here's another ballad of a fish that appeared upon the coast on Wednesday the fourscore of April, forty thousand fathom

above water, and sung this ballad against the hard hearts of
maids,                                              (IV, iv, 279-83)

cannot prevent one blast of January still to come—the wrath
of Polixenes, so singularly like the wrath of Leontes sixteen
years ago, when he throws off his disguise and becomes another example of the unaccountably vicious father, threaten-
ing to disinherit Florizel, hang the shepherd, and scratch
Perdita's beauty with briers (IV, iv, 427-51). Autolycus was
littered under Mercury, but this is some hairy god more
ancient than Jove and ten times more terrible in his caprice.
Time of course goes on and all parties are reconciled:
Polixenes with Florizel and Perdita, Leontes with Perdita and
Hermione, and the two kings with each other. But Shakespeare disappoints our expectation in one important respect.
The recognition of Leontes and his daughter takes place off
the stage; we only hear three gentlemen talking prose about
it (v, ii), and are denied the satisfaction of such a scene as
we might have supposed would crown the play. The reason
may be that Shakespeare was weary of a plot which already
had complicated itself beyond comfort; or that a recognition
scene appeared in his mind more due to Hermione, considering the age and degree of her sufferings, than to that "most
peerless piece of earth" Perdita. In poetic justice he gave it
to Hermione, and we have the business of a statue coming
to life while music plays (v, iii). But the poetry he actually
had written required that Perdita should have it. Perhaps he
could not imagine—though this itself is hard to imagine—what
Leontes would say. For Leontes had done what no words,
even Shakespeare's words, could utterly undo. Mamillius and
Antigonus had lost their lives, an oracle had been blas-
phemed, a wife had been slandered, love had been defiled.
The griefs of Pericles had been fate's doing, and those of
Posthumus had been an Italian fiend's. Those of Leontes had
been his own, and the reward he merited was a muted joy.

# THE TEMPEST

IF Shakespeare thought of "The Tempest" as the last play he would write he may have said to himself— silently, we must assume—that he could afford to let action come in it to a kind of rest; that its task was not so much to tell a story as to fix a vision; that the symbols he hitherto had defined his art by concealing might now confess themselves, even obtrude themselves, in measured dance and significant song; and that while he was at it he would reca- pitulate his poetic career. It is interesting to conjecture thus, but it is perilous. "The Tempest" does bind up in final form a host of themes with which its author has been concerned. It is a mirror in which, if we hold it very still, we can gaze backward at all of the recent plays; and behind them will be glimpses of a past as old as the tragedies, the middle com- edies, and even "A Midsummer Night's Dream." Or it is a thicket of resonant trees, in an odd angle of the Shakespear- ean wood, which hums with echoes of every distant aisle. And certainly its symbols expose themselves as their ancestors in Shakespeare seldom or never did. The play seems to order itself in terms of its meanings; things in it stand for other things, so that we are tempted to search its dark backward for a single meaning, quite final for Shakespeare and quite abstract. The trouble is that the meanings are not self-evi- dent. One interpretation of "The Tempest" does not agree with another. And there is deeper trouble in the truth that any interpretation, even the wildest, is more or less plausible. This deep trouble, and this deep truth, should warn us that "The Tempest" is a composition about which we had better not be too knowing. If it is one of Shakespeare's successes, and obviously it is, it will not yield its secret easily; or it has no secret to yield. Notwithstanding its visionary grace, its tendency toward lyric abstraction, it keeps that lifelike surface and that humor with which Shakespeare has always protected his meaning if he had one: that impenetrable shield off which the spears of interpretation invariably glance—or return, bent in the shaft and dulled at the point, to the hand of the thrower. It may well be that Shakespeare in "The Tempest" is telling us for the last time, and consciously for the last time, about the world. But what he is telling us cannot be simple, or we could agree that it is this or that. Perhaps it is this: that the world is not simple. Or, mysteriously enough, that it is what we all take it to be, just as "The Tempest" is whatever we would take it to be. Any set of symbols, moved close to this play, lights up as in an electric field. Its meaning, in other words, is precisely as rich as the human mind, and it says that the world is what it is. But what the world is cannot be said in a sentence. Or even in a poem as complete and beautiful as "The Tempest."

Separations and reconciliations are woven here within the circle of a remote and musical island where an enchanter, controlling the black magic of native witchcraft with the white magic of his liberal art, controls also a tempest until it brings to pass all things he has desired. The ship it founders on the shore, or seems to founder, carries his two chief enemies: his brother Antonio, whose treason has put the sea between them, and Alonso king of Naples, confederate to this treason. Prospero as duke of Milan had honored his brother with "confidence sans bound." But Antonio had abused his trust, and that is the first separation. The second has occurred likewise before the play begins, and nothing in the play can cure it. Alonso has lost his fair daughter Claribel by marriage to the King of Tunis, and indeed it is from that "sweet marriage" that he is returning, bound sadly home for Naples, when he suffers shipwreck on Prospero's island.

Alonso's loss of his remaining heir, his son Ferdinand, is temporary in so far as Prospero merely keeps them apart on the island until the separation has served its purpose, meanwhile entertaining the prince with the unearthly music of Ariel and with the charms of his own daughter Miranda; but it is permanent when Ferdinand and Miranda give themselves away to each other in love. And by the same blow, happy though it be, Prospero loses Miranda. The plot of "The Tempest" is a complex of separations—and, swiftly and harmoniously, of reconciliations, so that Gonzalo can say:

> In one voyage
> Did Claribel her husband find at Tunis,
> And Ferdinand, her brother, found a wife
> Where he himself was lost, Prospero his dukedom
> In a poor isle, and all of us ourselves
> When no man was his own.               (v, i, 208-13)

But we have known from the beginning that Gonzalo would have grounds for speaking so. Prospero's isle is not poor; it is rich and strange and full of fair noises, and the magic with which he controls it will maneuver all lives into peace. We know this not merely from his assuring Miranda in the second scene that the sea-storm has been "safely ordered" (29), or from Ariel's report that not a hair has perished (217), but from the sense we always have here that danger is not real, that artifice is disarmingly at work, and that woe is only waiting upon sea-change. Tides of understanding must "shortly fill the reasonable shore" (v, i, 79-82) when music like this music plays—constantly, and with such continuing sweetness that the one unregenerate person on the island can speak of "sounds and sweet airs that give delight and hurt not" (iii, ii, 145).

The hag-born Caliban is not deaf to the "thousand twangling instruments" that hum about his ears. He is, however, the lowest inhabitant of the play; the human scale which Shakespeare has built begins with him. The island as we have

it is among other things a microcosm of humanity, and its
meanest soul smells music rather than apprehends it; or re-
ceives it at any rate in his grosser senses. We know Caliban
first of all by his style, which may not be the "special language" an old critical tradition says it is, but which gives us a
creature complete in beastliness. His characteristic speech
does not open the mouth to music; it closes it rather on harsh,
hissing, or guttural consonants that in the slowness with
which they must be uttered express the difficult progress of a
mind bemired in fact, an imagination beslimed with particulars. Caliban has no capacity for abstraction, and consequently
for the rational harmonies of music and love.

> As wicked dew as e'er my mother brush'd
> With raven's feather from unwholesome fen
> Drop on you both! A south-west blow on ye
> And blister you all o'er!                    (i, ii, 321-4)

The second of these sentences is scarcely articulated; it is a
mouthed curse which no tongue's skill can refine.

> This island's mine, by Sycorax my mother,
> Which thou tak'st from me. When thou cam'st first,
> Thou strok'dst me and made much of me, wouldst give me
> Water with berries in 't, and teach me how
> To name the bigger light, and how the less,
> That burn by day and night; and then I lov'd thee
> And show'd thee all the qualities o' the isle,
> The fresh springs, brine-pits, barren place and fertile.
> Curs'd be I that did so! All the charms
> Of Sycorax, toads, beetles, bats, light on you!    (i, ii, 331-40)

"Thou strok'dst me and made much of me"—the second
word is a thicket of vile sound, and the m's that follow are
the mutterings of less than human lips.

> All the infections that the sun sucks up
> From bogs, fens, flats, on Prosper fall and make him
> By inch-meal a disease! His spirits hear me
> And yet I needs must curse. But they'll nor pinch,

> Fright me with urchin-shows, pitch me i' the mire,
> Nor lead me, like a firebrand, in the dark
> Out of my way, unless he bid 'em; but
> For every trifle are they set upon me,
> Sometime like apes that mow and chatter at me
> And after bite me, then like hedgehogs which
> Lie tumbling in my barefoot way and mount
> Their pricks at my footfall; sometime am I
> All wound with adders who with cloven tongues
> Do hiss me into madness.                    (II, ii, 1-14)

"Like hedgehogs which lie tumbling"—the tongue of the speaker is thick in his throat, his palate is untrained.

> Pray you, tread softly, that the blind mole may not
> Hear a foot fall.                           (IV, i, 194-5)

Out of its context this has been thought pretty, but its context is an island among whose pits and thistles Caliban roots more like a hog than a man. He knows every detail of the place but he understands nothing.

> I'll show thee every fertile inch o' the island. . . .
> I'll show thee the best springs; I'll pluck thee berries;
> I'll fish for thee and get thee wood enough. . . .
> I prithee, let me bring thee where crabs grow;
> And I with my long nails will dig thee pig-nuts;
> Show thee a jay's nest and instruct thee how
> To snare the nimble marmoset, I'll bring thee
> To clust'ring filberts and sometimes I'll get thee
> Young scamels from the rock.                 (II, ii, 151-76)

"I'll dig thee pig-nuts," he promises the drunken Stephano, ignorant that Stephano is not a god. It may not matter what relation Caliban bears to Montaigne's cannibal—whether he is an answer to the doctrine of the noble savage, or whether he supports the doctrine by showing how nature is degraded upon contact with culture—so long as one sees that in Prospero's mind, which is the only mind where he counts, he is uneducable. He cannot take any print of goodness; he has that in him which good natures cannot abide to be with; he is a born devil on whose nature nurture can never stick. The phrases are Prospero's, for it is only Prospero who has taken pains with this thing of deformity, and it is only he who cares that failure has been his reward. He has failed with Caliban, either because Caliban was incapable of becoming man or because there is no art, Prospero's or Shakespeare's, by which the inhuman can be made human. Caliban represents the lower limit, as Prospero to his own confusion forgets for a moment when he loses himself in a certain "vanity" of his art and entertains Ferdinand with the pageant of Iris, Ceres, Juno, and the Naiads. Remembering Caliban's plot against his life, and remembering even more the intractable nature of the beast, he starts suddenly and waves the pageant away —explaining to Ferdinand that it has melted into air even as the earth will dissolve into sleep when its dreamer ceases to dream:

> You do look, my son, in a mov'd sort,
> As if you were dismay'd. Be cheerful, sir,
> Our revels now are ended. These our actors,
> As I foretold you, were all spirits, and
> Are melted into air, into thin air;
> And, like the baseless fabric of this vision,
> The cloud-capp'd towers, the gorgeous palaces,
> The solemn temples, the great globe itself,
> Yea, all which it inherit, shall dissolve
> And, like this insubstantial pageant faded,
> Leave not a rack behind. We are such stuff
> As dreams are made on, and our little life
> Is rounded with a sleep.          (IV, i, 146-58)

Scarcely higher on the scale than Caliban stand Trinculo and Stephano—or reel, for they are drunken rascals past reform, and there is no promise for them, as there is for Alonso and Antonio, of "a clear life ensuing" (III, iii, 82). Alonso and Antonio will reach the reasonable shore and own themselves again. When they do they will find Gonzalo there, for he has never strayed away. The good old counselor who made it possible for Prospero to survive the voyage from Milan with his daughter and his secret books, who amuses three cynical gentlemen with talk of the golden age (II, i, 143-79), who seasons all of his discourse with a wise wit, and who upon recognizing Prospero can weep, has always been possessed of an honor which "cannot be measur'd or confin'd" (v, i, 121-2). He sits near the top of the scale, just beneath the honey-throated Ferdinand and his admired Miranda. The top is reserved for these young lovers who have yet to know the world, and who for that reason alone are its best lovers. Ferdinand is all gallantry and devotion, and the compliments he pays his island mistress are worthy of one who when she first saw him could say: "Nothing natural I ever saw so noble" (I, ii, 418-9). He had seemed to her almost divine, as if the upper human limit were more than reached in him. He continues to deserve her wonder, as she his:

> You, O you,
> So perfect and so peerless, are created
> Of every creature's best. . . . I
> Beyond all limit of what else i' the world
> Do love, prize, honour you.           (III, i, 46-73)

Miranda, as her name half tells, is all tears and wonder. Her pity is had before it is asked, since she is without guile; and she knows how to weep for joy when Ferdinand returns her adoration. And if Shakespeare was thinking of "The Tempest" as his last play he may have written a special meaning, not to say a special irony, into these now famous words:

> O, wonder!
> How many goodly creatures are there here!
> How beauteous mankind is! O brave new world,
> That has such people in 't!           (v, i, 181-4)

" 'T is new to thee," says Prospero quietly, noting that Miranda is more beautiful than any man she beholds, and more virtuous. The carcass of the world that age hands on to youth is suddenly not a carcass but a brave new goodly thing. There is mystery in that, and an irony which works either way, for both age and youth are as right as they are wrong.

Prospero is in one sense not measured on the scale, since he himself is its measurer. Yet he has human traits, one of which is his pride in his art and another of which is his sternness as he employs it. For he belongs among the strict elders of the later plays; his behavior not only toward Caliban but toward the delightful Ariel is harsh with threats and curses, and if his cruelty to Ferdinand is only feigned "lest too light winning make the prize light" (i, ii, 451-2), the feigner at least is master of the mood.

> My father's of a better nature, sir,
> Than he appears by speech.        (i, ii, 496-7)

But Miranda does not know her father perfectly. She perhaps does not follow the turnings of his great speech on dreams. She has never shared with him the secret knowledge to which he bids farewell as he breaks his wand and takes breath for a masterpiece of hymn new-harmonized from Arthur Golding's Ovid:

> Ye elves of hills, brooks, standing lakes, and groves,
> And ye that on the sands with printless foot
> Do chase the ebbing Neptune, and do fly him
> When he comes back; you demi-puppets that
> By moonshine do the green sour ringlets make,
> Whereof the ewe not bites; and you whose pastime
> Is to make midnight mushrooms, that rejoice
> To hear the solemn curfew; by whose aid,
> Weak masters though ye be, I have bedimm'd
> The noontide sun, call'd forth the mutinous winds,
> And 'twixt the green sea and the azur'd vault
> Set roaring war; to the dread rattling thunder
> Have I given fire, and rifted Jove's stout oak
> With his own bolt; the strong-bas'd promontory
> Have I made shake, and by the spurs pluck'd up
> The pine and cedar; graves at my command

Have wak'd their sleepers, op'd, and let 'em forth
By my so potent art. But this rough magic
I here abjure, and, when I have requir'd
Some heavenly music, which even now I do,
To work mine end upon their senses that
This airy charm is for, I'll break my staff,
Bury it certain fathoms in the earth,
And deeper than did ever plummet sound
I'll drown my book.                                    (v, i, 33-57)

And if she is giving him any attention at the end she probably does not guess what he means when he speaks of a retirement to Milan

where
Every third thought shall be my grave.
(v, i, 310-11)

The meaning may be Shakespeare's no less than Prospero's. If so, the ambiguity does admirably for an ending note.

Is Shakespeare Prospero, and is his magic the art with which he has fabricated thirty-seven plays? Is he now burying his book—abandoning the theater—and retiring where every third thought will be his grave? And does "The Tempest" so signify? Answers are not too easy. Shakespeare has never dramatized himself before, and it may not have occurred to him to do so now. Also, "The Tempest" is not a cantata; it is still a play, and it is ballasted with much life. It has snarling beasts and belching drunkards to match its innocent angels and white magicians. It contains two of Shakespeare's finest songs—"Full fathom five thy father lies" and "Come unto these yellow sands"—and two of his coarsest—"'Ban, 'Ban, Cacaliban" and "The master, the swabber, the boatswain, and I." And Ariel is more than an angelic musician; he is a mischief-maker, another Puck, unwilling at his work and restless under the burden of magic he bears. It can be doubted, in other words, that Shakespeare sat down solemnly to decorate his life's work with a secret signature. "The Tempest," pressed a little, yields this meaning as it yields most of the meanings ingenuity can insist upon, and yields it with grace. But a better signature was the play itself, which, if its author had been given to such exercises, he might have recognized as one of the most beautiful literary objects ever made. He would scarcely, however, have been so conscious of what he had done. He is more likely to have let the moment go with four simple words: Now I will rest.

# HENRY VIII

SHAKESPEARE'S rest could not have been interrupted long by "Henry VIII," even if he wrote
every word of it. It has become a tradition to say
that only five or six scenes are his, and that Fletcher, or possibly Massinger, is responsible for the remainder; although
one extreme theory gives him the entire work, and another
takes it all away. The question has interest, not because
"Henry VIII" is important in itself but because in any view
it is an imitation of Shakespeare; it is at the same time like
him and unlike him. And the question will not be answered
because in such cases we cannot know whether the poet has
imitated himself or been imitated by another.

A certain resemblance to Shakespeare's later plays is all too
obvious. Tempests, shores, flowers, music, and peace are incidental themes. Henry knows how to praise Katherine in
the idiom of Pericles and Florizel: she is "the queen of
earthly queens" (II, iv, 141), and her saint-like meekness is
most rare. And reconciliation is rampant—several dramas,
rather than one, busily develop it into a kind of orthodoxy.

Just there the resemblance ceases; or overleaps its limits
and lands in imitation. For the successive dramas in which
Buckingham, Katherine, Wolsey, and Cranmer submit their
wills to Henry's are not dramas of reconciliation. The theme
has been watered down; resignation is now the word, and its
repetition through a series of unmotivated surrenders suggests
machinery. Either Shakespeare has lost the impulse which
gave his final stories their mellow power, or some other poet
has never felt it. Three proud persons break suddenly and
bow before a dummy king who represents England, and a

fourth who has never been "unsound," Archbishop Cranmer, basks weeping in the sun of his accepted monarch. It is
like nine-pins going down, nor can we miss a tone of smugness in the proud ones as they pray. This is Buckingham:

> Go with me, like good angels, to my end;
> And, as the long divorce of steel falls on me,
> Make of your prayers one sweet sacrifice,
> And lift my soul to heaven. (II, i, 75-8)

This is Katherine:

> Remember me
> In all humility unto his Highness.
> Say his long trouble now is passing
> Out of this world; tell him, in death I bless'd him,
> For so I will. (IV, ii, 160-3)

And this is Wolsey:

> Nay then, farewell!
> I have touch'd the highest point of all my greatness;
> And, from that full meridian of my glory,
> I haste now to my setting. I shall fall
> Like a bright exhalation in the evening,
> And no man see me more. . . .
> I have ventur'd,
> Like little wanton boys that swim on bladders,
> This many summers in a sea of glory,
> But far beyond my depth. My high-blown pride
> At length broke under me, and now has left me,
> Weary and old with service, to the mercy
> Of a rude stream, that must for ever hide me. . . .
> O Cromwell, Cromwell!
> Had I but serv'd my God with half the zeal
> I serv'd my king, He would not in mine age
> Have left me naked to mine enemies.
> (III, ii, 222-457)

The smugness of their tone goes with a smoothness in their
verse such as Shakespeare had long ago outgrown. Not for
years had he let his lines roll like this, or ripened his meta-

phors to rottenness. "Highest point," "meridian," "setting," "bright exhalation in the evening"—there is too much of it by Shakespeare's final standard, and although it is excellent in its way it bears no resemblance to the unique elliptical poetry he had recently been writing. "Swim on bladders," "sea of glory," "high-blown pride," "rude stream"—any competent poet could have developed the image thus, just as any workman of 1612 or 1613 could have worked out the vegetable autobiography of Wolsey in terms of his tender leaves, his blossoms, his blushing honors, his greatness ripening, and his root nipped on the third day by a killing frost (III, ii, 352-8).

The style of any good poet moves from simplicity to congestion, and once this end is reached return is difficult if not impossible. If Shakespeare returned in "Henry VIII" he was performing an extraordinary feat. He had performed many feats in his history, but not this one, of which nevertheless he was perhaps capable. At the same time, however, and in the same play, he imitated—or someone did—his last nervous style. It crops out everywhere, not only in the scenes assigned to him but in some that are assigned to his collaborator.

> The tract of everything
> Would by a good discourser lose some life,
> Which action's self was tongue to.            (I, i, 40-2)

> Of her that loves him with that excellence
> That angels love good men with.            (II, ii, 34-5)

> And which gifts,
> Saving your mincing, the capacity
> Of your soft cheveril conscience would receive,
> If you might please to stretch it.            (II, iii, 30-3)

> For it is you
> Have blown this coal betwixt my lord and me,
> Which God's dew quench!            (II, iv, 78-80)

If your business
Seek me out, and that way I am wife in,
Out with it boldly.                          (III, i, 37-9)

Such a noise arose
As the shrouds make at sea in a stiff tempest,
As loud, and to as many tunes. . . . No man living
Could say "This is my wife" there; all were woven
So strangely in one piece.                   (IV, i, 71-81)

These are imitations in the sense that their virtue has no bulk,
their involutions no excuse. They may or may not have been
written by Shakespeare, but it does not matter. They do not
save the play for distinction any more than its gorgeous
pageants make up for an absence of drama, or than its external compliments to Oxford and Cambridge, Elizabeth and
James, have continued after three centuries to be interesting.
The two styles in "Henry VIII" are two currents of water,
one tepid and the other icy. The difference is to be noted,
but it is also to be noted that the water is never wine.

The style of certain passages in "The Two Noble Kinsmen" which criticism persists in suspecting to be Shakespeare's gives us a headier imitation of his brew.

Draw thy fear'd sword
That does good turns to th' world.           (I, i, 48-9)

O queen Emilia,
Fresher than May, sweeter
Than her gold buttons on the boughs or all
Th' enamell'd knacks o' the mead or garden! Yea,
We challenge too the bank of any nymph,
That makes the stream seem flowers! Thou, O jewel
O' th' wood, o' th' world, hast likewise bless'd a place
With thy sole presence.                      (III, i, 4-11)

Each stroke laments
The place whereon it falls, and sounds more like
A bell than blade.                           (V, iii, 4-6)

But it is imitation, and once again the identity of its contriver does not matter. The lines are charming in their oddity rather than beautiful in their strength; the syntax is wrenched, the syllables are curled, for no discoverable reason. The quaint series of little triumphs grows tiresomely long, together with a story which cannot be believed and whose two fine heroes talk like one gold-plated man. The shortness of breath in Shakespeare's later verse was a sign of seriousness and power; here after a while it is weakness, for this verse lives only within the phrase, dying at each fall to gasp again. Such cleverness is senseless, as Shakespeare in his right mind never was. It drones, as he never did. None of his styles was an end in itself as this one is. He wrote to further ends: to say things, to tell stories, to mingle lives with lives. His one great end he could never have wished to put into a few words. Nor did he need to, since his many words would last.

INDEX

# INDEX